FACTOR ANALYSIS
AND MEASUREMENT
IN SOCIOLOGICAL
RESEARCH

FACTOR ANALYSIS AND MEASUREMENT IN SOCIOLOGICAL RESEARCH

A Multi-Dimensional Perspective

Editors

David J. Jackson
and Edgar F. Borgatta

 SAGE Studies in International Sociology 21
sponsored by the International Sociological Association/ISA

For information address

SAGE Publications Ltd, 28 Banner Street, London EC1Y 8QE
SAGE Publications Inc, 275 South Beverly Drive
Beverly Hills, California 90212

British Library Cataloguing in Publication Data

Factor analysis and measurement in sociological
  research. — (Sage studies in international
  sociology; 21).
  1. Sociology — Statistical methods
  2. Factor analysis
  I. Jackson, David J.   II. Borgatta, Edgar F.
  III. Series
  301'.07'2   HM24   80-40746

  ISBN 0-8039-9814-7

First Printing

lw
3-10-81

CONTENTS

III   MEASUREMENT MODELS AND RESEARCH APPLICATIONS

FOREWORD

Reliable and theoretically meaningful measurement is a major prerequisite for sociological research. The systematic pursuit of this objective is essential for all phases of sociological research. The preliminary phases of concept formation and exploration, as well as more advanced stages of explicit model testing, require appropriate measurement strategies. The papers presented in this volume focus on the methodology and application of factor analysis and related multidimensional procedures as measurement strategies. Consideration is given to factor analysis as an exploratory tool, a method for testing the stability of measurement models across different populations, and as an integral part of structural equation models. Attention is given to both quantitative and qualitative variables. Related procedures such as non-metric scaling and latent structural analysis are also discussed.

David J. Jackson
Edgar F. Borgatta

INTRODUCTION: MEASUREMENT IN SOCIOLOGICAL RESEARCH

David J. Jackson
*National Institute of Mental Health,
Adelphi, Maryland*

Edgar F. Borgatta
City University of New York

From the way misunderstandings arise among persons and peoples, some may doubt that there is good communication in the use of languages. Still, generally people can make themselves understood, and the success in communication is attested to by massive production of printed materials, a fantastic tonnage of human output. The fact that communication occurs, however, does not mean that it involves words that are precisely defined in the meaning they carry — certainly not by standards that have come to be common to the sciences. So, for example, one may feel, quite reasonably, that communication has occurred in saying that another is highly alienated, just as one may feel that communication has occurred in saying that the length of an object was 1.1456 meters long. The operations corresponding to the latter are clear with regard to measurement, but this is not the case with the former.

The heritage of sociology is found in social philosophy, in essays and descriptions of cultures, and in myriad sources, but in general the language used has not been a precise language, but the common language. The idea of measurement of concepts common to sociology is relatively recent, although the ideas of counting to establish rates and amounts is fairly old. Demographic counts, for example, are parts of early considerations of suicide, of migration, of population projections, sometimes shared with economics and related disciplines. But even in the demographic and registration traditions it was the pragmatic arbitrary needs of governments that were the dominant considerations, not precision in terms of sociological concepts. In the social philosophic vein, however, there has not been a strong tradition of questioning the precision of the language used, nor for that matter the logic of the inference processes in arriving at conclusions. Theoretical expositions not based on precise use of language are likely to become polemic, and are likely to be subject to criticism from sources of equally imprecise language use. It is in this sense that the introduction of measurement into sociology and the social sciences begins to suggest that the possibility of cumulating knowledge, rather than tonnage of printed materials, is possible.

Progress in the development of measurement in the social sciences has not been uniformly distributed or equally accepted. For obvious reasons, educational psychology was interested in measurement problems, psychology with analysis of experimental designs, and economics with trend and regression analyses. Sociology, historically, has had a niggardly concern with measurement and data analysis, and even in the post-World War II period appeared to be hostile to analytic research procedures that went beyond ad hoc simple indices and tabular presentation. Even in the current period there is reference back to the 'Columbia Tradition' or the 'Chicago School,' the first referring primarily to procedures of using what has come to be called 'Tabular Analysis' and the latter being an orientation to case, community, and other studies not based on use of highly developed approaches to measurement of variables. Concomitantly, descriptions of persons concerned with more statistical or rigorous approaches were pejorative, and a term like 'factor analyst' was a fatal invective. Internationally, Americans in contrast to Europeans were seen as empiricists, less theoretical and more concerned with research, even if tabular analysis was the level of presentation.

The progressive shift for sociology has had a number of sources. A major thrust in the direction of use of numbers came from the sponsored concern in the Social Science Research Council in improving the mathematical knowledge of sociologists and psychologists in the 1950s, which may have had more of a propagandistic impact than anything else. But more important, some of the barriers among the disciplines may have eroded, and some of the techniques and skills from different disciplines diffused. The development of computers and the ability of even unskilled persons to become involved in statistical and other procedures certainly must have had great impact. For example, as late as 1960, doing a factor analysis using the complete centroid procedure required extraordinary computer access and knowledge if more than a 40×40 matrix was involved, and a principal components analysis of that magnitude was out of the question. The arrival in the late 1960s of user-oriented computer program packages appears to be an important historical influence in making disciplines conversant with the statistical and numerical procedures available and in use.

We thus arrive at the current period, with many other disciplines sharing an interest in statistics and methodology with sociology, and some of the concerns in this volume must be seen as having quite broad application in the social and psychological sciences. And, noticeably, themes and topics presented here will be found in books in other disciplines. Borrowing, it happens, leaves some of the history of development and the lore of use of procedures unknown, so it is not remarkable to find that procedures that are known to some continue to recur as questions of interest to the newly initiated; so it occurs that there are duplications of presentations that might have been of interest quite a few years ago to some, put to rest, and then when enough time has passed they are seen as a 'new' topic. Some of these issues occur in this volume, and some may find a topic familiar if they are well versed in the areas covered. Still, the importance of restatement and emphasis, as we will note below, is important.

With regard to measurement, it needs to be emphasized that there are two major issues that sociologists must address more directly than they have in the past. The first is that they must deal with development of *valid* measures to correspond to their theories if they presume to science. This is the notion that corresponding to a concept there is a clear meaning, only one meaning, and it is used in the same way consistently in the theoretical formulation. Corresponding to the concept, thus, there should be a specific set of operations, and in the ideal state the correspondence is direct (isometric) between concept and operations. In the social and psychological sciences, one cannot assume the correspondence, and so the factor analytic procedures that have developed have come as both challenges to the self-assured and disruptions to those who had already arrived at conclusions. For example, with the idea of alienation, how is it to be measured? If one looks at the uses, many suggested meanings may arise in the literature. Thus, many items may be suggested as indicators. If jointly measured, the items may reveal a pattern where five factors are found with good representation of items. If they are named, the naming follows the content as revealed (intuitively) to the analyst, and some of the factors may clearly not be alienation. The process, to that point, could eliminate some meaning and clarify; but, to the residual factors, say three, the analyst would have to look and say: if one of these is alienation, the other two are not, yet they seem to imply some of the content we would intuitively have thought associated with the concept from the way it has been used in the literature. So, probably, from that point on, assuming this has been a rather comprehensive study of the concept, the least that will face the analyst is naming the concepts corresponding to the factors as Alienation I, Alienation II, and Alienation III, and defining them specifically when using them. But what does this do to pre-existing theory? Unless by some fortunate accident the theorist has kept his concept having only one of the three meanings, the theory is virtually made uninterpretable by the advancement of knowledge about the measure. It is in this sense that advancement of sciences proceeds with the advancement of measurement, and theory only in a romantic belief anticipates empirical observation, at least at this level of science.

In approaches to validation related to both questions of measurement and factor analysis, some of the foibles of the social sciences become more visible. Thus, in the multi-trait, multi-method approach to convergent and discriminant validity, concepts of domains of measurement (approaches) are noted. It is not enough to identify a concept like assertiveness, but it is important also to know in what domain of measurement it exists, and further, by being located in the domain, there is also knowledge of *what it is not*. If the traits have been developed by factorial procedures, then more specific meaning can be given to what a variable is not. But, additionally, the procedure places emphasis on parallel measurement in independent approaches, and the prediction diagonal gives some immediate and often humbling information about the predictability of the measure.

Return to the question of reliability is natural when modest prediction numbers are observed, and a key to improvement is an emphasis on the reliability of the variables. This thus places the concerns of reliability and validity clearly into the arena of work with factor analysis. The many techniques associated with these concepts feed each other in the improvement of the science.

Implicit in the comments here is the emphasis that advancement of sociology is likely to be tied to improvement of measures within the science. However, not all thrusts go in that direction. Part of the advancement will come from burying obsolete and inappropriate procedures, or at least clarifying them. Routine computation of measures of reliability (consistency) appear finally to be making headway into the research literature. Dependence on confounded concepts, like the test-retest reliability, which reflects both consistency and stability of subjects, is hard to break in the style of work of sociologists from earlier generations. Similarly, the style of building indices on the basis of a set of interrelated items, put together in an ad hoc way according to face validity, without reference to factorial structure, still seems the method of choice for much of the sociological fraternity (or should it be sibernity?). Fewer researchers move in the direction of cumulative scaling, possibily as they get a sense of the model not being appropriate except in rather limited cases, but also as they note the limited and rare advantage of the procedure. But, almost as a cultural matter, the procedure hangs on with many sociologists who have not seen measurement in a broader context. So, many changes yet to come have to do with not merely adding to the skills of researchers, but subtracting some of the things that are done as carryovers of earlier innocence.

In this volume a number of topics are covered, and the issues presented cannot be seen as definitively put to rest. Measurement and factor analysis are not topics that have been exhausted; nor have the topics become comfortable in the use and lore of research in all places and times. The essays should be put in the perspective of international communication. Several of the essays grew out of presentations at the 1978 meeting of the International Sociological Association. The remaining essays were commissioned for this publication. One consequence of this international dimension is heterogeniety of methodological perspectives. The major common denominator of this set of essays is their recognition of the fundamental importance of measurement. Some topics will appear highly specific according to the titles, but the essays selected actually have broad implications for research. This is a sampling of a set of concerns that essentially become coincident with the whole field of knowledge that is sociology. Within the limitations of space and time available, this volume represents a hopeful contribution to noting an international convergence on the importance of the topics of measurement and factor analysis for sociology.

I

FACTOR ANALYSIS AND MEASUREMENT
IN EXPLORATORY RESEARCH

1

FACTOR ANALYSIS AS AN AID IN THE FORMATION AND REFINEMENT OF EMPIRICALLY USEFUL CONCEPTS

Alberto Marradi
University of Catania, Italy

I

Factor analysis is seen by most authors as just one of the many techniques of multivariate analysis. Traditional (Blalock, 1960; Morrison, 1967) as well as more modern (Cooley and Lohnes, 1971; Van der Geer, 1971) manuals in social sciences data analysis cover this subject after treating multiple correlation, partial correlation, and path analysis, and before treating canonical correlation. A general model has been proposed which unifies factor analysis and most other multivariate techniques under the heading 'analysis of covariance structures' (Jöreskog, 1970). The latter is a major technical achievement; however, the technical point of view results in concealing the peculiar methodological use to which factor analysis may be put, and for which it was indeed created (Spearman, 1904). One starts with one

Author's note. An earlier version of this paper was given at the Ninth World Congress of Sociology, Uppsala, August 1979. The author expresses his deep gratitude to Professor Philip E. Converse and Dr Lutz Erbring, of the University of Michigan, for critically reading and thoroughly discussing the paper.

set of variables and finds their linear combination(s) best predicting the variance in the set itself. The particular nature of the technique makes it inappropriate for the measurement of relations between phenomena; on the other hand, it makes it the ideal tool for exploiting relations between lower-level phenomena in order to summarize something they have in common, i.e. to measure a higher-level phenomenon.

While such high-level phenomena are of paramount interest for the social sciences, their measurement often presents severe problems, which either are given very inadequate solutions or are evaded by doing research on trivialities or keeping the discussion at a philosophical level. Factor analysis allows social scientists to bring many interesting contructs down to the empirical arena by measuring them in an adequate way, or — better — in a way that may be adequate if the algorithm is fed with accurately chosen and measured data, and the procedural phases are steered by a combination of semantic competence, experience with empirical research, familiarity with the substantive domain, solid epistemological foundations, and a good deal of common sense: the same qualities that are necessary meaningfully to perform any kind of data analysis.

By mentioning the capability of extracting the reduced number of variance-predicting linear composites from a set of variables, one stresses the side of factor analysis that retains the attention of statisticians and most psychometricians (see e.g. Hartley, 1954: 196; Henrysson, 1960: 14; Fruchter and Jennings, 1962: 238, 262; Harman, 1967, 4ff.; Morrison, 1967: 259; Maxwell, 1968: 275; Jöreskog, 1978: 453). Psychologists and social scientists object, however, that the linear combinations produced by factor analysis are interesting only in so far as they may be meaningfully interpreted in terms of underlying phenomena (see e.g. Burt, 1940: 18; Eysenck, 1953: 110-11; Rummel, 1967: 19-21; Butler, 1968: 356; Burt, 1973: 144). Thurstone (1947: 51) remarks that 'the problem is choosing the most fruitful set of parameters to describe the variation in a domain. These parameters represent scientific concepts. They are not merely numerical coefficients.' Cattell ventures the opinion that:

> economy of measurement in terms of substituting a few factor measures for a very large number of variable measures. . .which is so often cited by statisticians and psychometricians, is decidedly less important than the psychologists' argu-

ment, namely that the personality factors found by factor analysis are highly meaningful source traits...which are part of the basic scientific understanding of personality. [1962: 217-18]

Social scientists should not try to impose their view of factor analysis on statisticians; but they should not either borrow the latter's view, as they are called upon to exert some hard thinking about the opportunities the technique offers toward solving some peculiar epistemological problems of their disciplines.

The nature of such opportunities is missed by those who see 'factors as causal mechanisms accounting for the relationships among variables' (Mulaik, 1972: 362; similar statements in Eysenck, 1953: 107-8; Tucker, 1964: 110; Cattell, 1965b: 424; Brislin et al., 1973: 259; Kim and Mueller, 1978a: 7-8), and factor analysis as a special case in the family of techniques that search for variables causing a certain association between other variables to vanish (see e.g. Holzinger, 1940: 237; Maxwell, 1968: 276; McRae, 1970: 101; Weisberg, 1974: 743; Jöreskog, 1978: 453-5). On the other hand, a serious epistemological misunderstanding, or a gross terminological inaccuracy, is involved in stating that 'factor analysis...may be used...in the development of structural theories' (Mulaik, 1972: 10; also see Harman, 1967: 6, 268) or in the testing of hypotheses (see references in Section 5, where the point is amply discussed).

The above mentioned views seem to attest to an insufficient consideration of:

(a) the need for a relationship of indication between variables at different levels of abstraction. This semantic link has a function similar, though not identical, to the operational definition of concepts, which anchors them to the result of complex measurements; on the contrary, it should be sharply distinguished from a relationship, causal or otherwise, between variables at *the same* level of abstraction;

(b) the distinction between concepts, or variables, being the elements of scientific discourse, and hypotheses, or theories, being relationships established between these elements.

Factor analysis allows one to use statistical relationships between several lower-level variables as empirical evidence for or against the establishment of a semantic relationship of indication between these variables and an abstract concept, which may thus be measured and transformed into a variable with a high semantic extension and theoretical importance.

The various aspects of this downward relationship of indication and of its corresponding upward process of measurement are discussed in Sections 2 — 4 below. Their postulated relevance to the solution of peculiar problems in the social sciences earns them logical priority over a more widely appreciated feature of factor analysis, viz. the ability to supply the coordinates for the projections of a set of variables from a p-dimensional space onto a series of suitably chosen planes.

Through careful examination of these two-dimensional plots the social scientist can obtain a sufficiently correct perception of the p-dimensional configuration of variables, which in turn is isomorphic with the pattern of their empirically measured interrelations. It is up to the scientist to find conceptual reasons for the way variables actually cluster in the plots he is examining, and accordingly to interpret the variables in each cluster as indicators of different concepts.

Sections 5—8 suggest one particular manner of handling problems presented by the passage from the set of variables to the clusters of indicators. The link with the previous sections lies in the fact that each cluster, once its membership has been defined, should be submitted to a separate factor analysis in order to refine the measurement of the underlying concept. In other words, multiple-factor analysis may be construed as a preliminary to single-factor analysis.

Mathematical aspects and problems of factor analysis will not be discussed here, as they are exhaustively covered by dozens of specialized texts. After the Thurston school in the 1940s, Guilford (1952), Eysenck (1953), and a few others, the methodological debate on factor analysis has subsided, and technical problems have almost monopolized attention. By now, the average social scientist should have been exposed to more than his share of Procustes[1] rotations, and he may be willing to listen to a methodological argument again. At least, this is what the author hopes.

II

In the social sciences, a variable bearing some theoretical interest is seldom measurable through a direct question or stimulus. This is especially true when such variables are deep, general and enduring personality traits. Let's suppose we are interested in people's authoritarianism. It would be self-deceiving to measure this trait through questions like 'Are you (an) authoritarian?' This would measure something different from authoritarianism, i.e. the disposition to admit publicly one's authoritarianism, or the willingness to appear authoritarian. In general, indicators bearing a simple, textual resemblance to the term designating the trait are often fraught with strong suspicions of invalidity, i.e. of measuring something different from what they are supposed to measure. As a consequence, we are called upon to exert our semantic imagination, or informed common sense, in order to find questions and stimuli that may serve as indicators of our trait even though there is no textual resemblance between their wording and the term designating the trait.

The relationship of indication between the trait and the question is not warranted by a mechanical correspondence of terms, but by the scientist's judgment as to a more or less vast semantic overlap between trait and indicator. Thanks to this overlap, the question will obtain responses that are — for a majority of subjects — largely controlled by their positions on the trait that is being measured. However, the overlap is far from complete, because:

(a) The indicator has a much narrower referent than the general trait. It usually tends to elicit the respondents' attitudes or reactions toward some specific object, on the assumption that these attitudes are largely controlled by the trait. The indicator just picks one among the numerous objects that would be eligible. The trait's semantic extension includes attitudes toward each of these objects, and much more.

(b) On the other hand, the indicator also measures something other than the trait. The respondents' actual answers may be influenced by several other sources: personality traits different from that which we intend to measure; attitudes toward the question's object that depend upon some specific circumstances (life experiences, etc.) rather than upon general traits; misinterpretation of the question's meaning, or of some particular term; willingness to comply with the interviewer's supposed opinion; mere absent-mindedness. Moreover, what an answer looks like in data analysis also depends on coding and punching errors.

As a consequence, the validity of an item as an indicator of a general trait should always be questioned. Even when such validity is grounded on current theory and has been somehow confirmed by previous research, the specific features of a research design (population, sampling and interviewing techniques, questionnaire context, coding instruction, etc.) may bring about a different interplay of non-pertinent influences, as listed under point (b) above.

All these rather obvious facts are apparently forgotten by those who trust the measurement of a personality trait to a single indicator. In some circumstances this may be unavoidable (e.g. when no other suitable indicators are included in a data set of which one is doing secondary analaysis). At any rate, however, this case of 'force majeure' does not justify more than any other case the total identification between an abstract trait and an indicator whose semantic extension is patently narrower and whose validity is, or should be, in question. Yet, many social scientists bestow upon their indicators all the semantic richness of their concepts, and lightheartedly use these enlarged referents in their comments and theorizing (Timasheff, 1947: 209; McRae, 1970: xi).

The more general and semantically rich a concept is, the more numerous its indicators should be in a research design. The advantages of this procedure are manifold: different questions tap different facets of the same concept; idiosyncrasies and misunderstandings connected to a specific indicator are less damaging; errors tend to balance away. A plurality of indicators for the same concept is likely to disturb only those who attribute to the whole of science that semantic definiteness and rigidity which has been reached only by some sections of physical science, after centuries of struggle about concepts and their proper operational definitions. In the early phase of a science (and probably in any phase of the social sciences, whose objects vary significantly over time and space) a plurality of indicators for the same concept is a physiological rather than a pathological state, and should be blessed in so far as it alerts the scientist to the autonomy of his concepts vis-à-vis his measuring instruments, and to the gap dividing the two.

III

The choice of indicators for a concept is a responsibility the scientist may never renounce in favor of some algorithm. Theory and previous research may help him, but the final judgment as to what indicators are likely to be valid in a given context is always with him, and he should not abdicate it in favor of ready-made batteries of questions or tests. At any rate, even the most informed and careful selection of indicators is marked by an unsuppressible element of arbitrariness. This I want to underline, in view of a later development of my argument.

Moreover, the validity of an indicator may not be proved in an 'objective' way even a posteriori, i.e. by algorithms applied to the data gathered. We can objectively measure reliablity, which tells us whether our instrument is consistently measuring the same thing, but we cannot possibly tell what sort of thing it is. Of course, the low reliablity of an indicator is strong evidence against its validity, but the converse is not true. As Deutscher put it,

> measurement can be consistently in error as well as consistently correct, and therefore a high degree of reliability can be achieved anywhere along the continuum between absolute invalidity and absolute validity. . . . Any mathematical formula which expresses validity as a direct function of reliability, or vice versa, must be in error. [1969:34]

When we deal with a set of indicators for the same concept, what has been said of reliability (measured through test-retest correlations) applies to inter-item correlations as well. High correlation coefficients tell us that our indicators are measuring much the same thing, without formally proving anything as to its nature. While validity is never positively proved, if some items show systematically lower correlations with others, their validity as indicators of that 'same thing' is — at least within the limit of the research in question — disproved.

Therefore, visual inspection of a matrix of correlation coefficients among indicators of the same concept should be resorted to by researchers having no acquaintance with, or computational access to, factor analysis, or willing to anticipate its results. According to Borgatta (1959: 523), 'the factorial structure of a matrix may be anticipated quite directly by looking at the arrangements of correlations of variables.' At any rate, several flaws in one's choice of indicators may be detected through that simple means.

An obvious remedy for such flaws is the discarding of one or more indicators from the list. Seldom, however, is the correlation matrix so neatly arranged that little doubt is left as to what to discard and what to retain. Often the coefficients decline gradually from highest to lowest, and their pattern looks irregular. Therefore, visual inspection is frequently insufficient to define clearly a subset of indicators to be discarded as presumably invalid.

Factor analysis can perform that task with superior efficiency, by substituting a simple vector of coefficients correlating each indicator with a factor for the dispersive matrix of coefficients correlating each indicator with every other. A certain amount of information is lost in this reduction; but the very nature of the technique assures that what is lost tends to coincide with the idiosyncratic or erratic components of each indicator. In other words, we tend to lose precisely what is irrelevant to our purpose of measuring a theoretically interesting concept.

The above statements need to be immediately qualified: they are true insofar as only one meaningful factor is extracted from a correlation matrix. A set of indicators, or subsets thereof, may measure several interesting concepts, as will be seen in Section 5; Sections 3 and 4, however, are devoted to the simpler case of one factor only.

Let us take a closer look at this factor. It has no real existence in our data apart from its correlations with each indicator, which in turn derive from the pairwise correlations of each indicator with any other in the set. If an indicator shows higher-than-average correlations with the others, its correlation with the factor ('factor loading') will also turn out to be higher than for other indicators.

This makes sense intuitively: let us imagine the concept as the center of a semantic space, and its indicators as points scattered around that center, at distances inversely proportional to their validity. We want to infer the distances between the points and the center (which we cannot measure) from the distances between any couple of points (which we can measure: they are the inverse of the correlations between the corresponding indicators). If a point is located nearer the center, its average distance from other points will be smaller (i.e. its average correlation higher) than is true for more distant points. Therefore, close correlation with other indicators is the best evidence available of small distance from the concept.

Again, all this needs to be qualified, both to prevent an objection and to further our understanding of the epistemological background. The objection is: let Figure 1 be the two-dimensional projection of a semantic space, where an asterisk represents the concept, and letters represent the indicators; indicators C and D have the smallest average distances from others, but indicators G and H are located nearest the asterisk.

FIGURE 1

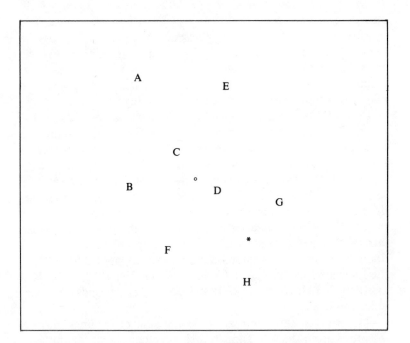

The answer to the objection is that the asterisk in Figure 1 may happen to display exactly the semantic position of the concept we have in mind relative to the indicators we have chosen; but there is no way to know it, because there is no way 'objectively' to locate a concept we have in mind within a space defined by indicators that have been measured through actual operations. Factor analysis will locate the ideal center of the space at the centroid of the points representing the indicators, which is uniquely determined by their correlations (Thurstone, 1947: 151ff.). This centroid (small circle in Figure 1) is by definition closer to the indicators having higher average correlations with other indicators in the chosen set, and therefore it cannot be placed where the asterisk would have it placed.

This argument should lead us to a better appraisal of the whole question of validity. If we could 'objectively' locate a concept in the space defined by actually measured indicators, the factor loading would be an exact measure of validity of the corresponding indicator — at least, given our sample, and the techniques used in gathering and factoring the data.[2] But neither factor analysis nor any other technique can ever establish an objective link between the contents of a researcher's mind and of a data matrix. Therefore, we must be satisfied with measuring the distance between each indicator and that centroid we ourselves implicitly locate when we choose our indicators, and measure them in the field.

These distances are expressed by a vector of factor loadings. Indicators having larger (positive or negative) loadings should be given prevalence in the interpretation of the factor: careful evaluation of their semantic contents will very often lead to acknowledging that we have measured something that differs to a greater or lesser degree from what we wanted to measure. This need not induce us to abandon our general concept: only, insofar as we want to use it — as measured by that particular analysis — in further analyses of the same data set (see Section 8, point e), we are called upon to rename it, by emphasizing aspects semantically closer to the indicators having larger loadings (Gouldner, 1957: 445; Harman, 1967: 133; contra Guttman, 1955: 79; on grounds of factor indeterminacy).

On the other hand, indicators having smaller loadings may be discarded from the set. Though their invalidity is not definitively demonstrated, surely the concept cannot be simultaneously (i.e. on the same data set) measured by them and by indicators having higher loadings, because it would be measured through divergent, inconsistent means. The threshold beyond which a loading is to be judged small should not be defined in advance, as it depends on the nature of the data, the technique by which they have been gathered, the accuracy in error-checking, etc. A sharp drop in the loadings' magnitude is a better cutting point than any predetermined numerical threshold. Semantic differences between the discarded and the retained indicators should also be evaluated.

IV

If we decide to discard one or more indicators from the set, we cannot just retain the rest of factor loadings at their previous values. When we remove one item from the list we also remove a row and a column from the correlation matrix. Though other correlations are left unchanged, the whole configuration of inter-item distances is affected to a certain degree, also depending on the number of indicators that are left untouched. Therefore, the factor loadings must be re-computed from the reduced correlation matrix (Smith, 1974: 506). Assuming we are satisfied with the new list of indicators and their associated loadings, what we have made is an informed decision as to which of an initial set of items are to be considered — given our population and our measuring and computing techniques — indicators of the same concept.[3] Depending on the semantic contents of the retained items, somehow weighted by their loadings, we also judge whether our original understanding of that concept needs a more or less substantial revision.

A vector of factor loadings is the first important result of a factor analysis. A majority of students devote most of their attention to the mathemathical refinement of techniques whereby such a result is arrived at (see e.g. Lawley, 1940; Guttman, 1953; 1954; Fruchter, 1954; Rao, 1955; Kaiser and Caffrey, 1965; Harman and Jones, 1966; Jöreskog, 1967; Lawley, 1967; Browne, 1968; Clarke, 1970; Jöreskog and Goldberger, 1972; Schönemann and Wang, 1972; Tucker and Lewis, 1973; Bentler, 1977). Some also focus on the extent to which this result (i.e. the close association of those indicators with, and in, a factor) can be generalized from one population to others; when there is more than one factor (see Sections 5—8), this is known as the problem of invariance to the factor structure (Thurstone, 1945; 1947: 324ff.; Ahmavaara, 1954; Ahmavaara and Markkanen, 1958; Jöreskog, 1971; Mulaik, 1972: 337ff.; Please, 1973) and will not be dealt with here.

Until recently, students and users of factor analysis have paid surprisingly little attention to a third avenue of interest, namely the measurement of individual scores on the general trait through individual scores on the indictors. Heerman stated (1964: 379) that 'factor analysis does not seem very useful in describing the individual subject...this is not necessarily a major objective of factor analysis.' A few years later, McDonald and Burr could remark:

> In the past thirty years or so the theory of common factor analysis has undergone a tremendous amount of development...but very little attention has been given to the correlative problem of determining factors scores...the usual objectives of factor analysis are commonly considered to be attained when one has an interpretable factor structure. [1967: 381]

A very similar statement is found in Harman (1967: 345), who himself discusses the topic in a rather rash and unsatisfactory last chapter of his classic treatise (1967).

Several authors maintain that factor scores should not be computed owing to mathemathical indeterminacy of factors (as opposed to principal components). Factor indeterminacy does not 'bear on the practical utility of factor analysis as a research tool as long as it is used to study the structure of variables without attempting to estimate a person's factor scores' (Schönemann and Wang, 1972: 89). Similar theses have been argued by Guttman (1955), Harris (1967), and others. Green (1976: 263; italics mine) ventures the opinion that 'many factor analysts...ignore factor scores because they hesitate to *verify* so *nebulous* a construct as a rotated factor by seeking scores on it as if it were a *real variable.*'

The last quotation is particularly representative of a statistician's point of view. The initial measurements are assumed to be true-to-reality, and the attention is therefore concentrated on the mathemathical exactitude of subsequent analyses. If some transformation is less than mathemathically exact, then its results are 'nebulous.' But how more nebulous and fraught with errors of every kind are the 'real variables!' Whoever is aware of the bluntness and distortion inherent in data gathering procedures in the social sciences should greet the computation of factor scores, no matter if mathemathically imperfect, as a giant step toward correct measurement. A score resulting from an ably performed factor analysis is a much more sensitive and foolproof assessment of one's position on a trait than a raw score on any 'real variable.'

By this I do not mean that any technique for computing factor scores is equally good. This point has indeed been made by Sewell (1941: 284), Alwin (1973: 206-8), and Kim and Mueller (1978a:51), alleging that different computational criteria yield scores that correlate very highly with each other (Alwin brings evidence, but based on three indicators only). At any rate, at least three criteria are liable to serious methodological criticism:

(a) to simply take the scores on a single indicator — provided it is easily measured and has a high factor loading — as scores on the general trait (Rummel, 1967: 442): this amounts to wasting most of the information obtained through a factor analysis;

(b) to simply sum the scores on all the indicators having a high loading, without weighting them (see e.g. Thurstone, 1947: 514). Prior standardization of the scores is viewed as optional by Rummel (1967: 172)! According to Alwin (1973: 194), these 'factor-based scores are perhaps the most common approach to index construction in sociology'; that choice is reasonable 'if the researcher...has...little prior experience with the particular set of items sampled' (1973: 205). This point is developed by Kim and Mueller (1978b: 71-2): 'The conservative stance is to view the structures found by factor analysis as only suggestive, indicating some clustering in the data but no more.' Yet, this commendable caution is misguided, because equal weighting of items is no less arbitrary than differential weighting, and it is certainly more arbitrary if it disregards available evidence as to differential validity of items as indicators of a concept;

(c) to weight the scores on each indicator by the corresponding factor loading (see e.g. Fruchter, 1954: 205; Cattell, 1957: 287ff.; Blalock, 1960: 620; Cattell, 1965a: 105; Teune, 1968: 137). However, using factor loadings as weights in building factor scores is like using zero-order correlation coefficients as weights in a regression equation: each among a set of closely correlated predictors is individually credited with an influence that it shares with other members of the set, and the solution is largely redundant.

Let us translate this in terms of factor analysis. Ideally, we would like every facet of the general trait to be adequately represented in its measurement, and choose — or should choose — indicators accordingly. Covering the whole concept's semantic span usually entails picking indicators at a certain semantic distance from one another. But the public's perception of a semantic space is seldom the same as the researcher's: unexpected couples or trios of indicators tend to appear, which — for reasons discussed in Section 3 — draw the centroid in their own direction, and away from other more semantically isolated indicators. As a consequence, indicators too close to one another turn up artificially high loadings, while comparatively isolated indicators have their loadings depressed.

Thus, a facet of the general trait that happens to be closely measured by two or three indicators would be greatly emphasized within the overall factor score because each of these indicators is heavily loaded; conversely, there will be a twofold handicap for facets measured by only one less heavily loaded indicator. Using factor loadings as weights entails magnifying the consequences of the unavoidably unequal representation of facets in the basketful of indicators we have submitted to factor analysis. On the other hand, those consequences are reduced if we use weights obtained by regressing the factor on its indicators, i.e. a perfect equivalent of a regression equation's beta weights.[4] Such weights, currently called 'factor score coefficients', only assign to each indicator a contribution to an inferred factor which is not shared by other indicators in the battery. For every indicator, the factor score coefficient is smaller than the factor loading; however, the reduction is usually lesser for comparatively isolated indicators than for tightly clustered ones.

Some of the tightly clustered indicators may turn out to be credited with only a very small autonomous contribution to the measurement of the concept, since each is barely different from a linear combination of other indicators. The same may happen to an apparently isolated indicator, whose smaller factor loading was the consequence of a large error variance. Whenever a factor score coefficient falls below a certain threshold (for which a numerical value cannot and should not be defined in advance), the analyst must not hesitate to drop the corresponding indicator, since this simplifies both the computation of factor scores and the interpretation of the concept he is trying to measure.

If one or more indicators are discarded, the vector of factor score coefficients in the vector are satisfactorily high, but the analyst judges that the indicators are too numerous, he may experiment with various subsets of indicators in order to find out whether more economical solutions exist that he deems satisfactory from a semantic point of view. In any case, insight into the domain of empirical reference of a concept is gained if several alternative solutions are explored rather than halting in worship before the first computer printout.

Summing up, a researcher wishing to measure a deep personality trait, or general value orientation, or any similar object, should go through the following steps:

(a) select a list of suitable indicators and measure them in the field;

(b) compute a matrix of pairwise correlation coefficients between the indictors, and obtain a vector of factor loadings through factor analysis;

(c) consider the loadings' magnitude in order to better articulate his understanding of the concept, and to discard less correlated indicators if that is semantically plausible; repeat steps (b) and (c) until satisfied with the solution;

(d) compute a vector of factor score coefficients for the retained indicators;

(e) consider the coefficients' magnitude in order to see whether some indicators may be dropped; repeat steps (d) and (e) with different subsets of the retained indicators;

(f) select a preferred solution, by balancing considerations of economy and of adequate coverage of the semantic space;

(g) compute a factor score for each individual, through the formula

$$F_i = C_1 S_{1i} + C_2 S_{2i} + \ldots + C_n S_{ni}$$

where C_1 is the factor score coefficient for indicator 1, and S_{1i} is the score of individual i on indicator 1.

Only steps (b), (d), (g) consist of mathemathical manipulations and may be trusted to a computer; steps (a), (c), (e), (f) involve the researcher's subjective appraisal of a complex interplay of theoretical, semantic, and technical considerations. This side of factor analysis is either concealed or begrudgingly acknowledged in the texts; many authors would openly deny the legitimacy of steps (e) and (f), as detracting from the 'scientific' status of the procedure. But even step (b) involves a choice among several techniques for extracting factor loadings. Moreover, the deeper intrusion of subjective judgment into neat technical automatism occurs at step (a) (selection of indicators), which could not possibly be trusted to a computer — though some researchers may perform it as routinely and blindly as a computer would.

While steps (c), (e), (f) entail choices among alternatives that technical evidence has already considerably reduced, the initial selection of indicators entails a choice among theoretically countless alternatives. Even the most 'objective' conduct (i.e. worshipping the computer printout instead of using it as a ground for wise decisions) cannot mend the unbounded subjectivity of the first step. As a consequence, we are perfectly justified in reducing the initial list when some technical manipulation has made it clear that some indicators would bring largely inconsistent or redundant contributions to the measurement of our concept. If we hesitate in reducing the list, what we are really worshipping is the most subjective and uninformed of our choices rather than 'objective' mathemathical results.

The whole matter might appear under a totally different light if technical steps were viewed as useful aids toward a better informed subjective judgment rather as the sanctuary of science, to be guarded against contamination by any non-axiomatic forms of knowledge. Of course, the subjective decisions as well as the reasons for and against each of them should be submitted to the scientific community along with the results of the analysis. Unfortunately, as Eysenck (1953: 108) and Kruskal (1970: 55) deplored, review editors and publishers tend to cut down reports of methodological preliminaries, and few readers are really prepared to appreciate them. This is precisely what strips the terms 'intersubjectivity' of most of its meaning. At any rate, the whole report by the researcher should testify to his consciousness of the ample subjective components in his results. For instance, he should never lose sight of the disti. .tion between the concept as he conceives it and as he has managed to measure it.

V

In the previous sections, discussion has been limited to a single factor measuring a single trait, in order to confer analytical clarity to the argument. This may also describe the actual development and outcome of some factor analyses, if only a few semantically close indicators are considered, or if the analyst is inclined to disregard additional factors as they show up to disturb his convictions about the presence of a single factor in a given domain.[5] However, a majority of factor analytic studies end up with several interpretable and theoretically relevant factors, because the battery of tests or indicators is designed to measure, or happens to measure, more than one general trait.

A distinction is currently being made between exploratory and confirmatory — or hypothesis-testing — factor analysis (e.g. Henrysson, 1960: 56ff.; Child, 1970: 8; Mulaik, 1972: 9ff., 362ff.). The former type obtains when the researcher would not venture any forecasts on the nature and structure of factors that will be extracted from his matrix. The latter obtains when he sets forth an explicit hypothesis on such nature and structure, and treats factor analysis as a test that will either confirm or disconfirm his expectations.

A first comment about this position concerns the improper use of the term 'hypothesis'.[6] In the philosophy of science this term designates statements concerning the relationships between two or more concepts, or variables; the empirical existence, and forms of measurement, of such concepts are logically prior to any discourse on the relationship between them. But in factor analysis, it is precisely the separate empirical existence and adequate means of measurement of certain concepts — not their mutual relationship — that is in question. True, existence and measurability are ascertained through manipulation of relationships between possible indicators of those concepts; but indicators, qua indicators, are placed at a lower level of abstraction. And that makes a lot of difference. Of course, in common parlance the term 'hypothesis' has a much wider, and vaguer, connotation than in the philosophy of science. But, at least in this instance, the adoption of the wider connotation is rather dangerous, in that it parallels — and attests to — an insufficient awareness of the epistemological distinction between techniques intended to measure concepts (thereby turning them into variables), and techniques intended to measure, or estimate, relationships between variables.

A second remark is that a sharp discrimination between exploratory and confirmatory uses of factor analysis, while it is well grounded both in epistemology and in statistical technique (Jöreskog, 1966; 1969), neither portrays the present state of affairs in empirical social research, nor seems to be a desirable target for the near future. Social scientists using factor analysis for their empirical research goals (as distinguished from models-developing statisticians and psychometricians) may be ranked along a continuum of awareness of the concepts they intend to measure, with a gradually shifting balance of emphasis upon indicators on one side, and concepts (or 'hypotheses', as some would call them) on the other side.

At one extreme of this continuum stand those who punch all the data (the term is purposely chosen, because they seldom have a clear idea of the concept-indicator relationship, and tend to think in terms of data) at their disposal, throw them into a computer and 'let the results (or: the data) speak for themselves.' This approach to factor analysis should be described as 'blind' rather than 'exploratory,' and is exactly what Mulaik has in mind when he speaks of the 1950s and early 1960s as the era of blind factor analysis (1972: 9) and what Eysenck already condemned as 'blind empiricism' (1953: 108), or Armstrong (1967) vividly portrayed as 'Tom Swift and His Electric Factor Analysis Machine.' Examples are particularly numerous among the analyses of process-produced political data published in the mid-1960s (Rummel, 1963; Adelman and Taft-Morris, 1965; Gregg and Banks, 1965; Rummel, 1966a; Rummel, 1966b; Russett, 1966; Tanter, 1966). As anyone who has looked critically at the international collections of this kind of indicators must have remarked, many of the 'hard' data considered by these data-worshippers do not meet even the minimal requirements as to reliability (in a non-technical sense) and level of measurement; use of r with categorical data is not so uncommon as it is absurd. Small wonder that such users of factor analysis have trouble interpreting their computer's factors, and resort instead to the ritual exhibition of page-wide matrices of factor loadings, all duly carried to fifth decimal. Such matrices are their end product; as they cannot really tell what it is they have measured, they instinctively restrain from thinking of individual scorers on their computer-generated artifacts, and consequently seldom if ever carry on to the computation of factor scores.

At the other end of of the continuum are a few who entertain a very firm idea of what concepts are useful in describing a given domain, and, not being prepared to give up their idea even in the face of contrary evidence, claim confirmation by resorting to verbal acrobatics in the interpretation of factors. According to Humphreys (1968: 282), 'any behavioral scientist of any modest degree of ingenuity can rationalize the random grouping of any set of variables' (the same opinion is voiced by Linn, 1968: 39). This may be detected by a critical reading, but it runs the risk of no sanction worse than an occasional bitter review or letter to the editor. For most readers, what goes on record is that the analyst's 'hypothesis' has been 'confirmed.' On the other hand, the actual results are also published, thus making alternative interpretations possible.

Things are worse if confirmation-oriented analysts profit by the manifold opportunities that factor analysis offers to sophisticated users who wish to steer its course in a given direction. The number of factors to be extracted and rotated, the rotational criterion, the discarding of some indicators rather than others, are among the decisions that may be made in such a way as to favor a particular outcome. The advent of confirmatory factor analysis has added as powerful a tool as target rotation, by which a matrix of factor loadings derived from real data may be rotated into maximum possible congruence with another matrix, established a priori by the analyst. Hurley and Cattell already (1962: 260) said of their 'Procrustes':[7] 'this program lends itself to the brutal feat of making almost any data fit almost any hypothesis.' In the following years objective goodness-of-fit tests have been developed; but the array of rotational programs has grown so rich, and consequently the choice so ample, that one tends to agree with Levine (1977: 41) when he says that 'most readers would not be happy with a researcher who claims the validity for his hypothesis after having forced his data to fit this hypothesis. In some way, such target rotation forces one's empirical data to fit the target.'

Lawley (1958), Jöreskog and others who worked on the confirmatory model of factor analysis intended to place the technique under the aegis of hypothesis-testing, considered to be the unique paradigm of scientific enterprise. However, this development will be mature when the profession is sufficiently aware as to appreciate and demand a detailed description of all the methodological and technical steps through which a certain result is arrived at, and thereby to exert a real intersubjective control. Until that time, placing emphasis on a confirmatory function of factor analysis may lead many into committing sins for which no punishment is to be feared, because little trace of them, besides the outcome, is likely to appear in print. Similarly, a greater methodological awareness should be reached before an exploratory function is singled out at no risk of encouraging blind factor-fishing expeditions.

It is comforting to note, however, that most users of factor analysis are neither unfailing confirmationists nor blind factor-fishers. They select their indicators with reference to some idea they have in mind about what relevant dimensions exist in a given domain. This idea is something different from a criterion of mere availability of indicators, but it is also less rigid and precise than a 'hypothesis', whose formal confirmation or disconfirmation is sought. Common sense, if not hampered by misconceived falsificationism, suggests to a good many users an approach that is essentially the same as Thurstone outlined some years ago. He maintained that the theoretically important things in a factor analysis take place in the researcher's head before the analysis, when indicators are selected, and after it, when factors are interpreted (Guilford,

1964: 163). His position 'stands in contrast to...haphazard
...feeding of data into computer' (Mulaik, 1972: 340). Yet, he
warned 'on the basis of considerable experience, that a factor
analysis does not necessarily reproduce the categories that constitute the preconceptions of the investigator' (Thurstone, 1947:
340) and ascribed much of the scientific interest aroused by the
technique to the fact that 'the underlying order in a domain can be
discovered without first postulating it in the form of a hypothesis'
(1947: 56).

When Thurstone spoke of the explanatory nature of factor
analysis, he had in mind the mature and subtle approach described
above. The researcher's image of the concepts he is going to
measure need be no more precise than is necessary to permit a
meaningful choice of indicators. Any greater degree of formaliza-
tion may divert the researcher's attention from the meaningful interpretation of whatever results come out, to the search for a yes-no
verdict to his favored 'hypothesis.'

Since an exploratory (as distinguished from blind) attitude still
appears to prevail among the users of factor analysis, and if one
agrees that a rigid hypothesis-testing framework is at least
premature, it follows that the several points at which the researcher's intervention, decision, interpretation are needed should be
openly dealt with, rather than underplayed or concealed. At these
points the researcher needs methodological assistance in order to
make the needed decisions in such a way as best to discover and
understand what is in the data, and nothing else. But here is
precisely where he is abandoned by the technical literature. The
classical manuals devote most of their space and attention to a
detailed description of eigenvalue algorithms and similar topics,
whose utility for the average user has been greatly reduced by the
availability of pre-packaged computer programs. The specialized
journals like *Psychometrika* almost exclusively deal with abstruse
mathematical niceties, which are miles away from the grasp and interests of the average social scientist.

Sections 3 and 4 have dealt with the points at which the researcher must or may intervene when the goal of his factor analysis is to
measure one single concept. Sections 6—8 deal with the same
points in the case of more than one concept.

VI

Several aspects of the problem, and the way they are mutually related, should be considered before choosing the indicators to be submitted to a factor analysis:

(a) the extension of the semantic domain we want to chart by singling out and measuring concepts within it;

(b) the level of abstraction of the concepts we want to measure;

(c) the number of indicators we want to factor-analyze;

(d) the a priori strength of the semantic link we are drawing between concepts and indicators;

(e) the degree of textual similarity between the concepts, as we imagine them before the analysis, and their respective indicators;

(f) the degree of association, as measured by a factor loading, sufficient to hold an item a valid indicator of a concept (see Section 3).

Of course, a formal decision is needed only concerning point (c), while it is hardly conceivable about points (a), (b), (d). However, more or less consciously, sooner or later, some decisions are made about all the points, affecting and/or being affected by all others. Awareness of some obvious relations between the aspects might help to make such decisions in a wiser and more consistent way.

If (a) (the domain's semantic extension) is large, and (c) (the number of indicators) is not particularly high, then (b) (the concepts' level of abstraction) will also be high, and (f) (the threshold above which a factor loading is considered proof of a semantic relation between concept and indicator) will tend to be low. It is likely that these relations do not hold if (e) (concept-indicator's textual similarity) is high. This means that, for each concept that we imagine as relevant to the domain, we have chosen a set of indicators so worded (or otherwise arranged) as to maximize the probability of their clustering together. Using the same terms, or the same sentence structure, for indicators of the same set is an obvious means of bringing about this outcome. Another device is exploiting response sets by submitting indicators of the same set close together rather than randomizing them throughout the larger battery. If (e) is kept high, through these or subtler means, (b) can be made as low as desired, no matter how large (a) is, and (f) will probably be high. Factor-analytic results will easily be shown to 'confirm the researcher's hypothesis' about the conceptual structure of the domain. If such cheap confirmation is not sought, then the joint factoring of indicators with high (e) is of little use, and the sets pertaining to each concept should rather be factored separately.

The joint factoring of items that we consider indicators of different concepts makes sense only if there is a sizable possibility that they cluster in a way different from what we have imagined. A high (e) (textual similarity within sets) makes this possibility artificially low. However, it is naturally low if (a) is large and (b) is kept low: a wide semantic domain will not be uniformly covered by low-level concepts, which will probably have high (d) (close semantic link with their indicators). We will know a priori that indicators cluster around their designated concepts, rather than spreading over the semantic space; factoring them together will probably be a useless preliminary.

Factor analysis has a real exploratory function when indicators appear to be spread uniformly enough to leave real uncertainty about their actual clustering. This entails that concepts in turn need be semantically contiguous enough to cover the total semantic space they encompass; it also entails that (d) should not be too high, that (e) should be as low as possible, and that we cannot expect to keep (f) too high.

The plan to cover a large semantic domain (large (a)) with many low-level concepts (low (b), which usually implies high (d)) requires a very large (c). Yet, too many indicators have two consequences: a huge amount of computing (which is no more an insuperable barrier, but still a financial burden), and greater difficulty in disentangling one concept from another.

A plausible conclusion is that in an exploratory (in Thurstone's sense) factor analysis the first key decision is to be made either on the concepts' level of abstraction (b) or on the the extension of the semantic domain (a). Either of these determines the other, and strongly affects the number of indicators (c) and the strength of the concept-indicator link, both a priori (d) and as measured by a factor loading (f). The two polar models are shown in Figure 2. Most actual models are intermediate between the two poles. They either implicitly follow the relational principles portrayed by the graphs or meet with some kind of difficulty.

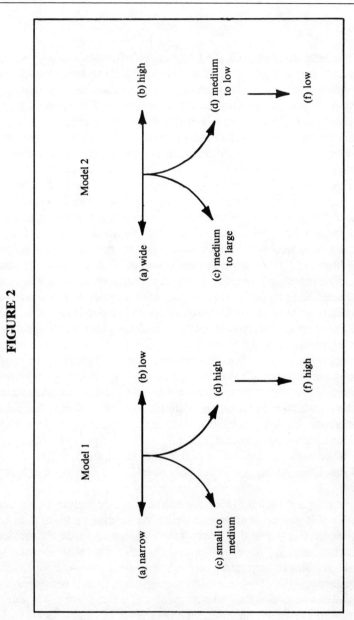

FIGURE 2

VII

The first decision following the choice of indicators concerns the techniques of factoring. The merits of each technique have been widely discussed in the literature. While I am very sympathetic to some arguments behind the alpha technique (Kaiser and Caffrey, 1965), in this discussion it is proper to refer to the most widely used procedure, principal factors. A careful study by Browne (1968) has shown that principal factors give slightly less precise estimates of factor loadings than maximum likelihood estimates (Lawley, 1940; Jöreskog, 1967), but with far less computation. As regards the vexed question of communalities, Harman has remarked (1967: 83) that 'for all-but-very-small sets of variables the resulting factorial solutions are little affected by the particular choice of communalities in the principal diagonal of the correlation matrix,' and Velicer (1972) supports Harman's opinion with empirical evidence.

The subsequent decision is about the number of factors to be extracted and rotated. It is rather common practice to rotate as many factors as are extracted, but this may be avoided if rotation is performed in a separate computer run. Depending on the prevalent view of factor analysis, the decision about how many factors to interpret is not given separate treatment, and this had led to confusion between the criteria that should guide the two steps, which indeed are totally different. When factors are extracted and rotated, the paramount preoccupation should be not to distort the factor structure by underestimating the communalities or in other ways. This occurs (Guilford, 1952: 27) if too few factors are extracted, as for instance, according to some authors (Cattell, 1858; Cattell, 1966; Brislin et al., 1973: 272-80), when Kaiser's criterion is followed.

Kaiser's criterion (1958) states that a factor should be retained only if it gathers a greater share of the general variance than one (standardized) variable contributes. Its critics made the obvious remark that the same cutting point is being used with any number of variables in the matrix. It could be added that here we have an instance of the above mentioned confusion, in that considerations related to the substantive intepretation of a factor are made to impinge on a technical decision. On the other hand, it also seems highly questionable to link the number of factors with the number of cases, as it is done when loadings or residuals are somehow compared with the standard error of a zero correlation coefficient for the given sample size (Harman and Jones, 1966; see also Linn, 1968). The so-called scree test (Cattell, 1966) seems an easy and very defensible solution, as it takes only the patterning of eigenvalues into account, independently from both subjective semantic appraisal and irrelevant considerations of sample size. A comparison of stability in rotational results with a different number of factors is advisable if a very safe solution is sought (Thorndike, 1970).

Whatever criterion is followed in determining how many factors to extract, it has little to do with the number of factors that should be interpreted. This decision must be controlled by non-technical considerations, related to the analyst's understanding and aims. Factors having smaller eigenvalues are often formed by one or two indicators plus error variance gathered from the others. The researcher should mention their existence, but he is perfectly free to drop them with the corresponding indicators, which turn out to be so idiosyncratic. As a general principle, 'there is no single true number of factors for any set of data... the researcher is free to retain or dismiss factors if his knowledge of the domain he is studying and his personal judgement warrant the change' (Brislin et al., 1973: 270).

An almost universally worshipped totem is the proportion of variance explained. It represents both a measure of success of a given factor analysis, and the main reference point in deciding whether an additional factor should be interpreted, i.e. given the status of a concept. Thurstone was particularly keen on exorcizing this taboo:

> the principal purpose of factor analysis is to identify one or more underlying factors... that produce the differential performances or other individual differences, even if the discovery of such a factor or factors should account for only a part of the test variances in any particular test battery... the question of whether these factors account for all, or only a part, of the variances of the particular tests that we happen to use is, then, a secondary matter for the scientific problem. [1947: 179-80]

And he pushed further:

> a factor study may be a major scientific contribution if it reveals only a single clear factor which can be given a fruitful and provocative interpretation, even if all the other factors in the same study prove to be entirely indeterminate. Furthermore, such a factorial result might be of fundamental significance even if, say, only a fourth or a third of the variance of the crucial tests is accounted for by the factor in question. [1947: 340]

While we should extract and rotate as many factors as are technically necessary for a safe solution, we have to interpret only as many as we are able, or deem relevant. Therefore, we need have no other reference point than a matrix of factor loadings, or — better — a series of plots. Each plot represents the projection of all variables from a p-dimensional space on the plane defined by two factors. It gives the same information as the corresponding vectors of loadings, but with far greater efficacy. It was by looking at plots that Thurstone developed his notion of simple structure, which opened the way to rotational procedures and led to a much greater utility of multiple-factor analysis for psychologists and social scientists.

'The simple structure concept was Thurstone's solution to problems posed by the statistical concepts of sample and supply and as such represented a radical departure from statistical thinking' (Butler, 1968: 355). Small wonder statisticians in the 1940s and 1950s were annoyed by the success obtained among researchers (see e.g. Eysenck, 1953: 112) by the concept of simple structure, or — in Kaiser's words — by the 'inflexible devotion to Thurstone's ambiguous, arbitrary, and mathematically unmanageable qualitative rules for his intuitively compelling notion of simple structure' (Kaiser, 1958: 188; also see Carroll, 1953: 23-4).

What is obtained by looking at the plots is an immediate insight into the way indicators cluster in the semantic space. Of course a plot represents that space from one point of view, thus blurring or concealing aspects that are clearly evidenced by other plots. Therefore, pairwise plots of all important (i.e. having sizable eigenvalues) factors need to be inspected before the structure of that space is fully understood. In my view, this is the crucial step in factor analysis, because the respective position of indicators in the space is the only empirical result of the analysis, while the location of reference axes is arbitrary. Locating the reference axes is only a necessary step to obtain representation of the indicator-points, as is true for any system of axes and points. The former may and must be altered in order to improve representation of the latter.

As a consequence, it is at the actual clustering of indicators, as portrayed in the plots, rather than at reference axes that we should look when singling out factors for interpretation, refinement, and further use. The advantage inherent in so doing is clear. Each reference axis is orthogonal to all previously defined axes, since it is extracted from a matrix of residual correlations. This constraint confers a high degree of rigidity to the whole system of axes, which encounters obvious difficulties in fitting a configuration of points freely clustering in a *p*-dimensional space. A technique of orthogonal rotation such as Varimax has been developed in order to improve the fit by maximizing the variance of squared loadings for each factor (Kaiser, 1958), which has the effect of drawing the reference axes as near as possible to the indicator-vectors. As this simplifies the task of interpreting factors represented by orthogonal reference axes in terms of actual indicators, Varimax has been largely adopted by researchers trying to reconcile the search for meaningful factors with a fidelity to the technical requirement of orthogonality.

However, while technical considerations are sovereign in their place, there is no reason why they should intrude into the semantic part of the analysis. Once more this point is effectively made by Thurstone:

> Among statisticians and psychologists there is a rather general belief that if human traits are to be accounted for by any kind of factors, then these factors must be uncorrelated. This belief has its origin in the statistical and mathematical convenience of uncorrelated factors and also in our ignorance of the nature of the underlying structure of mental traits... Height and weight are two useful measures of body size, even though they are correlated. If we should use, instead, two linear combinations of height and weight which are uncorrelated in the general population, we might find such measures more convenient in statistical theory... but they would be awkward to think about. [1947: 139]

The techniques of oblique transformation[8] offer a fallacious alternative, in that they remove the constraint of orthogonality only to replace it by other constraints, less straightforward and less perceived but no less binding. In the various formulas there always is an arbitrary parameter which actually determines the degree of obliqueness in the solution: (b) for Promax (Hendrickson and White, 1964), (c) for Harris and Kaiser's method (1964), (d) for Direct Oblimin (Jennrich and Sampson, 1966), γ for Carroll's Indirect Oblimin (see Harman, 1967: 325-6), and so on. Several authors (Hakstian and Abell, 1974: 442-4; Kim and Mueller, 1978b: 38; Harman, 1967: 334) rank oblique transformation techniques in order of increasing, or decreasing, obliqueness of the produced solution; this amounts to denying the assertion that such techniques provide empirical information on the amount of actual correlation between factors.

The only way to obtain this information is to abandon the idea that the final factors need in any way be connected with the references' axes that are drawn as a result of the first factor analysis of the entire battery of indicators. The drawing of reference axes may be considered as no more than a prerequisite of two-dimensional representation of the vectors' configuration. When inspection of two-dimensional representations has induced a satisfactory understanding of the structure of the semantic space, the function of the reference axes may be considered accomplished, and it is the clustering of indicators as it appears in the various plots that should retain the attention.

In other words, whenever a gathering of indicator-vectors in a certain portion of space is confirmed by the relevant plots, there exists something to be interpreted. The complex of such 'somethings' will usually coincide neither in quantity nor in quality with the complex of references axes as drawn through any single technique of factoring and rotation. Indeed, talking about a 'complex' of reference axes sounds odd, because we have rather a 'system' of reference axes, with necessary interrelations as defined by the particular technique. But we do have a complex, a set — not a system — of concepts.

VIII

The choice of defining factors to be interpreted on the basis of the points' configuration has vast ramifications. While these are obviously intermingled, I will try to examine them separately and in logical order:

(a) The analyst must appeal to his judgment in order to decide what condensation of points is sufficiently tight and consistent across plots to be defined a cluster and call for interpretation.

(b) He also has to resort to his judgment in order to assign each indicator to one cluster, or possibly to none, or to more than one. In dubious cases, he may compare distances from the clusters' centroids, but he will nevertheless have to define such centroids subjectively. This topic will be further discussed under point (c) below.

Points (a) and (b) are likely to disturb most statisticians because 'a scientific methodology cannot be dependent on subjective operations' (Harman, 1967: 293), though there is at least one distinguished statistician who does not share this view of science: 'without protection from a facade of irrelevant computations. . . sociologists will have to use their brains. In my view, science will not suffer' (Hogben, 1957: 21). Harman is consistent with his own views when he states (1967: 250): 'The frame of reference, the configuration of points representing the variables being of lesser significance.'

In fact, an approach based on the configuration of points rather than of reference axes brings subjective intervention more visibly to the surface. However, even in the most classical of factor analyses, indicators are assigned to this or that factor on the basis of their loadings. This means that an arbitrary threshold is stipulated below which a loading on one factor is judged too low. Other more or less arbitrary thresholds prevent factors from being extracted or rotated. Values smaller than 1 are substituted in the main diagonal of the correlation matrix. All these subjective interventions are avoided only by principal component analysis, which pursues an exact mathemathical transformation of the correlation matrix, and is therefore considered rather a different technique than a subspecies of factor analysis.

(c) When a rich battery of indicators is factor-analyzed, it usually happens that one or two clearly defined clusters show up, while a few points appear isolated and many others swarm about in the p-dimensional space, with different plots possibly supplying divergent indications as to their memberships in clusters. Each clearly defined cluster will be submitted to a separate single-factor analysis as described in Sections 3 and 4 above: interpretation of the factor will be refined in view of the loadings' magnitude; possibly some indicators will be dropped; when a satisfactory solution is found, factor scores will be computed for every individual.

Indicators that appear spatially isolated from the rest may be dropped. Small clusters may also be dropped, if good reasons are given for so doing; for example, textual similarity (see Section 6, point (c)) between two or three indicators may produce a cluster that is semantically uninteresting. In the latter instance, however, one indicator from the cluster should be retained for the further steps described below.

All indicators that are neither isolated nor clearly belonging to a cluster should be pooled and resubmitted to factor analysis. The removal of already defined clusters and of isolated indicators might be described as a decompression of the semantic space, which often has the effect, in my experience, of evidencing some additional clusters that were obscured in previous representations. Each cluster defined through re-pooling will of course be submitted to a separate single-factor analysis, like the originally defined clusters.

However, a certain number of indicators is likely to 'remain in the swarm', i.e. to take positions that prevent their safe allocation to a cluster. Depending on their number, spatial configuration, and semantic content, the analyst will then have to choose among several alternatives. He may drop the entire set of left-over indicators, stating that they do not allow any concept to be clearly recognized. If some left-over indicators are not too distant spatially and semantically, he may explore the possibility of considering them as belonging to a single cluster, by trying to find a conceptual interpretation for the supposed underlying factor. Alternatively, he may experiment with different allocations of the remaining indicators to clusters, by permitting overlapping memberships and generally relaxing the requirement that clusters be sharply differentiated in space, provided they are semantically consistent.

Of course a situation like this offers great latitude to a confirmation-oriented analyst (see Section 5), while he will find greater difficulties in artfully bringing about a confirmation of his theses when sharply differentiated clusters have shown up. A researcher who is aware of the exploratory and intersubjective (as distinguished from both objective and subjective) nature of science will openmindedly explore cues contained in the results, but will feel an obligation to remind his readers of the decreasing robustness of factors that needed increasing amounts of manipulation to be defined.

(d) After the discussion of point (c), it should be clear that a researcher may experience greater difficulties in interpreting the results of a factor anlaysis if he sticks to his original idea of the conceptual dimensions relevant to a certain domain. In Sections 3 and 4 it has been remarked that in single-factor analysis the researcher's understanding of the concept he is trying to measure should be refined and articulated, and sometimes substantially revised, in view of the factor loadings' magnitude. Yet, it is hardly conceivable that the factor loadings of the chosen indicators could exhibit patterns that would entail a wholesale rejection of the original concept.

On the contrary, this may happen, and indeed it rather frequently does, in multiple-factor analysis. Suppose the battery has been formed by joining the items composing several 'scales' that have a consolidated conceptual interpretation in the literature. Suppose, further, that the indicators coming from the same scale take widely distant positions in every plot, and unequivocally belong to different clusters. The conclusion that they do not measure the same thing, at least as regards the population being analyzed, is inevitable. Using a metaphor, we might say that the scale has 'blown up.' Two different degrees of negative consequences may be drawn from this finding:

(i) the concept should have been measured using an at least partially different set of indicators. In this case, factor analysis performs the important function of refining and improving the stock of indicators of a given concept, by eliminating those items that have proved invalid, at least within a given context;

(ii) the concept itself is scarcely useful in that particular context, as it does not favor a meaningful categorization and understanding of attitudes, abilities, acts, behaviours. This consequence should be drawn with considerable caution, and perhaps only after repeated failures with different sets of indicators and in different subgroups of a population.

At any rate, the rejected concept should no longer be used in the analysis of the data set of which the factor-analyzed items are a part. It may be retrieved at a different level of abstraction, i.e. as an aspect of a different concept. When some of the supposed indicators of concept A are part of the cluster that is being interpreted as measuring concept B, it is perfectly reasonable that part of the meaning of concept A be incorporated in the meaning of concept B. Only in artificial languages are the borders between concepts and concept watertight.

The possibility of a concept in the researcher's mind finding no empirical counterpart in a cluster of indicators is matched by the possible formation of a cluster having no ready conceptual counterpart in the researcher's mind. Like the operationalist in Blumer's ironic picture (1940: 711), the social scientist has managed to 'isolate some stable content (yielded as a result of some particular mensurative procedure)'; but he should not 'regard the concept as any symbol that refers to this content.' Rather, he will have to exert his sociological imagination in order to find a conceptual dimension capable of plausibily unifying the indicators' semantic contents. Familiarity with the cultural system and/or the modal personality of the subjects to which the data pertain will be a powerful aid in correctly re-constructing the reasons why the subjects react in a similar way to that set of stimuli.

These considerations, emphasizing the role of background knowledge and interpretative ability, show how trivial and misplaced is the protest against 'concepts being formed by the computer.' This is wrong even in the case of blind factor-fishers, who do *not* form concepts if they just reproduce computer printout.

A wiser rema⸳˙ concerns the reversal of the concept-indicator relationship as we are used to thinking of it. If normally we first form a concept and then look for its suitable indicators, what we may have here — so to speak — are indicators in search of a concept. This is indeed a distinguishing feature of factor analysis, in Thurstone's words (1947: 56), 'probably the characteristic of factor analysis that gives it some interest as a general scientific method.' It could be noted, however, that a similar reversal also takes place in secondary data analysis, whenever researcher B gets cues from the data-gathering categories and/or empirical findings or researcher A, and uses some of the latter's variables as indicators of a concept he may have formed by developing these cues.

Everything considered, we form our concepts by drawing from our social and personal fund of experiences. While it would be foolish to think that the analysis of a computer printout can replace this patrimony, it definitely can become a part of it, and therefore give its peculiar, and occasionally decisive (though never exclusive), contribution to concept formation. Factor analysis performs its function 'by focussing concept formation on certain actual replication patterns requiring to be explained' (Cattell, 1965b: 425). Blumer himself admitted that 'what is needed is a working relation between concepts and the facts of experience wherein the former can be checked by the latter, and the latter ordered anew by the former' (1940: 709).

(e) The approach to the definition of factors outlined under points (c) entails that, whenever the membership of a cluster is enumerated, the indicators involved be submitted to a separate factor analysis.[9] Their net contributions to the measurement of the factor are determined through the procedure summarized at the end of Section 4, which is independently applied to each cluster. As a consequence, *there will be no constraint on the relationship between factors,* as is the case with current factoring techniques. The information offered by a correlation coefficient between two separately measured factors is empirical rather than analytical. A matrix of such correlation coefficients may be submitted to a second-order factor analysis in order to explore the possibility of measuring concepts at a higher level of abstraction.

Finding second-order factors, however, is by no means the commonest or most interesting use of factor scores. A factor score is the weighted sum of an individual's scores on a series of indicators. As the weights are many-digit decimals, a vector of factor scores is something formally very close to continuous measurement.[10] Therefore, factor scores are technically ideal variables in data analysis.

NOTES

1. Procustes is not a mispelling for Procrustes; rather, it is the other way around. Procustes was a mythical pre-Roman bandit who fitted his prisoners to the length of his bed by stretching them or cutting them to size. Hurley and Cattell (1962) smartly labelled after him some kind of transformation of a matrix into another (target) matrix; but they added an 'r'. The mispelled name has enjoyed great fortune, and nobody — as far as I know — has checked it.

2. Statisticians have produced a large array of factoring techniques. Their relative merits will be appraised only when relevant to the purpose of the present

paper. When not otherwise specified, implicit reference is made to the technique known as principal factors, with Varimax rotation.

3. Such a decision, and the evidence behind it, may be of great help for further research using this concept. New indicators may be substituted for those that were discarded as invalid, and some of them may prove to be good. This cumulation of experiences should lead to an increasingly better empirical definition of concepts, but it has taken place too rarely in the social sciences.

4. The regression method of estimating factor scores is ascribed to Thomson by some authors (Maxwell, 1968: 279; Saris et al., 1978: 91) and to Thurstone by others (McDonald and Burr, 1967: 382; Tucker, 1971: 427). Less widely used methods of estimation have been proposed by Bartlett (1937), and by Anderson and Rubin (1956). The various methods are compared in Horn (1965), Glass and McGuire (1966), Harris (1967), McDonald and Burr (1967), Tucker (1971), Saris et al. (1978).

5. The classic proponent of this approach is Charles Spearman, who fathered many of the earliest developments of factor analysis in order to demonstrate the presence of a single factor in all tests of intelligence (1904; 1927).

6. This improper use is very common among writers on factor analysis: Guilford (1952: 36), Eysenck (1953: 107), Cattell (1965a: 208), Humphreys (1968: 282), to mention just a few classics.

7. See note 1 above.

8. The expression 'oblique transformation' should be preferred to the current 'oblique rotation', which is contradictory (Gruvaeus, 1970: 493).

9. Similar points have been made in the recent literature. Burt (1973: 159) suggests 'to run separate...factor analyses of indicants of each theoretical concept separately' in order to eliminate 'interpretational confounding.' Smith (1974: 505-6) underlines that 'the use of factor analysis for forming an index' implies 'a separate analysis of just the set of presumed indicators to determine item weighting and evaluate validity.'

10. A strictly continuous measurement of empirical phenomena is obviously not feasible, as it would imply recording figures with an infinite number of digits. Social science variables that are currently called 'continuous' often are very poor approximations to actual continuity, and should rather be called metrical.

REFERENCES

Adelman, I. and C. Taft-Morris (1965) 'A Factor Analysis of the Interrelationship Between Social and Political Variables and Per-Capita Gross National Product,' *Quarterly Journal of Economics,* vol. 79: 555-78.

Ahmavaara, Y. (1954) 'The Mathematical Theory of Factorial Invariance Under Selection,' *Psychometrika,* vol. 19: 27-38.

Ahmavaara, Y. and T. Markkanen (1958) *The Unified Factor Model.* Stockholm: Almqvist & Wiksell.

Alwin, D.F. (1973) 'The Use of Factor Analysis in the Construction of Linear Composites in Social Research,' *Sociological Methodology and Research,* vol. 2: 191-214.

Anderson, T.W. and H. Rubin (1956) 'Statistical Inference in Factor Analysis,' *Proceedings of the 3rd Berkley Symposium on Mathematical Statistics and Probability,* vol. 5: 111-50.

Armstrong, J.S. (1967) 'Derivation of Theory by Means of Factor Analysis, or Tom Swift and His Electric Factor Analysis Machine,' *The American Statistician,* vol. 21: 17-21.

Bartlett, M.S. (1937) 'The Statistical Conception of Mental Factors,' *British Journal of Psychology,* vol. 28: 97-104.

Bentler, P.M. (1977) 'Factor Simplicity Index and Transformations,' *Psychometrika,* vol. 42, no. 2: 277-95.

Blalock, H.M. (1960) *Social Statistics.* New York: McGraw-Hill. Pages refer to the Italian translation of 1970.

Blumer, H. (1940) 'The Problem of the Concept in Social Psychology,' *American Journal of Sociology,* vol. 45: 707-19.

Borgatta, E.F. (1959) 'On Analyzing Correlation Matrices: Some New Emphases,' *Public Opinion Quarterly,* vol. 22: 516-28.

Brislin, R.W., W.J. Lonner, and R.M. Thorndike (1973) *Cross-Cultural Research Methods.* New York: Wiley.

Browne, M.W. (1968) 'A Comparison of Factor-analytic Techniques,' *Pyschometrika,* vol. 33: 267-334.

Burt, C.L. (1940) *The Factors of the Mind: An Introduction to Factor Analysis in Psychology.* London: The University of London Press.

Burt, R.S. (1973) 'Confirmatory Factor Analysis-Analytic Structures and the Theory Construction Process,' *Sociological Methods and Research,* vol. 3: 131-90.

Butler, J.M. (1968) 'Descriptive Factor Analysis,' *Multivariate Behavioral Research,* vol. 3: 355-70.

Carroll, J.B. (1953) 'An Analytic Solution for Approximating Simple Structure in Factor Analysis,' *Psychometrika,* vol. 18: 23-38.

Cattell, R.B. (1957) *Personality and Motivation Structure and Measurement.* Yonkers, N.Y.: World Book.

Cattell, R.B. (1958) 'Extracting the Correct Number of Factors in Factor Analysis,' *Educational and Psychological Measurement,* vol. 18: 791-838.

Cattell, R.B. (1962) 'Personality Assessment, Based Upon Functionally Unitary Personality Traits, Factor Analytically Demonstrated,' pp. 198-219 in Stanley Coppersmith (ed.), *Personality Research.* Copenhagen: Munksgaard.

Cattell, R.B. (1965a) 'Factor Analysis: An Introduction to Essentials. I: The Purpose and Underlying Model,' *Biometrics,* vol. 21: 190-215.

Cattell, R.B. (1965b) 'Factor Analysis: An Introduction to Essentials. II: The Role of Factor Analysis in Research,' *Biometrics,* vol. 21: 405-35.

Cattell, R.B. (1966) 'The Scree Test for the Number of Factors,' *Multivariate Behavioral Research,* vol. 1: 245-76.

Child, D. (1970) *The Essentials of Factor Analysis*. London: Holt, Rinehart & Winston.

Clarke, M. R. B. (1970) 'A Rapidly Convergent Method for Maximum-Likelihood Factor Analysis,' *British Journal of Mathematical and Statistical Psychology*, vol. 23, part 1 : 43-52.

Colley, W. and P. R. Lohnes (1971) *Multivariate Procedures for the Behavioral Sciences*. New York: John Wiley.

Deutscher, I. (1969) 'Looking Backward: Case Studies on the Progress of Methodology in Sociological Research,' *American Sociologist*, vol. 4: 34-42.

Eysenck, H. J. (1953) 'The Logical Basis of Factor Analysis,' *American Psychologist*, vol. 8: 105-14.

Fruchter, B. (1954) *Introduction to Factor Analysis*. Princeton: Van Nostrand.

Fruchter, B. and E. Jennings (1962) 'Factor Analysis,' pp. 238-65 in H. Borko (ed.), *Computer Applications in the Behavioral Sciences*. Englewood Cliffs, NJ: Prentice-Hall.

Glass, G. and T. O. McGuire (1966) 'Abuses of Factor Scores,' *American Educational Research*, vol. 3: 297-304.

Gouldner, A. W. (1957) 'Cosmopolitan and Locals: Towards an Analysis of Latent Social Roles,' *Administrative Science Quarterly*, vol. 2: 444-80.

Green, B. F. (1976) 'On the Factor Score Controversy,' *Psychometrika*, vol. 41: 263-6.

Gregg, P. M. and A. S. Banks (1965) 'Dimensions of Political Systems: Factor Analysis of "A Cross-Polity Survey",' *American Political Science Review*, vol. 59: 602-14.

Gruvaeus, G. T. (1970) 'A General Approach to Procrustes Pattern Rotation,' *Psychometrika*, vol. 35: 493-505.

Guilford, J. P. (1952) 'When Not to Factor Analyze,' *Psychological Bulletin*, vol. 49: 26-37.

Guilford, J. P. (1964) 'Some New Looks at the Nature of the Creative Process,' in N. Frederiksen and H. Gulliksen (eds), *Contributions to Mathematical Psychology*, New York: Holt, Rinehart & Winston.

Guttman, L. A. (1953) 'Image Theory for the Structure of Quantitative Variates,' *Psychometrika*, vol. 18: 277-96.

Guttman, L. A. (1954) 'Some Necessary Conditions for Common-Factor Analysis,' *Psychometrika*, vol. 19: 149-61.

Guttman, L. A. (1955) 'The Determinacy of Factor Score Matrices, with Implications for Five Other Basic Problems of Common Factor Theory,' *British Journal of Statistical Psychology*, vol. 8: 65-81.

Hakstian, A. R. and R. E. Abell (1974) 'A Further Comparison of Oblique Factor Transformation Methods,' *Psychometrika*, vol. 39: 429-44.

Harman, H. H. and W. H. Jones (1966) 'Factor Analysis by Minimizing Residuals (Minres),' *Psychometrika*, vol. 31: 351-68.

Harman, H. H. (1967) *Modern Factor Analysis*. Chicago: University of Chicago Press.

Harris, C. W. (1967) 'On Factors and Factor Scores,' *Psychometrika*, vol. 32: 363-79.

Harris, C. W. and H. F. Kaiser (1964) 'Oblique Factor Analytic Solutions by Orthogonal Transformations,' *Psychometrika*, vol. 29: 347-62.

Hartley, R. (1954) 'Two Kinds of Factor Analysis,' *Psychometrika*, vol. 19: 195-203.

Heerman, E. F. (1964) 'The Geometry of Factorial Indeterminacy,' *Psychometrika*, vol. 29: 371-81.

Hendrickson, A. E. and P. O. White (1964) 'Promax: A Quick Method for Rotation to Oblique Simple Structure,' *British Journal of Statistical Psychology*, vol. 17, part 1: 65-70.

Henrysson, S. (1960) *Applicability of Factor Analysis in Behavioral Sciences: A Methodological Study*. Stockholm: Almqvist & Wiksell.

Hogben, L. T. (1957) *Statistical Theory: the Relationship of Probability, Credibility, and Error*. New York: Norton.

Holzinger, K. J. (1940) 'A Synthetic Approach to Factor Analysis,' *Psychometrika*, vol. 5: 235-50.

Horn, J. L. (1965) 'An Empirical Comparison of Various Methods for Estimating Common Factor Scores,' *Educational and Psychological Measurement*, vol. 25: 313-22.

Humphreys, L. G. (1968) 'Factor Analysis: Psychological Applications,' pp. 281-7 in *International Encyclopedia of the Social Sciences*, vol. 5.

Hurley, J. R. and R. B. Cattell (1962) 'The Procrustes Program: Producing Direct Rotation to Test a Hypothesized Factor Structure,' *Behavioral Science*, vol. 7: 258-62.

Jennrich, R. I. and P. F. Sampson (1966) 'Rotation for Simple Loadings,' *Psychometrika*, vol. 31: 312-23.

Jöreskog, K. G. (1966) 'Testing a Simple Structure Hypothesis in Factor Analysis,' *Psychometrika*, vol. 31: 165-78.

Jöreskog, K. G. (1967) 'Some Contributions to Maximum Likelihood Factor Analysis,' *Psychometrika*, vol. 32: 443-82.

Jöreskog, K. G. (1969) 'A General Approach to Confirmatory Maximum Likelihood Factor Analysis,' *Psychometrika*, vol. 34: 183-202.

Jöreskog, K. G. (1970) 'A General Method for Analysis of Covariance Structures,' *Biometrika*, vol. 57: 239-51.

Jöreskog, K. G. (1971) 'Simultaneous Factor Analysis in Several Populations,' *Psychometrika*, vol. 36: 409-26.

Jöreskog, K. G. and A. S. Goldberger (1972) 'Factor Analysis by Generalized Least Squares,' *Psychometrika*, vol. 37: 243-60.

Jöreskog, K. G. (1978) 'Structural Analysis of Covariance and Correlation Matrices,' *Psychometrika*, vol. 43: 443-77.

Kaiser, H. F. (1958) 'The Varimax Criterion for Analytic Rotation in Factor Analysis,' *Psychometrika*, vol. 23: 187-200.

Kaiser, H. F. and J. Caffrey (1965) 'Alpha Factor Analysis,' *Psychometrika*, vol. 30: 1-14.

Kim, J. O. and C. Mueller (1978a) *Introduction to Factor Analysis: What It Is and How To Do It*. London: Sage, University Papers 07-013.

Kim, J. O. and C. Mueller (1978b) *Factor Analysis. Statistical Methods and Practical Issues*. London: Sage, University Papers 07-014.

Kruskal, W. (1970) 'Statistics, Public Policy, and Data Fallibility,' pp. 48-56 in W. Kurskal (ed.), *Mathematical Sciences and Social Sciences*. Englewood Cliffs, NJ: Prentice-Hall.

Lawley, D. N. (1940) 'The Estimation of Factor Loadings by the Method of Maximum Likelihood,' *Proceedings of the Royal Society of Edinburgh*, vol. 60: 64-82.

Lawley, D. N. (1958) 'Estimation in Factor Analysis Under Various Initial Assumptions,' *British Jounrnal of Statistical Psychology*, vol. 11:1-12.

Lawley, D. N. (1967) 'Some Results in Maximum Likelihood Factor Analysis,' *Proceedings of the Royal Society of Edinburgh*, vol. 67: 256-64.

Levine, M. S. (1977) *Canonical Analysis and Factor Comparison*. London: Sage, University Papers 07-006.

Linn, R. L. (1968) 'A Monte Carlo Approach to the Number of Factors Problem,' *Psychometrika*, vol. 33: 37-71.

Maxwell, A. E. (1968) 'Factor Analysis: Statistical Aspects,' pp. 275-81 in *International Encyclopedia of the Social Sciences*, vol. 5.

McDonald, R. P. and E. J. Burr (1967) 'A Comparison of Four Methods of Constructing Factor Scores', *Psychometrika*, vol. 32: 381-401.

McRae, D. (1970) *Issues and Parties in Legislative Voting. Methods of Statistical Analysis*. New York: Harper & Row.

Morrison, D. F. (1967) *Multivariate Statistical Methods*. New York: McGraw-Hill.

Mulaik, S. A. (1972) *The Foundations of Factor Analysis*. New York: McGraw-Hill.

Please, N. W. (1973) 'Comparison of Factor Loadings in Different Populations,' *British Journal of Mathematical and Statistical Psychology*, vol. 26: 61-89.

Rao, R. C. (1955) 'Estimation and Tests of Significance in Factor Analysis,' *Psychometrika*, vol. 20: 93-111.

Rummel, R. J. (1963) 'Dimensions of Conflict: Behavior Within and Between Nations,' *General Systems Yearbook*, vol. 8:1-50.

Rummel, R. J. (1966a) 'The Dimensionality of Nations Project,' pp. 109-29 in R. L. Merritt and S. Rokkan (eds), *Comparing Nations*. New Haven, Conn.: Yale University Press.

Rummel, R. J. (1966b) 'Dimensions of Conflict: Behavior Within Nations, 1946-1959,' *Journal of Conflict Resolution*, vol. 10: 65-73.

Rummel, R. J. (1967) *Applied Factor Analysis*. Evanston, Ill.: Northwestern University Press.

Russett, B. M. (1966) 'Discovering Voting Groups in the United Nations,' *American Political Science Review*, vol. 60: 327-39.

Saris, W. E., M. De Pijper, and J. Mulder (1978) 'Optimal Procedures for the Estimation of Factor Scores,' *Sociological Methods and Research*, vol. 7: 85-106.

Schönemann, P. H. and M. M. Wang (1972) 'Some New Results on Factor Indeterminacy,' *Psychometrika*, vol. 37: 61-91.

Sewell, W. H. (1941) 'The Development of a Sociometric Scale,' *Sociometry*, vol. 5: 279-97.

Smith, K. W. (1974) 'On Estimating the Reliability of Composite Indexes Through Factor Analysis,' *Sociological Methodology and Research*, vol. 2: 485-510.

Spearman, C. (1904) 'General Intelligence Objectively Determined and Measured,' *American Journal of Psychology*, vol. 15: 201-93.

Spearman, C. (1927) *The Abilities of Man*. London: Macmillan.

Tanter, R. (1966) 'Dimensions of Conflict: Behavior Within and Between Nations, 1958-1960,' *Journal of Conflict Resolution*, vol. 10: 41-64.

Teune, H. (1968) 'Measurement in Comparative Research,' *Comparative Political Studies*, vol. 1: 123-38.

Thorndike, R. M. (1970) 'Method of Extraction, Type of Data, and Adequacy of Solutions in Factor Analysis,' *Dissertation Abstracts* 2970-B.

Thurstone, L. L. (1945) 'The Effects of Selection in Factor Analysis,' *Psychology*, vol. 10: 165-98.

Thurstone, L. L. (1947) *Multiple-Factor Analysis: A Development and Expansion of the Vectors of Mind*. Chicago: University of Chicago Press.

Timasheff, N. S. (1947) 'Definitions in the Social Sciences,' *American Journal of Sociology,*' vol. 53: 201-9.

2

SELECTING A DATA ANALYSIS
MODEL FOR FACTORIAL
ECOLOGY RESEARCH

David J. Jackson
National Institute of Mental Health,
Adelphi, Maryland

Edgar F. Borgatta
City University of New York

INTRODUCTION

Factorial ecology is a particular approach to the investigation of residential differentiation of sub-units of urban areas. The name 'factorial ecology' was first applied to this endeavor in the mid-1960s (Sweetser, 1965a, b). There are three distinctive facets of this research tradition: (1) an overarching interest in the differentiation of residential areas within a metropolitan community: this focus of interest is, of course, not unique to factorial ecologists; (2) the extensive use of official census data and geography as a primary source of variables and units of analysis; (3) the routine application of common factor analysis and component analysis procedures to explore census data.

While there are antecedents, a major stimulus of factorial ecology as a distinct research tradition was the social area analysis

---

Authors' Note. We wish to acknowledge with appreciation Harold F. Goldsmith for his encouragement and thoughtful comments on an earlier version of this paper.

research of Shevky, Williams and Bell (Shevky and Williams, 1949; Shevky and Bell, 1955). For vaguely specified theoretical reasons, these researchers deduced that there were three major dimensions of urban differentiation, i.e. social rank (economic status), urbanization (family status), and segregation (ethnic status). A major portion of research in this realm has been designed and interpreted in terms of these three assumed dimensions. It should be realized that, while factorial ecologists generally take these three postulated dimensions into account, few would claim any allegiance to the related theoretical underpinnings of social area analysis.

The systematic study of urban differentiation has a history of over 50 years. Its roots are the University of Chicago's urban ecologist of the 1920s, its trunk is the Shevky, Williams and Bell research on social areas, and its branches are formed by the present sociologists and geographers pursuing factorial ecology. What is the quality of the fruit of this tree? R. J. Johnston offers this conclusion:

> By far the major finding, common to a majority of studies, irrespective of the location and cultural context of the relevant city, is the generality of Shevky and Bell's three-dimensional model of the bases to residential area differentiation. This must, in part, reflect the data used, the variables collected by census authorities and made available for small areas, and the inference that Shevky and Bell derived their theory concurrently with their experimentation with census data. Yet, within this constraint, there can be no doubt that socioeconomic status, family status/life cycle, and ethnic status are consistently major determinants of where people live, irrespective of the degree of institutional intrusions to the processes of residential location. [1976:217].

Johnston continues his assessment of the findings of factorial ecology by noting a number of post Shevky-Bell developments:

(1) identification of area mobility-related dimensions (McElrath, 1965; Schmid and Tagashira, 1965; and Murdie, 1969);

(2) identification of 'clusters of dimensions' related to the original three dimensions described by Shevky and Bell. Some researchers report finding different segregation dimensions for different ethnic groups (Murdie, 1969) and multiple family status dimensions; Anderson and Bean (1961) isolated a dimension with high loadings of life-style variables (dwelling type, dwelling tenure, marital status) and a family composition dimension (fertility, working females).

Parkes (1973) reports evidence for the division of socioeconomic status dimension into 'wealth' and 'occupational status' for Newcastle, NSW;

(3) identification of dimensions representing specialized areas such as a 'skid row' dimension for Seattle (Schmid and Tagashira, 1965).

This summary of factorial ecology findings by Johnston might lead one to conclude that factorial ecology has arrived at a mature state of development, having resolved most of the basic issues associated with its application and interpretation. This is at best an over-optimistic assessment of the accomplishments of factorial ecology.

A CRITIQUE OF FACTORIAL ECOLOGY

In spite of the relatively long history of factorial ecology, there is no systematic account of the methodological strategy of this research enterprise. There are several introductory discussions of the aims and methodology of factorial ecology. However, they fail to go much beyond a review of alternative techniques for analyzing census tract or related data. Sweetser attempted to spell out a systematic approach to data reduction (Sweetser, 1976) to futher the objectives of factorial ecology. However, he fails to provide any rationale for his approach other than that it seems to work.

Hunter's methodological critique of factorial ecology (1972) is perhaps the most systematic assessment of the methodology of factorial ecology which also offers feasible recommendations. His discussion focuses on the issue of alternative calculation routines which may, and often do, generate somewhat different results. In some ways, his critique and recommendations are a transfer of similar views which the Harrises expressed with respect of psychological research (Harris and Harris, 1971). Hunter states:

Since factorial ecologists typically employ only one initial and one derived solution in their studies, and since it is known that the results one obtains can vary considerably across factor models, it is possible — even likely — that many of the substantive conclusions which have emerged from their research would not have been reached if different factor models had been used. Since most studies have used the same factor model — principal factor, coupled with varimax rotation — it is possible that the consensus which currently exists among factorial ecologists concerning the nature of social differentiation within urban areas is to some degree a function of the fact that they have tended to use the same statistical procedure.... Only those common factors which appear to be method-independent can be identified with any confidence as important underlying variables. [1972: 109]

Any factors that are not method-independent, according to Hunter, should be viewed as possible artifacts of a particular solution. Hunter also recommends 'solving' the factor score problem by calculating the scores for image factors or 'principal component' scores, since in these cases the scores are linear functions of the observed variables.

There are three major flaws in Hunter's critique and recommendations.

(1) He fails to take account of the difference between the common factor model and methods of estimating the parameters of the model. There is only one common factor model, while there are various algorithms for estimating the parameters of the model. While component procedures such as principal components or image analysis (Schönemann and Steiger, 1976; McDonald, 1977; Jöreskog, Klovan and Reyment, 1976) may be modified to be models, in most applications they are tautological data transformations. Contrary to Hunter's assertion, there is now, but to a somewhat less extent than in the early 1970s when Hunter wrote his critique, a general consensus that maximum likelihood procedures under rather general conditions are the best alternative for estimating the parameters of a common factor model. In a similar fashion, Hunter confuses important issues by emphasizing the difference in numerical results of common factor analysis and component procedures rather than focusing on conceptual differences between these two classes of data analysis methods. For example, under certain analytically specified conditions, i.e. when the common factor model fits the data and unique variances are all equal, the results of a common factor analysis and incomplete 'principal component' analysis are 'identical' (Anderson and Rubin, 1956). There is also some evidence that these two major approaches (common factor, image and principal components) under some conditions give very similar results empirically (Velicer, 1972). While it may be important to consider the results of factorial ecology investigations with

alternative methods, it may be a serious mistake to accept the common denominator of different procedures as equally relevant to the objectives of the data analysis. This brings us to our second comment on Hunter's critique.

(2) Hunter fails to take adequate account of the research objectives of factorial ecology. It is of singular importance to have a clear understanding of the research objectives of factorial ecology in considering the relative merits of alternative methods of analysis. It is also important to distinguish between ultimate objectives, which may not admit of a direct approach, and more immediate and tractable objectives.

(3) Our final comment on Hunter's critique is that it is also limited in usefulness, since he fails to take account of the special properties of census tract data. The historical origins of these methods of analysis are closely linked with the psychology of mental abilities and personality. Most of the literature on the use and interpretation of these methods is closely associated with research on individuals. There is a sufficient degree of differences between individual and aggregate data that factorial ecologists need to exercise caution in adopting procedures from psychology. In any event, any assessment of the relative appropriateness of these alternative methods must be informed by the characteristics of census tract data.

In the following pages, we will outline a perspective on the methodology of factorial ecology. The discussion is organized around this question: what are the relative merits of common factor analysis and component procedures for factorial ecology research? We will highlight the central analytic differences between these alternative procedures and evaluate them in terms of the basic objectives of factorial ecology and some important properties of census tract data.

THE RESEARCH OBJECTIVES
OF FACTORIAL ECOLOGY

The generally declared objective of factorial ecology is the investigation of residential urban differentiation. Factor analysis and related procedures have been considered useful tools for pursuing this interest. In the actual application of factor analysis to census data, there are two constrasting, but not necessarily unrelated, research objectives, i.e. 'parsimonious' data reduction, and the measurement of 'fundamental' latent variables which account for residential differentiation. While these objectives are clearly present in most factorial ecology investigations, any explicit strategy for achieving them or specified criteria for assessing progress towards their realization is strikingly absent. At times, one gets the impression that there is an almost naive faith that common factor or component analysis will, as if by magic, produce fundamental latent variables or a scientifically important data reduction.

We argue that a clear distinction should be made between these two goals of data reduction and the discovery and measurement of latent variables. The present task for factorial ecology is definitely beyond any ad hoc data reduction, but still far short of discovering fundamental latent variables. Neither of these objectives is currently appropriate for factorial ecology as a scientific endeavor. A more important task demands our attention. Prior to spelling out the nature of this recommended task, however, we call the reader's attention to our perspective, which we imagine is shared by other factorial ecologists, on the long-range goals of factorial ecology. This perspective is only implicitly present in the factorial ecology literature; however, attempting to make it more explicit will help highlight the rudimentary and tentative character of present ventures in factorial ecology research.

Ultimate Objectives of Factorial Ecology

To a considerable extent, the work of factorial ecologists stems from the assumption that there is a process that generates a structure to residential location. At the present time, we have only nebulous ideas regarding the details of the dynamics of this process. It is hoped that the results of factorial ecology will contribute to the conceptualization and understanding of this process.

This process is thought to operate in terms of:

(1) household units;
(2) properties of household units;
(3) residential units (physical structures, dwelling units);
(4) properties of residential units;

(5) connected sets of residential units (all residential units in an enclosed physical area of a city);

(6) derived (aggregated) properties of residential units in a connected set of residential units;

(7) derived (aggregated) properties of household units in a connected set of residential units;

(8) externals caused by industrial and commercial processes, laws, development policies, etc.

At this time, the first four of these concepts require no further comment. However, 'connected sets of residential units' (5) does. A connected set of residential units is all residential units in a city enclosed (bounded) by a series of connected line segments. All of the residential units in a city comprise a connected set of residential units. The same is true of the residential units within a census tract, a neighborhood, a block group, etc. A set of mutually exclusive and exhaustive connected sets of residential units can be constructed to partition the set of all residential units in a city. The tracting of a city is an example of such a partitioning. Since, at any particular point in time, the number of residential units is finite, there is a finite number of ways to partition a city. It is a basic assumption of factorial ecology that the residential location process is of such a nature that certain connected sets have special properties. If an appropriate partitioning of a city were accessible, the growth and development of the residential structure of cities could become more intelligible. An issue of major importance to the maturing of factorial ecology is the development of principles for identifying optimal partitioning connected sets of residential units. An issue of similar importance is the systematic and explicit integration of partitioning principles with a specification of the residential location process. To date, factorial ecologists have, with little hesitation, accepted official census tracts as viable approximations. This issue has been recognized, but addressed only from an empirical perspective (i.e. the analysis of different levels of census aggregation), rather than from any analytic perspective which ties the partition of a city to the process assumed to generate residential structure.

We now turn to a consideration of derived properties of the residential units and household units within a connected set of residential units. These are derived properties in the sense that they are mathematical functions of the properties of residential or household unit properties. Most census tract characteristics reported by the Census Bureau are examples of derived properties of either residential or household units. For the most part, factorial ecologists have limited themselves to units and derived properties defined and measured by official census-takers. The set of possible derived measures is infinite: how does one sensibly select from this pool of possible aggregated measures? Availability and cost are important considerations, but hardly defensible criteria for designing scientific research. It would be unfair to assert that availability and cost were the only criteria guiding the selection of measures for factorial ecology research; however, they have played an inordinate role. What is needed is a set of rules developed from and supported in terms of the specification of the residential location process. One might consider the trial-and-error strategy of trying different measures and retaining those that 'work.' This is certainly a defensible strategy in the absence of any better alternative. However, to be useful it must be applied in a systematic manner and in the context of explicit pr ciples which guide one's decision as to whether a measure is 'working' or not.

In the above discussion, we made reference to the need for factorial ecology research to be guided by the postulated residential location process. In a sense, these are pointless recommendations in the absence of an explicit and rigorous specification of this process. One of the hoped-for outcomes of factorial ecology research is information that may be used to conceptualize and understand the residential location process. We must make do with what we have. The development of factorial ecology must be an iterative procedure — a procedure in which data are initially collected, analyzed, and interpreted on the basis of vague and implicit principles. In the course of the interpretation of the data more explicit principles are developed which guide subsequent research. The cycle is repeatedly pursued. With each iteration, we strive for more explicit and systematic principles to guide research while at the same time evaluating tentative principles in terms of their ability to order and explain empirical observations.

At the present time, it would be wise systematically to explore census data in terms of the objectives of factorial ecology. While other alternatives should be considered, we are still sufficiently unsure of how to specify optimal units of analysis and variables to recommend, assuming the costs of any other alternative. Consequently, we need an explicit strategy for systematically exploring census data. It may well be that this is a cul de sac and nothing of lasting scientific importance will come of it. Only time and careful research will tell.

Parsimonious Data Reduction

Judged from this ultimate long-range interest of factorial ecology, the parsimonious data reduction approach seems inefficient. There are potentially hundreds of different measures of census tract characteristics available for analysis. It might at first seem desirable to use data reduction techniques to make this set of data more manageable. It has generally been found that a large proportion of the variance of standardized variables describing tracts can be accounted for in terms of a few linear combinations (components) of the observed variables. Is this parsimonious data reduction? It is, of course, a data reduction, but is it parsimonious? From a scientific perspective, there are a number of serious problems with this simplistic data reduction approach.

There is a high degree of arbitrariness in this procedure. It accomplishes a data reduction only for a particular set of variables which describe a particular urban area at a particular point in time. Different initial sets of variables may lead to very different linear composites. These composites may not have the same data reduction properties with respect to the same urban area at different points in time or different urban areas. Consequently, a simplistic data reduction approach provides no conceptual apparatus for a systematic investigation of urban areas across time and cities. However, this is both a theoretical and an empirical question which no one, to our knowledge, has systematically addressed. It is a theoretical issue in that the specification of a set of 'important' properties is basically a theoretical question. It is, at the same time, an empirical issue in that it involves an empirically falsifiable hypothesis.

A parsimonious data reduction implies some criteria by which the parsimony of the data reduction may be evaluated. The ratio of principal components with eigenvalues greater than unity to the total number of principal components is far from being a reasonable criterion, in and of itself, for evaluating the scientific importance of a data reduction. This criterion is too dependent on the particular set of measures selected for analysis.

If data reduction is not the primary objective for factorial ecology, then what is the objective? Is the primary objective of factorial ecology the discovery of fundamental residential differentiation variables?

Discovery of Fundamental Latent Variables

This is be a laudable but poorly timed objective. We can only make guesses, shots in the dark, in attempting this task. The major source of available and standard data for systematically pursuing factorial ecology is official census data. Dynamic processes of residential location and urban development may not be revealed in terms of census tracts. Consequently, it seems unwise to devote time and resources to seeking to discover fundamental causal variables in terms of census tract data. We are not recommending that we forget about this theoretical interest, but only that we place it in proper perspective. At the present time, it is of secondary importance. Considerable investment of resources would be required to make a convincing case that any of the 'factors' currently discussed in the literature are in some meaningful sense 'fundamental', or even that they correspond to real variables.

The Present Task of Factorial Ecology

If the proper objective of factorial ecology is not parsimonious data reduction as such or the development of measures of fundamental latent variables as such, what should it be? The objective we advocate is modest, but far from simple to accomplish. It is in some ways most in keeping with ongoing factorial ecology, with the trappings of fundamental variables and parsimonious data reduction removed. We should seek to discover the conditions under which sets of observed variables display a non-trivial pattern of association (structure) across different cities and the same city at different points in time. In short, the primary task is to discover empirically stable structures of covariation. After a case has been made for the existence of stable, non-trivial patterns of covariation for particular sets of variables under specified conditions, there will be a firmer foundation for substantive-theoretical interpretation of these empiricially stable patterns. From this perspective on factorial ecology, the construction of scores is, at best, a secondary concern. Although often both interesting and in some respects useful, score construction is not presently a fundamental criterion for the design of factorial ecology research.

The Meaning of Stable Covariance Structures

Prior to turning to a brief consideration of some relevant properties of census tract data, we wish to present a few observations on the significance of stable covariance structures. While we have little hesitation in endorsing the scientific importance of establishing the existence of stable structures, the significance of such structures, if they exist, is not a simple issue.

Sets of variables that display a stable pattern of covariation suggest the possibility of a functional unity of the involved variables; i.e., each member of the set tends to change in a similar fashion. The set of variables covary as a unit. There are a number of different alternative explanations of this functional unity. We shall only suggest a few at this time.

Trivially Redundant Content

A set of measures with a stable structure may be empirically and theoretically trivial if the covariation is due to analytic dependencies between the measures. For example, a set of five alternative measures of fertility which share very similar parts in their operational definition may have a stable covariance structure. However, this stability would to some extent be a trivial consequence of the shared parts, not a reflection of some empirical unity of covariation. Some sets of measures used in factorial ecology research are of this type.

Common Causal Antecedents

A stable covariance structure may be due in part to the measures having a common causal antecedent (or set of correlated common causal antecedents).

Developmental Unity

Growth processes may be expressed in terms of stable covariance structures under certain conditions. For example, a set of anatomical and physiological measures on a class of organisms at different stages of maturation may form a stable covariance structure. The consistently high and positive correlations between such measures as height, body weight, length of forearm, etc., may be represented as a size factor. However, this pattern is due to a common developmental process, not some latent causal variable such as size. The size of an organism does not cause body weight or height.

Causal Dependencies Between Variables

A set of variables that are causally interrelated would, under some circumstances, display a stable covariance structure. For example, the stable associations between some housing characteristics and some household characteristics are undoubtedly due to some extent to causal dependencies between these variables. If the type of housing in an area is changed in an appropriate manner, a change in the characteristics of the households that take up residence in the area may be observed.

Unimagined Processes that Generate Stable Covariance Structures

In the early part of this century, Spearman's general factor theory of human abilities seemed to be a compelling causal explanation of the stable patterns of covariance in ability measures. The *g*-factor as a latent causal variable seemed to be the only possible alternative. However, Godfrey Thomson (1919; 1939) was able to construct a 'bond' sampling process model of the functioning of the brain which could also account for the observed stable covariance structures (Maxwell, 1977). It is of interest to note that Thomson's theory in all likelihood would not have been developed in the absence of Spearman's causal model, which called attention to an important general empirical pattern. We should be open to the possibility that some now unknown model of urban change can account for the stable patterns of covariation among census tract variables. The systematic demonstration of the existence of these assumed stable covariance structures may make an important contribution to the development of such a model.

If there are stable patterns of covariation for certain sets of census variables under specified conditions, they may be due to combinations of any and all of the above possibilities. At the present time, we have no sound a priori grounds for explaining stable patterns of covariation between census tract variables. The stable patterns that are presently thought to be present in census tract data may to a significant extent be due to trivial and artifactual reasons.

SPECIAL PROPERTIES OF CENSUS TRACT DATA RELEVANT TO FACTORIAL ECOLOGY

Factorial ecologists have a negligible degree of control over the official census tract data available for systematically pursuing their research objectives. Factorial ecology is secondary analysis; we are committed to making the most of available census tract data. By taking explicit and systematic account of relevant properties of tract data, we will be able to design more informative data analyses. But what are the relevant properties of census tract data that require special attention?

Given that we anticipate the use of common factor or component procedures, we suggest this definition of relevant properties of census tract data. Any property of census tract data that is apt to have a systematic and predictable effect on the results of a component or common factor analysis is a relevant property.

As an example of a relevant data property, consider an example from another area of research. Much of the literature on component and factor analysis is developed within the context of continuous measures and multivariate normal distribution theory. Psychologists were quick to realize that when these methods were extended to data that poorly approximated these assumptions, special allowances needed to be taken. One of the important properties of normally distributed variables is that the mean and variances of these variables are functionally independent. However, if one is analyzing dichotomous variables, i.e. where the only admissible scores are zero or unity, a metric problem arises. In this case, there is a functional dependency between the means and variances of the measures. When phi-coefficients are analyzed using common factor analysis, or principal component analysis, a 'spurious' factor (component) can emerge. This factor (component) will have loading roughly proportional to the means of the dichotomous variables (Lawley, 1944; Maxwell, 1977). If one desires, analytic procedures may be used to remove this factor (component) from the correlation matrix prior to the analysis. A similar set of issues is to be found in the psychological literature on factor analysis, e.g. the power of tests, method factors, response sets, and ipsative items. Similar issues need to be addressed by factorial ecologists in their investigations of census tract data. While there is a rudimentary awareness of these issues, as evidenced by the occasional use of nonlinear transformations of certain variables prior to an analysis, its importance needs to be highlighted and systematically explored. We now call attention to a few of these properties of census tract data.

Census Tracts as Samples

In most factorial ecology studies, there is no apparent sense in which the data under analysis is a sample. There are some instances in which the tracts under analysis do form a sample from a larger universe of census tracts (Borgatta and Hadden, 1976); however, in most cases, the investigator has data on all the tracts of interest. One might consider conceptualizing all the tracts for a particular metropolitan area as a sample of alternative areal units. Tracts, at best, have only an approximate conceptual meaning in terms of the guidelines the Census Bureau recommends to local tract committees. An actual set of tracts might be viewed as a sample from the set of boundaries that alternative tract committees might have generated. It is of some importance to know the extent to which factorial ecology results are contingent upon the definition of areal units. This is an avenue of investigation that has been explored to some extent.

There is also another meaningful sense in which tract observations may be viewed as a sample. This is the reliability perspective. Some tract measures are unreliable owing to sampling procedures in data collection. Tract measures are based on samples of different size. In the 1970 Census there were 5, 15, 20 and 100 percent sampples. In general, we would expect measures based on 5 percent sample to be less reliable than those based on 100 percent sample (the population). Since sample sizes vary by the total population in tracts, the reliability of measures will also vary by the total population of tracts. There are, of course, other sources of non-random measurement error owing to reporting, data processing errors, and allocation procedures. After more careful consideration, it may be decided that this sampling source of unreliability is of minor significance. However, consideration needs to be given to this property, since it is a known source of error.

Unreliability of Tract Variables

In the previous section, it was suggested that methods of data collection by means of samples of households and structures within tracts involves some degree of measurement error. There are also other sources of measurement error that should be considered. Response error is undoubtedly present at the individual household and enumerator level. Missing data owing to suppression may be represented to some degree in terms of unreliability. There are other data processing sources of potential measurement error. While the Census Bureau strives to maintain high standards, their procedures are not designed to maximize reliability for the somewhat nebulous interests of factorial ecology. For example, the weighting of some item counts may also have unanticipated effects on the reliability of tract measures. This question of reliability is related to the communality estimates reported in factorial ecology investigations. It is not unusual to find some measures with communalities approaching unity for correlation matrices. Are the data really this reliable, or are there other neglected properties of tract data that account for these questionably large communalities? At this time we wish only to indicate that this is an issue requiring consideration.

Complex Variables

Most of the variables constructed to represent household and housing unit properties of census tracts are complex variables in the sense of involving more than a single content. The typical factorial ecology variable is a rate with respect to some sub-populations of the tract; e.g., 'low occupation status (males)' is the number of males employed in low status occupations divided by the total number of employed males. This is a ratio of a sub-sub-population to a sub-population of a tract. Sets of variables may be ratios with identical or very similar denominators, e.g. youth dependency ratio and elderly dependency ratio. An examination of the scatter diagram of pairs of these variables will often show a striking departure from a linear association. This type of data raises serious data analysis and interpretation problems. It may lead to 'factors' that reflect the analytic structure of the data, i.e. nonlinear aspects of the association between variables. Factorial ecologists have not been totally insensitive to these issues; witness the occasional use of nonlinear data transformations. We need not only to become more sensitive to these complexities, however, but to investigate systematically their implication for the analysis and interpretation of census tract data.

Consider the following examples. The distribution of occupations of males within tracts may be represented by three variables, X, Y, Z, corresponding to proportions low, moderate and high occupational status. From a traditional factorial ecology perspective, these three variables would be seen as indicators of a social status 'factor.' Notice that within a tract these three variables will sum to unity. A model of these three variables as a linear function of a hypothetical social status variable (f) would have this form:

$$X_1 = a_1 f + e_1$$
$$X_2 = a_2 f + e_2$$
$$X_3 = a_3 f + e_3.$$

Since $X_1 + X_2 + X_3 = 1$, there is a functional dependency between each of the residual terms and the hypothetical variable. From this perspective, the correlation between any pair of the X variables will be due to common dependency on the hypothetical variable, the covariation of the residual variables with the hypothetical variable, and the covariation of the two residual variables. Apart from a set of rigid and unfounded assumptions, the parameters and various covariance terms of this model could not be estimated. Our point is that variables of this sort have functional (definitional) dependencies that need to be explicitly taken into account in the design of factorial ecology research. The strategy of including only linearly independent sets of variables based on a common distribution fails to remove the functional dependency between these variables. We presently have no recommendation on how to handle variables of this type; however, we suspect that a reasonable solution is to be found in a simple transformation that represents the whole distribution rather than any set of nonlinear transformations of parts of the distribution, e.g. probits of X_1 and X_2. Another aspect of the complexity of census tract data is the fact that various parts of measures are based on different samples of households. There is a possibility that these differences may be expressed in terms of 'method factors' (components) when common factor analysis and/or component procedures are used for analysis of tract variables containing parts from different samples.

Undefined Tract Variables

It is possible to construct census tract variables that are undefined for some tracts or have only an arbitrary definition. Any variable that has some sub-population as a base is not defined for any tract for which this sub-population is absent. For example, medium rent of Negro occupied units is not defined for tracts that are 100 percent non-Negro. 'Percent families in poverty' is not defined for tracts that have no family households. This raises the question of just what variables and types of tracts are appropriate for a factorial ecology investigation. This is another issue that requires explicit consideration. Regardless of the field of application, the results of a common factor or component analysis are not simple to interpret in terms of their scientific significance.

ANALYTIC PROPERTIES OF COMMON FACTOR ANALYSIS AND COMPONENT ANALYSIS

In order better to answer the question of whether common factor analysis or component analysis is more appropriate for pursuing the objectives of factorial ecology, we will briefly review the properties of the common factor analysis model and two alternative versions of component analysis, i.e. incomplete standardized principal components and rescaled image analysis. We will then call attention to some analytic relations between the three methods of analysis. In the last section of this paper we will explicitly confront the question of which method is more appropriate for factorical ecology.

Common factor analysis, rescaled image analysis and incomplete standardized principal components analysis are three similar, but distinct, representations of y, a $(p \times 1)$ vector of observable variables, and Σ, the $(p \times p)$ matrix of the covariances of y. In all three cases, y and Σ have the following form:

$$Y = \Lambda \xi + e$$
$$\Sigma = \Lambda \Phi \Lambda^1 + \Psi$$

where ξ is a $(k \times 1)$ vector of primary independent variables; e is a $(p \times 1)$ set of secondary (residual) variables; Λ is a $(p \times k)$ matrix of coefficients; Φ is the $(k \times k)$ matrix of the covariances of ξ; and the covariances of the residuals are represented by the $(p \times p)$ matrix Ψ. These variables (ξ, e), Λ, and covariance matrices, are defined (conceptually and operationally) in distinct ways for each of the three representations. In order to highlight the similarities and differences between these three representations, we impose the following restrictions: (1) our comparisons are stated in terms of a population; (2) the primary independent variables (ξ) are considered to be uncorrelated (orthogonal); (3) all variables (ξ, e, Y) are considered to be centered; i.e, the means of all variables are equal to zero.

The following points summarize some of the most important similarities and differences between these three representations.

Model Versus Transformation

If the number, k, of primary independent variables satisfies Lederman's (1937) inequality,

$$k < (2p + 1 - \sqrt{8p+1})/2$$

then the common factor representation is a falsifiable model. This model states that Ψ is diagonal and positive definite and the covariances between ξ and e are zero. If the y vector has a multivariate normal distribution, maximum likelihood procedures (Lawley and Maxwell, 1963) are available for estimating Λ and Ψ parameters for a given value of k and testing the fit of the estimated model.

Both component representations are special transformations of Σ which may be used to *define* ξ and e as linear transformations of the observed variables (y). In the case of the common factor model,

ξ and e do not have a unique definition in terms of y, Λ and Ψ. This is not to say that they cannot be calculated when the model is true and y, Λ, and Ψ are known (Guttman, 1955). There is an infinite set of alternative values of ξ and e which satisfy all of the requirements of the model. While this does not, in principle, discount the scientific value of the common factor model, it does pose special problems for the interpretation and defense of this model. This is especially true for exploratory common factor analysis. In a similar manner, the fact that ξ and e are linear transformations of y for the two component representations does not automatically elevate them to some superior status. Their application and interpretation also requires rationalization.

Conceptual Definitions of Independent Variables

All three representations of y and Σ have distinct conceptual definitions of ξ and e. These conceptual definitions lead to similar but distinct operational definitions of ξ, e, Λ and Ψ in terms of three different eigen-decompositions of Σ or a rescaling of Σ.

Common Factor Model

The principles of partial correlation are used to define ξ conceptually. The elements of ξ are defined as k orthogonal latent variables such that the partial correlation between any two y variables is zero when the effect of the vector of ξ variables is partialled out; i.e., the primary independent variables in ξ account for all of the covariation between the observed variables. The secondary or residual variables (e) are considered to be sources of variation in the observed variables that are mutually uncorrelated with each other and uncorrelated with the primary independent variables. The residual terms are also considered to represent the aggregation of random errors of measurement of the y variables and other sources of variation specific to a particular y variable. Consequently, the following would not be inconsistent with this interpretation of ξ and e. A k factor model adequately represents y_1 (a $(p_1 \times 1)$ vector of random variables) and y_2 (a $(p_2 \times 1)$ vector of random variables). However, $k+2$ primary variables are required adequately to fit $(y_1^1; y_2^1)$. This could be accounted for in terms of specific sources of variation in y_1 and y_2 variables being additional common sources when the two sets of variables are included in the same analysis.

Incomplete Standardized Principal Components

The first principal component of a set of variables, y, is the linear combination of y with a unit length weight vector and maximum variance; i.e.,

$$x_1 = \lambda_1^1 y$$

such that

$$\lambda_1^1 \lambda_1 = 1$$

and Var (x_1) = maximum. The second principal component has a similar definition but is also required to have zero covariance with the first principal component. Subsequent principal components are defined to have unit length weighting vectors, maximum variance and orthogonal to all previous components. The number of principal components with variance greater than zero is equal to the rank of the observed covariance matrix, Σ, which is typically equal to the number of variables. Consequently, principal components are, by definition, designed to be othogonal-linear combinations of the observed variables with maximum variances. Sometimes principal component analysis is characterized as being distinct from common factor analysis by stating that the principal components are designed to account for the variance of the observed variables, while common factor analysis is oriented toward accounting for the covariance of the observed variables (Lawley and Maxwell, 1963). This is a somewhat misleading statement. The covariances of the observed variables also contribute to the definition of the principal components. It would be more accurate to say that principal components are defined to account for the total variance of the variables while common factors account for just the common variance of the observed variables. Consequently, any random measurement error variance of the observed variables will have some part in defining the principal components. The exact nature of this role, however, is not clearly understood.

The principal components are transformed into an incomplete standardized principal component analysis by rescaling the first k components to have unit variance and defining a 'residual component' as the sum of the $(p-k)$ principal components with the smallest variances. The value of k is typically defined as the number of principal components with variances greater than unity. The motivation for this modification is typically to approximate a common factor model representation. If the observed covariance matrix, Σ, does have a common factor structure and the unique (residual) variances are all equal, there is a sense in which this is a good approximation. The columns of the Λ matrix for the common factor model and the incomplete standardized principal component representations would be proportional. However, other properties would not be the same; e.g., the residuals of the component representation would still be correlated. However, when the unique variances of the common factor model are not equal, there is no analytically determined degree of similarity between the two Λ matrices. There is some empirical evidence that, when k is small relative to p, the two Λ matrices are similar, at least for some sets of data (Harris and Harris, 1971; Velicer, 1972). This is not to say that there is in general no practical difference between the two representations when k is small relative to p.

Image Analysis

Multiple correlation is the key concept used to define image variables. The image (a_j) of an observed variable y_j with respect to a set of variables in the vector y is defined as the least squares estimate of y_j from the remaining variables in y. For example, let

$$y_j = \sum_{i=1}^{p} \beta_{ji} y_i + \varepsilon_j \qquad (\beta_{jj} = 0)$$

be the least square regression equation for predicting y_j from the remaining $(p-1)$ observed variables. The image of y_j is

$$\sum_{i=1}^{p} \beta_{ji} y_i \qquad (\beta_{jj} = 0)$$

and the anti-image is ε_j.

Image analysis was originally proposed by Guttman (1953), but little attention was given to this representation until Harris (1962) identified a number of theoretically interesting relationships between image analysis and canonical common factor analysis. Nevertheless, image analysis has still received little practical application.

Guttman (1953) demonstrated that, if the common factor model were true for k factors for p variables and the ratio of k to p approached zero as the number of variables increased without limit, then the matrix of image covariances (G) approached $\Sigma - \Psi$ (common factor representation). This, of course, implies that in the limit the covariances of the anti-images are equal to the covariances of the corresponding common factor residuals. This is equivalent to stating that image analysis and common factor analysis are equivalent representations of Y and Σ when

$$\lim_{p \to \infty} \frac{k}{p} = 0$$

for indefinitely large p. This result suggests that G would be an appropriate matrix to factor when k is small relative to p. Harris's paper (1962) demonstrates that the eigenvectors of $S^{-\frac{1}{2}} G S^{-\frac{1}{2}}$ and $S^{-\frac{1}{2}} \Sigma S^{-\frac{1}{2}}$ ($S = (\text{diag } \Sigma^{-1})^{-1}$) are equal and their eigenvalues are functionally related. This insight leads to Harris's recommendations to approximate the common factor representation by factoring $S^{-\frac{1}{2}} G S^{-\frac{1}{2}}$, the rescaled image covariance matrix. This procedure is essentially a rescaled incomplete standardized principal component analysis of $S^{-\frac{1}{2}} G S^{-\frac{1}{2}}$. The details of this method are summarized in other sources (Harris, 1962; Kaiser, 1963; Mulaik, 1972).

Independent Variables

While all three representations have a similar linear form, the primary and secondary independent variables (ξ and e) for common factor analysis are inherently hypothetical within the limits of the model. The corresponding ξ and e variables for the two component representations are linear functions of y. In all three cases, the covariances of ξ and e variables are zero; however, the covariance of the residuals (e) is a diagonal matrix by definition for the common factor model and in general non-diagonal for the two-component representation, i.e. correlated residuals.

Metric Invariance

The metric invariance properties of these three representations are of major importance. The common factor model and rescaled image representations are, in a sense, scale-free. If an analysis of y and Σ lead to Λ, an analysis of Dy, where D is a diagonal matrix, and $D\Sigma D$ will lead to $D\Lambda$. The parameters are scale transformations for different scalings of the observed variables. When the metric of the y variables is of no inherent significance, it is highly desirable to have a method of analysis that is not dependent on the scaling of the variables. The parameters of the principal component representation are not 'scale-free.' The general practice of standardizing the variance of all variables to unit variance does not adequately avoid this problem.

Having summarized the major properties of these three representations, we are now prepared to deal with the question of which approach is most appropriate for the interests of factorial ecology.

SELECTING A DATA ANALYSIS METHOD
FOR FACTORIAL ECOLOGY

We now return to our initial question: is common factor, principal components, or image analysis more appropriate for factorial ecology? Recalling that the assumed objective of factorial ecology is the discovery of stable covariance structures across cities and time, none of these methods in terms of their standard conceptualization presented in the previous section would appear to be ideally suited to factorial ecology.

Common factor analysis is conceptualized in terms of assumed latent variables. Incomplete standardized principal components and rescaled image analysis are presented as approximations of common factor analysis, which supposedly avoid some problems associated with the common factor model (the number of factors (communality estimation) and indeterminant factor scores). We would argue that these advantages are more apparent than real. For example, Kaiser argues that k (the number of eigenvalues of $S^{-\frac{1}{2}}GS^{-\frac{1}{2}}$ greater than unity) should be retained for rotation and interpretation. He presents four different arguments for this recommendation (Kaiser, 1963). Each argument presupposes that the common factor model is true. If we reject the common factor model's latent variable conceptualization, we have no grounds for employing any of these procedures unless we are prepared to offer some appropriate alternative interpretation of these procedures. We will strive to do this in the following discussion.

Any covariance matrix of more than a few variables presents a major challenge to a researcher attempting to identify possible important patterns of association. This challenge is greatly magnified when the task requires one to establish that there are similar patterns of association present in multiple covariance matrices. Consequently, it is no surprise that factor ecologists have adopted methods such as common factor or component analysis for analyzing covariance matrices. These methods may be employed effectively without any appeal to latent variables or fundamental variables that supposedly account for observed covariance. The major contribution of these procedures is that they facilitate the recognition of patterns of association that may not be easy to detect or describe in a   w covariance matrix. In some way, these procedures are analogous to mathematical notation. Many mathematical relations that would be extremely complex to represent and difficult to demonstrate using scalar algebra notation become rather simple when matrix notation and manipulation rules are employed. Definite patterns of association that might not be recognized in a covariance matrix may become obvious when appropriate transformations are applied to the covariance matrices.

If we were to find that there were trivially small differences between the matrices of covariances between a set of y variables for two cities, this would be sufficient evidence that there was a stable covariance structure between these variables for this set of cities. We would not even be required to describe the nature of the patterns of association. However, if we find that there are striking differences between the covariance matrices, this would not discount the hypothesis that there is some unrecognized stable pattern(s) present. A transformation of the covariance matrices to correlation matrices might be sufficient to disclose the stable pattern(s). This simple metric transformation may also prove to be inadequate for accenting stable patterns of association across cities. Failing to find evidence for stable covariance structures at the covariance or the correlation level using simple procedures, principal component analysis might be used to define reference axes for representing the covariance structures for the purpose of describing patterns of association stable acoross cities. If

$$\Sigma = PBP$$

is a principal component type decomposition of Σ,

$$C = (\text{diag } \Sigma)^{-\frac{1}{2}} PB^{\frac{1}{2}}$$

could be interpreted as a matrix of correlations between the observed variables and the p orthogonal reference axes. A failure to find similar C matrices based on the observed covariance matrices for two different cities might lead to a consideration of a similar analysis based on the observed correlation matrices. Notice that in this analysis principal component-type procedures are used to define orthogonal reference axes which may disclose stable patterns of covariation. We need make no appeal to the principal components of the observed variables as some sort of fundamental variables. However, in later stages of the development of factorial ecology we may wish to calculate components based on this type of analysis. The reader's attention is also called to the fact that we have not used any arbitrary rule for discarding those reference axes associated with principal components with small variances. If our purpose were to construct a relatively small set of composites to approximate the information in the initial set of p variables, some sort of cut-off rule would be useful. However, this is not our present purpose. If we were to find stable patterns across cities for reference axes associated with small eigenvalues, would we want to ignore them just because the variance of the associated component is small? We think not. However, it would be a welcomed reduction in complexity if we did have some justification for reducing the dimensionality of the observed covariance matrix. Setting this issue aside for the moment, we return to our search for stable covariance structures.

With respect to our declared purpose, the reference axes associated with the principal components definition is rather arbitrary. It may or may not lead to the recognition of similar patterns of association. Any rotation, orthogonal or oblique, that leads to the recognition of patterns of association that are stable across cities would be appropriate. 'Simple structure' criteria as expressed in Varimax or Promax rotation procedures could be employed. Their use need not be based on any belief that these rotations lead to substantively important structures that indicate the presence of 'fundamental' latent variables. If a set of variables is composed of subsets of variables which highly correlate within a subset and have a smaller degree of association with variables in other subsets, simple structure rotation procedures will aid in the recognition and description of such patterns. Blind faith, however, should not be placed in these mechanical procedures to automatically point out stable patterns of covariation.

While we feel that the analysis suggested in the last few paragraphs is reasonably appropriate for the objectives of factorial ecology, it does have a number of undesirable properties. These procedures are dependent upon the scaling of the observed variables. This is an especially serious limitation when our major objective is the comparison of structures across different cities for which the variances may be radically different. Another drawback is that the above analysis of p variables requires the examination of p reference axes. It would be desirable to have a rank reduction and scale-free procedure that was consistent with our research objectives and the known properties of census tract data. This would suggest a reconsideration of image analysis or common factor analysis since both are in a sense 'scale-free' and rank reduction procedures. Since rescaled image analysis as presented by Harris and Kaiser is inherently an approximation to common factor analysis, we would require an independent justification of this procedure for our purposes or an appropriate rationale for common factor analysis.

Consider the following representation of y, a $(p \times 1)$ vector of centered observed variables

$$y = c + s + r$$

The $(p \times 1)$ vector, r, represents the aggregation of all sources of random disturbances on the elements of y. When the number of census tracts is sufficiently large, it would not be unreasonable to consider the elements of r to be uncorrelated and approximately normally distributed. This interpretation would not be appropriate if Σ, the $(p \times p)$ covariance matrix, were not positive definite.

The $(p \times 1)$ vector s represents a part of the y that contributes to the variance of observed variables, but not the covariances of observed variables. The remaining part, c, is a $(p \times 1)$ vector of common parts, i.e. parts of observed variables which covary. The s

and r vectors are by definition uncorrelated with each other and the vector of common parts. In the following discussion we will combine s and r as a residual vector. While the distinction between the specific and error parts will have no consequences for the following development, the concept of a vector of specific parts is useful for accounting for some observed phenomena. This representation leads to the following covariance structure of y.

$$\Sigma = \Omega + \Psi$$

Ψ is a diagonal matrix of residual covariances while Ω is a matrix of the covariances of common parts. The residual covariance matrix, Ψ, is of rank p by definition. The rank of Ω is k. The technical literature on factor analysis enables us to state that

$$\alpha < k$$

where α is Guttman's 'best' lower bound on the number of common factors (the number of positive eigenvalues of $R - S$, where $S = [\text{diag } (\Sigma^{-1})]^{-1}$. Maximum likelihood procedures would be optimal for estimating Ψ for given values of k. These procedures, as Browne (1967) and Howe (1955) have demonstrated, may be justified apart from any distribution assumptions. If k is permitted to be sufficiently large, a Ψ can always be found which makes Ω of rank k. Since our primary interest is to find a minimum number of reference axes for representing the covariance structure of our observed variables which is consistent with our provision for unique and random error variance in the observed variables, the minimum k consistent with $\Sigma - \Omega$, being a good approximation of a diagonal matrix will satisfy our purposes. The maximum likelihood definition of Λ, where $\Omega = \Lambda\Lambda^1$, would be used to define the correlations between the p observed variables and the k reference axes. Simple structure rotations, orthogonal or oblique, could be used to help identify patterns of covariation.

The major advantages of using maximum likelihood procedures for defining Λ and Ψ relative to a rescaled image analysis or an incomplete standardized principal component analysis would be that these ML common factor analysis procedures assure us that $\Sigma - \Omega$ will be optimally close to a diagonal matrix for a given value of k. In any event, $\Sigma - \Omega$ should be examined for residual patterns of association when any of these three methods are used to define Λ.

While we are inclined to recommend the use of *ML* common factor analysis procedures for defining our reference axes, any of these procedures could be effectively used. Any one of them that contributes to the establishment of evidence that a particular pattern of covariation is stable across cities and time would further the objectives of factorial ecology. The crucial issue is not to locate 'factors,' that are common across different methods of 'factor analysis,' as Hunter has argued, but to establish the presence of stable patterns of covariation across cities and time. Any technique that helps to achieve this object is its own best defense.

SUMMARY AND CONCLUSION

In the previous sections of this paper we have argued that there is a need for a coherent and systematic specification of the methodology of factorial ecology. Three bench-marks are suggested for guiding the development of this specification: (1) the specification should be consistent with the fundamental long-range and present objectives of factorial ecology; (2) it should take account of special properties of census tract data which complicate their analysis and interpretation; (3) this specification should assess the technical properties and application of methods of analysis in terms of the basic objectives of factorial ecology and relevant properties of census tract data.

We assert that the fundamental present objective of factorial ecology is the discovery of stable patterns of covariation between census tract variables across cities and time. Once we have established in a convening manner the existence of stable patterns of association, our task is to interpret these patterns. Several alternatives (type of interpretations) are suggested.

We outline a few of the relevant properties of census tract data that need to be considered for their effect on the selection of measures, methods of analysis, and interpretation. After reviewing some of the relevant properties of incomplete standardized principal components, rescaled image and common factor analysis, we conclude that the prevalent latent variable assumptions of these procedures are not in keeping with our knowledge of tract variables and basic objectives. Consequently, we outline an alternative rationale for the use of these procedures in factorial ecology research.

While this discussion is only an initial attempt to specify and interpret the methodology of factorial ecology, we are confident that its general direction of development is sound. We anticipate providing a more detailed specification of the methodology of factorial ecology in the future.

REFERENCES

Anderson, T. W. and L. L. Bean (1961) 'The Shevky-Bell Social Areas: Confirmation of Results and a Reinterpretation,' *Social Forces*, vol. 40: 119-24.

Anderson, T. W. and H. Rubin (1956) 'Statistical Inference in Factor Analysis,' pp. 111-50 in *Proceedings of the Third Berkeley Symposium on Mathematical Statistics and Probability* (J. Neyman, ed), vol. V. Berkeley: University of California Press.

Bargmann, R. E. (1957) *A Study of Independence and Dependence in Multivariate Normal Analysis*. Chapel Hill, NC: University of North Carolina, Institute of Statistics (Mimeograph series no. 186).

Borgatta, E. F., and J. K. Hadden (1976) 'The Analysis of Social Areas: A Critical Review and Some Empirical Data,' in *The Outlook Tower*, J. V. Ferreira and S. S. Jha (eds). Bombay: Populat Prakashan Privat Limited.

Browne, 'M. W. (1967) 'Fitting the Factor Analysis Model,' *Research Bulletin* 67-2. Princeton, NJ: Educational Testing Services.

Browne, M. W. (1968) 'A Comparison of Factor Analytic Techniques,' *Psychometrika*, vol. 33: 267-334.

Guttman, L. (1953) 'Image Theory for the Structure of Quantitative Variates,' *Psychometrika*, vol. 18: 227-96.

Guttman, L. (1954) 'Some Necessary Conditions for Common Factor Analysis,' *Psychometrika*, vol. 19: 149-61.

Guttman, L. (1955) 'The Determinacy of Factor Score Matrices with Implications for Five Other Basic Problems of Common-factor Theory,' *British Journal of Statistical Psychology*, vol. 8: 65-81.

Howe, H. G. (1955) 'Some Contributions to Factor Analysis,' Report no. ORNL-1919, Oak Ridge, Tenn.: Oak Ridge National Laboratory.

Harris, C. W. (1962) 'Some Rao-Guttman Relationships,' *Psychometrika*, vol. 27: 247-63.

Harris, C. W. (1964) 'Some Recent Developments in Factor Analysis,' *Educational and Psychological Measurement*, vol. 24: 193-206.

Harris, C. W. (1967) 'On Factors and Factor Scores,' *Psychometrika*, vol. 32: 363-79.

Harris, M. L. and C. W. Harris (1971) 'A Factor Analytic Interpretation Strategy,' *Educational and Psychological Measurement*, vol. 31: 589-606.

Hunter, A. A. (1972) 'Factorial Ecology: A Critique and Some Suggestions,' *Demography*, vol. 9: 107-18.

Johnston, R. J. (1976) 'Residential Area Characteristics: Research Methods for Identifying Urban Sub-areas Social Area Analysis and Factorial Ecology,' pp. 193-237 in *Spatial Processes and Form*, vol. 1, D. T. Herbert and R. J. Johnston (eds). New York: John Wiley.

Jöreskog, K. G. (1963) *Statistical Estimation in Factor Analysis*. Stockholm: Almqvist & Wiksell.

Jöreskog, K. G. (1966) 'Some Contributions to Maximum Likelihood Factor Analysis,' *Research Bulletin*, 66-41. Princeton, NJ: Educational Testing Services.

Jöreskog, K. G. (1967) 'Some Contributions to Maximum Likelihood Factor Analysis,' *Psychometrika*, vol. 32: 443-82.

Jöreskog, K. G., J. E. Kolvan and R. A. Reyment (1976) *Geological Factor Analysis*. New York: Elsevier.

Kaiser, H. F. (1963) 'Image Analysis,' in *Problems in Measuring Change*. C. W. Harris (ed.). Madison: University of Wisconsin Press.

Lawley, D. N. (1944) 'The Factor Analysis of Multiple Item Tests,' *Proceedings of the Royal Society Edinburgh*, vol. 62: 74-82.

Lawley, D. N. and A. E. Maxwell (1963) *Factor Analysis as a Statistical Method*. London: Butterworths.

Lederman, W. (1937) 'On the Rank of the Reduced Correlational Matrix in Multiple Factor Analysis,' *Psychometrika*, vol. 2: 85-93.

McDonald, Roderick P. (1977) 'The Indeterminacy of Components and the Definition of Common Factors,' *British Journal of Mathematical and Statistical Psychology*, vol. 30: 165-76.

McElrath, D. S. (1965) 'Urban Differentiation: Problems and Prospects,' *Law and Contemporary Problems*, vol. 30: 103-110.

Maxwell, A. E. (1977) *Multivariate Analysis in Behavioral Research*. New York: Halsted Press.

Mulaik, Stanley A. (1972) *The Foundations of Factor Analysis*. New York: McGraw-Hill.

Murdie, R. A. (1969) *Factorial Ecology of Metropolitan Toronto, 1951-1961*, Research Paper No. 116, Department of Geography. Chicago: University of Chicago Press.

Parkes, D. N. (1973) 'Formal Factors in the Social Geography of an Australian Industrial City,' *Australian Geographical Studies*, vol. 11: 171-200.

Rao, C. R. (1955) 'Estimation and Tests of Significance in Factor Analysis,' *Psychometrika*, vol. 20: 93-111.

Rozeboom, W. W. (1965) 'Linear Correlations Between Sets of Variables,' *Psychometrika*, vol. 30: 57-71.

Schmid, C. F. and K. Tagashira (1965) 'Ecological and Demographic Indices: A Methodological Analysis,' *Demography*, vol. 1: 194-211.

Schönemann, P. H. (1971) 'The Minimum Average Correlation Between Equivalent Sets of Uncorrelated Factors,' *Psychometrika*, vo. 36, 21-30.

Schönemann, P. H. and J. H. Steiger (1976) 'Regression Component Analysis,' *British Journal of Mathematical and Statistical Psychology*, vol. 29: 175-89.

Schönemann, P. H. and M. Wang (1972) 'Some New Results on Factor Indeterminacy,' *Psychometrika*, vol. 37: 61-91.

Shevky, E. and W. Bell (1955) *Social Area Analysis: Illustrative Application and Computational Procedure*. Stanford: Stanford University Press.

Shevky, E. and M Williams (1949) *The Social Areas of Los Angeles*. Los Angeles: University of California Press.

Sweetser, F. L. (1965a) 'Factorial Ecology: Helsinki, 1960,' *Demography*, vol. 2: 372-85.

Sweetser, F. L. (1965b) 'Factor Structure and Ecological Structure in Helsinki and Boston,' *Acta Sociologica*, vol. 8: 205-25.

Sweetser, F. L. (1969) 'Ecological Factors in Metropolitan Zones and Sectors,' pp. 413-56 in *Quantitative Ecological Analysis in the Social Sciences*. M. Dogan and S. Rokkan (eds). Cambridge, Mass.: MIT Press.

Sweetser, Frank L. (1976) 'Towards a General Typology of Australian Urban Neighborhoods,' (A working paper). Canberra, Australia.

Thomson, C. H. (1919) 'On the Cause of Hierarchical Order among Correlation Coefficients,' *Proceedings of the Royal Society*, A, vol. 95: 400-8.

Thomson, Godfrey H. (1939) *The Factorial Analysis of Human Ability*. Houghton-Mifflin Company, Great Britain.

Tucker, L. R. (1964) 'Recovery of Factors from Simulated Data,' paper read at a joint meeting of the Psychonomic Society and the Psychometric Society, Niagara Falls, Ontario, October 1964.

Velicer, Wayne F. (1972) 'An Empirical Comparison of Factor Analysis, Image Analysis, and Principal Component Analysis,' PhD dissertation, Purdue University, Lafayette, Indiana.

Wirth, L. (1938) 'Urbanism as a Way of Life,' *American Journal of Sociology*, vol. 44: 1-24.

3

A NON-METRIC MULTI-DIMENSIONAL SCALING OF URBAN SERVICES AND URBAN POPULATIONS

William G. Howard
Central Texas Health Systems Agency,
Austin, Texas

David R. Heise
University of North Carolina

Factor analytic studies repeatedly have identified four key dimensions among the demographic and socioeconomic characteristics of urban populations: size, wealth, age, and racial composition (see reviews by Berry, 1972; Hadden and Borgatta, 1965; Howard, 1973). Theoretical fruitfulness of such typological work depends on relations between these dimensions and other substantive distinct variations in cities. If such relations exist, then the dimensions constitute a system of 'natural classification' for cities in the sense that 'the determining characteristics are associated, universally or in a high percentage of all cases, with other characteristics, of which they are logically independent' (Hempel, 1952:53).

This paper explores relations between the character of a city's

Authors' Note. Data were coded with funds from N. S. F. Grant No. 1-0-160-3296-XA056; we were grateful to Gordon DeFriese for abetting the coding project. Extensive computer programming aid was received from the staff of the Institute for Social Science Research at the University of North Carolina Collection, and William Powell, Curator of the University's North Carolina Collection, provided helpful information concerning individual cities.

population and the kinds of commercial and professional services offered in the city. The concern here is to develop an independent typology of service structures and then to see whether its dimensions relate to demographic dimensions of cities. Thereby we address the question of the 'naturalness' of city classifications based on population characteristics; but we also provide a coherent description of systematic variations in service structures which may be of interest to urban sociologists and urban planners.

POPULATIONS AND SERVICES

A relationship between urban population types and city services is expected because particular types of persons may be inclined to perform certain activities; certain activities may be performed predominately by restricted types of persons; and the performance of one activity may depend on performances of other activities. These ideas, elaborated below, guide our analytic procedures and our interpretations of results.

One might imagine a 'person space', in which the distance between two individuals is defined in terms of the number of daily activities that they share. Persons with similar statuses and roles would cluster near one another in such a space, and the coordinates of the space might define dimensions of contrasts in actor types. As a beginning supposition, we presume that an urban individual's activities can be indexed to a large degree in terms of habitat — especially whether town or city — and by the person's socioeconomic status, age, and race. Since the populations of cities have been found to vary in terms of similar variables, it might be inferred that variations exist in daily activities in different cities.

Most activities require supporting activities from others, and urbanites in particular exist in a web of interdependencies such that they cannot attend to bodily needs, relax, or work without services and goods provided by others. Moreover, supporting actions by others have two special features in cities: many are offered as commercial or professional services; and there is typically a substantial division of labor, with specialized organizations servicing and provisioning classes of activities (e.g., grocers support everyday maintenance of bodies and households; cinemas support entertainment activities). Consequently, the activities in cities should be reflected to a large degree in the presence of commercial and professional service institutions; and the demands of different kinds of populations engaging in different classes of activities should generate qualitative variations in the types of service institutions that are present in different cities.

A city's institutions are determined not only by the internal demands of the population but also by the city's specialized contributions to a larger inter-urban network of dependencies, and most cities contain one or more industries with extra-community clients. Because such industries are not dependent solely on the demands of the city's own population, they 'distort' the service structure, making the incidence of some organization disproportionately large, relative to what would be expected theoretically on the basis of demands in the local population. However, such industries generate their own relations between population and service structure because the peculiar activities involved in an industry ordinarily must be performed by special classes of persons. Industries sometimes are located because of an available labor force (e.g. factories in the American South); or the required labor force may be recruited from afar (as in educational centers); or it may be generated by more or less stable socialization processes (as happens to some degree in cities historically involved with extraction, heavy industry, or tourism). The net effect in any case is that specialized industries may generate unusual concentrations of certain person types in the local population. Thus here again — but for a different reason — a correlation is to be expected between the composition of a city's population and the organizations in the city.

By the above reasoning, each point in the 'person space' should be associated with a set of unique services demanded by such people and with a set of industries that employ such people, so the existence of the person space implies a corresponding service space. However, service organizations also develop interdependencies among themselves, and this consideration leads to supplementary expectations of structure among services. To take a single example, a city specializing in tourism should have a large incidence of hotels, restaurants, and entertainments, which in turn may generate demand for commercial laundries, food wholesalers, and talent agencies (to name just a few possibilities). Thus, service environments are structured not merely by their relations to populations having different compositions but also internally to some degree by the elaboration of interdependent service organizations. Consequently, some of the organizations in a city may have little direct relation to the composition of a population in terms of servicing that population or employing a significant portion of it, but the presence of such organizations still should be correlated with population type because they support the key services or industries that *are* linked to population composition.

PROCEDURES

The logic of defining the structure of service environments is as follows. A sample of cities is examined, and, taking one pair at a time, we ask the degree to which the two are similar in the sense of providing the same services, or different in the sense of providing distinct services. By quantifying the similarity assessment, we should be able to rank pairs of cities in terms of their relative degrees of similarity. And theoretically, this information on relative similarity can be used to define a space wherein each city is a point and dissimilarities among cities are represented as distances among the points. Points at opposite ends of such a space indicate contrasting cities, which is to say, contrasting service environments. Hopefully these contrasts can be characterized in some sensible way to define the dimensions of the space.

This is precisely the kind of problem that is the focus of nonmetric multidimensional scaling, and the scaling approach is adopted here using program POLYCON (Young, 1972; 1973). The POLYCON program is especially valuable for present purposes because, besides scaling the service environments, it also provides a means for assessing the correspondence between the service-environment structure and the urban population dimensions, using the latter as 'targets' for rotating the service-environment coordinates.

This research builds on a pilot study (Howard, 1973) of 13 North Carolina cities. The reader is referred to the report of that work for a more detailed review of the city classification literature and also for details concerning coding decisions employed during data collection.

SAMPLE OF CITIES

In 1970 North Carolina had 38 cities with populations of 10,000 or more, and classified telephone directories were available for 35 of these. These 35 cities constitute the sample of service-environments used in this study. Because of North Carolina's heterogeneity, this sample includes numerous agricultural and industrial towns, two small seaports, a mountain city, three military bases, a university complex, and several governmental centers. Thus, while it is neither a random nor a systematic sample from the universe of cities, this set can be presumed to tap much of the diversity present in small cities (the largest city had a population of 241,215 in 1970 — the date for all further demographic characterizations).

Some of the cities are geographic neighbors, raising the question of whether they are distinct environments except in a formal administrative sense. They are treated as distinct entities here under the assumption that functional specialization may occur in neighboring towns, thereby creating distinct service environments.

DATA SOURCE

Services offered in a city were determined from the classified section (the 'yellow pages') of the city's telephone directory. The directory classifications were used as the basis for grouping organizations in terms of the similarity of their services, and the prevalence of a given kind of service within the city was indexed by counting the number of distinct dialings within each classification. The Southern Bell manual (1971) lists 7,615 distinct classifications, and local additions provided another 333, giving a total 7,948 classifications that were used as the coding categories in this study. Thus the basic data matrix was 35 cities by 7,948 services with number-of-listed-dialings entered in each cell. Of course, a majority of the entries in the matrix were zero since most cities offer only a portion of the total range of services, as must be the case if they are distinct service environments.

The service data were coded from the 1970 edition of the telephone directory for each city, except that the 1969 edition was used for Sanford and the 1971 edition was used for Albermarle, Greenville, Roanoke Rapids, Statesville, and Thomasville.

Substantial economic motivations ensure that the listings of commercial services are exhaustive within each city. The adequacy of listings in some professional areas without traditions of advertising (e.g. medicine, religion, law, education) depends on the thoroughness of the local telephone company bureaucracy in assigning classifications. Our impression is that the presence/ absence of such services is adequately represented, though the number of classified dialings may underestimate the relative prevalences of these activities. The major limitations of the data set are that it does not index illicit activities, occasional services (e.g. concerts or street vending), or services that are offered on a non-public basis (e.g. homemaking, certain entertainments, and some counseling and charitable services that occur within larger organizations).

To our knowledge, the categories used in the yellow pages have not been designed so much as evolved, and thereby one can question their adequacy in grouping similar services. One consideration here is the sheer number: with thousands of categories available, rather fine distinctions can be made so that discrepant services need not be grouped together. These categories are applied by experienced personnel in telephone company offices and are subject to annual correction by the clients themselves, so the system is probably used with a fair degree of discrimination and accuracy. Moreover, the system is basically successful, being in wide use by the general public, suggesting that it does in fact contain information about service groups. On the other hand, the use of some highly specialized categories may be erratic, especially in smaller towns where an organization may be one of a kind. And the system surely does not reflect the full range of services offered in multi-faceted organizations like department stores or universities, especially when the organization itself does not request cross-listing in multiple categories. Finally, there are some local variations in the form of classifications (e.g. 'Druggist' versus 'Pharmacies'), so that to some degree dissimilarities in listings may represent differences in culture rather than differences in services.

CODING

The following procedures and conventions were followed in coding the materials. First, the service environments of the various cities were defined by all exchanges that were available as local service. Long-distance operators and the exchange maps in the front of the directories were consulted to identify local exchanges. Then the basic procedure was to go through the yellow pages from start to finish, listing by code number the classifications that were present and the number of dialings listed in each category. Ambiguities in the interpretation of multiple listings led to the adoption of the following special coding conventions in an attempt to draw out the basic underlying service structure and to eliminate overlapping listings by the more successful or aggressive businesses, i.e. businesses that paid to have more listings than the one free listing given to them by their local telephone company. When the same firm was listed as having a number of different locations each with a different dialing, the several dialings were counted separately. When the same firm listed several different departments in the same location but with different dialings, only one of the dialings was counted. When a single switchboard dialing was given for several different professionals, e.g. physicians, the different professionals were counted as different dialings. When several dialings were given for a single professional, a single dialing was counted.

The physical location of many of the business listings is outside the city limits of the city proper and even within the boundaries of smaller satellite cities in some instances. Therefore, what is under consideration here is some notion of a 'service community' as defined by the boundaries of the local telephone service. Since the goods and services of the major cities involved are routinely offered to the populations of the various satellite cities through local telephone service and vice versa, the demographic indicators used as target variables relate to county data although the text refers to 'cities.'

SIMILARITY COEFFICIENTS

The performance of 16 different similarity coefficients was examined in exploratory work; the sources and the formulas for these coefficients are reported in Howard (1973). Fourteen of the coefficients are defined in terms only of co-occurrences of services (rather than also considering frequencies of each service in each city), and non-metric scaling analyses based on these 14 coefficients produced just three distinct patterns of results.

In the first pattern, all cities scaled onto a single dimension, and a city's position on this dimension correlated almost perfectly with its population size. All four of the coefficients producing this pattern compared the number of services present in one city but not in the other to the total number of services that were coded in the study. The results indicate that absolute number of non-shared services is more a function of city sizes than anything else, in that larger cities always provide more services than smaller cities.

The second pattern was two-dimensional, with coordinates on one dimension corresponding closely to city size while the second dimension seemed to index the distinction between central cities and suburbs. All nine of the coefficients in this group compared the number of services occurring in two cities to the number of services occurring in either city. The results probably are best interpreted as indicating that, again, smaller cities have fewer services than larger cities, and satellite cities have fewer services than central cities of the same size.

The third pattern was a two-dimensional solution with one dimension corresponding roughly to city size and the second dimension corresponding roughly to the blue-collar versus white-collar composition of the population. The single coefficient giving this pattern indexes dissimilarity to the extent that the services in one city do not constitute a subset of the services in the other, so it is relatively insensitive to one city merely having more services than another and correspondingly more sensitive to qualitative differences in the kinds of services offered.

The analyses reported here were conducted using the coefficient that produced the third pattern above. This coefficient was introduced by Kulczynski (see Sokal and Sneath, 1963, Chapter 6), and is calculated by the following formula:

$$C = \frac{1}{2}\left[\frac{n_{AB}}{n_{AB} + n_{A\bar{B}}} + \frac{n_{AB}}{n_{AB} + n_{\bar{A}B}}\right]$$

where n_{AB} is the number of services present in both city A and city B; $n_{A\bar{B}}$ is the number of services present in city A but not city B; and $n_{\bar{A}B}$ is the number of services present in city B but not A. The first term in the brackets gives the proportion of services in city A that are shared with city B. If all A's services were present in B, then that proportion would be 1.0, indicating high similarity even if there is a size discrepancy so that B has more services. Similarly, the second term in the brackets is the proportion of B's services that are also present in city A. The overall coefficient value is the average of these two proportions. The coefficient does not eliminate size effects (because if services in one city are a subset of the other's, then one proportion will be 1.0 but the other proportion will be less than 1.0), but it does attenuate size effects enough to allow other kinds of discrepancies to appear. In comparing North Carolina cities, the values of this coefficient ranged from 0.47 (Chapel Hill and Thomasville) to 0.72 (Charlotte and Greensboro).

Analyses also were run using coefficients that had produced the other two patterns. Essentially the same results were obtained with 35 cities as had been obtained with 13 cities, and the results are not reported here.

SCALING AND TARGETING

The 35×35 table of similarity coefficients was entered in a POLYCON non-metric multidimensional scaling analysis as a square symmetric matrix with unspecified diagonal. The model designated that the solution should be in Euclidian space of four or less dimensions. Kruskal's Stress formula one, which utilized squared distances as the normalization constant, was chosen to aid in the determination of minimum dimensionality (see Kruskal, 1964 and Young, 1972; 1973 for an elaboration of the various Stress coefficients).

POLYCON provides the option of rotating a solution's axes in order to maximize their conformance with a set of target coordinates. Since the central question in this study concerns the degree to which dimensions of service structure correspond to dimensions of population composition, target coordinates were devised by characterizing the surrounding county of each city in terms of demographic variables (US Bureau of the Census, 1970a, b, c). The actual target vector was standardized to values between -1.0 and $+1.0$ by use of the following formula:

$$t_i = \frac{2X_i - (X_{max} + X_{min})}{X_{max} - X_{min}}$$

where t_i is the target coordinate of city i on demographic variable X when the original value of city i on that variable is X_i, the smallest observed value among the 35 cities is X_{min}, and the largest observed value is X_{max}.

RESULTS

Two dimensions were required to represent the contrasts in service structures among the 13 cities in the pilot study, so it was anticipated that two or more dimensions would be required for the 35 cities in the present study. The values of Kruskal's stress (see Young, 1972: 80-4) for the one-, two-, three-, and four-dimensional scaling solutions were 0.31, 0.18, 0.13, and 0.11, respectively, and this pattern of reduction in stress suggests that at least three dimensions are required here. Because stress coefficients only help to define the minimum dimensionality that is required for an adequate scaling solution, both the three- and the four-dimensional solutions are examined below.

The central theoretical question is whether the dimensions found in scaling services relate to demographic dimensions — that is, do the cities' characteristics as service environments correlate with their characteristics as population concentrations? Since the derived axes of a multidimensional scaling solution in Euclidian space have no intrinsic significance, it is to be expected that these axes must be rotated to develop their correspondence with demographic dimensions. Here, the necessary rotation was conducted by converting the demographic characteristics of the cities into a set of coordinates defining 'target' axes, and a scaling configuration was rotated to a maximal correspondence with these target dimensions in a least-squares sense. This approach leaves the scaled configuration of cities intact, changing only the orientation of axes through the configuration. Moreover, the axes are rotated under constraints of orthogonality for both the service-structure dimensions and the target dimensions. Thus correlations between the rotated axes and the target axes test correspondence between the service-environment space and the demographic space.

Size, wealth (median income), life-cycle (median age), and racial composition (percent non-white) of the city populations were used to generate target coordinates for rotations of the scaling solution. To examine the three-dimensional scaling solution, different sets of target coordinates were constructed from the four demographic variables by trying all combinations of three, and the service configuration was rotated to match each of these target combinations. Product-moment correlations between the city coordinates on the corresponding target dimensions are presented in the top part of Table 1.

TABLE 1
Correlations between rotated coordinates and target coordinates, when using different combinations of target dimensions (N = 35 cities)

Rotation	Population	Target based on cities Median family income	Median age	Percent non-white
1	—	0.74	0.41	0.49
2	0.67	—	0.41	0.59
3	0.59	0.73	—	0.52
4	0.67	0.73	0.42	—

	Population	Median family income	Aged 10-30	Percent non-white
5	0.65	0.71	—	0.52
6	0.66	0.70	0.59	—
7	0.77	0.75	0.51	0.50

First, it may be noted that all of the correlations in Table 1 are significantly different from zero ($p<0.05$), which provides unequivocal support for the expectation that the service profiles of cities are related to their demographic compositions. A closer examination of Table 1 reveals that city size and median family income are the two best predictors of a city's relative position in the service space, so these are presumed to define two of the demographic dimensions most related to services. When services are scaled in three dimensions, it is ambiguous from the results in the top part of Table 1 whether the third demographic dimension should be identified in terms of the racial composition variable or the life-cycle variable (rotation 3 versus rotation 4): the squared correlation coefficients summed over three dimensions are almost the same for both rotations.

Further examination of the data indicated that three cities had populations much larger than the rest so that they were excessively determining the rotation of a service axis to correspond to city size. To even out the contribution across all cities in the sample, a new population target variable was defined in terms of the logarithm of population. Moreover, the life-cycle variable (measured above as median age) appeared susceptible to a variety of reconceptualizations that might relate more closely with service structures. This possibility was explored by constructing six different variables dividing each city's population into 10-year age brackets over the range of 0 to 60 years and a seventh variable to include person aged 60 or more. Correlations were computed between these age variables and the coordinates on the third dimension obtained in rotation 4 to see if these age-related coordinates of the service space might be better explained by a life-cycle indicator other than median age. The following pattern of correlations was obtained: age 0-9, $r = 0.21$; age 10-19, $r = 0.25$; age 20-29, $r = 0.34$; age 30-39, $r = 0.17$; age 40-49, $r = 0.12$; age 50-59, $r = 0.09$; age 60 and up, $r = 0.08$ (the fact that all the correlations are positive indicates that coordinates on the third service dimension in rotation 4 retain some correlation with population size). This pattern suggests that it is not simply average age that is relevant to service structures, but rather the proportion of the population that is under 30 years of age. Accordingly, two new indicators of life cycle were constructed: proportion of the population under 30 years of age, and proportion of the population aged 10-29 years. The latter index showed the highest correlation with the coordinates of dimension three in rotation 4, so it was retained as the desired life-cycle indicator. It will be referred to as a measure of the 'youthfulness' of a population.

The results of rotating the axes of the three-dimensional scaling solution to correspond with targets defined in terms of log-population, median family income, youthfulness, and percent non-white are presented in the second part of Table 1. The correlations between service coordinates and the size and income targets are essentially comparable to what was obtained before. However, the use of log-population does permit a better fit to be obtained when the size dimension is used as a target with income and percent non-white. The re-defined life-cycle variable yields a substantially better fit than does median age. Indeed, utilizing log-population, median income, and percent youth as targets results in the greatest degree of fit yet obtained.

The size-wealth-youthfulness dimensions seem to provide a well grounded basis for describing the contrasts in service structures across these cities, yet a fit almost as good was obtained in the alternative rotation, where the racial composition target was substituted for youthfulness. This was taken as a signal that a four-dimensional solution for the service space might show contrasts corresponding to all four target variables. Thus, the axes of the four-dimensional scaling solution were rotated to fit all four demographic dimensions. The correlations between these service-space axes and the demographic target coordinates are presented in the bottom row of Table 1. The fit on the size and wealth dimensions increases notably in this solution, and respectable levels of fit also are obtained for both the youthfulness and racial compostion variables. Thus the four-dimensional solution is theoretically interpretable (even though the stress coefficient is not much less than for the three-dimensional solution); this solution reveals a very substantial correspondence between population composition and city services, and it suggests that variations in city services reflect population variation on all of the major demographic factors that have been identified repeatedly in factor-analytic studies of cities' demographic characteristics.

Each city's position in the service environment space was predicted from its profile of demographic characteristics, using four regression equations for translating demographic variables into predicted service coordinates. Distances between the predicted and observed positions were calculated. The mean distance between predicted and observed points was 0.65 and the standard deviation of these distances was 0.38 (these figures can be compared with the maximum distance between two cities in the service space — 3.31 for Chapel Hill and Thomasville). The standard deviation was inflated by one city (Thomasville), which was more than four standard deviations away from its predicted position. Subjective impressions by the second author (who visited 22 of the cities in the sample) seemed to support the notion that the deviant city 'looks' smaller, poorer, older, and more homogeneously white than demographic data suggest. However, rescaling the cities with Thomasville deleted did not imporve the fit with demographic variables. Moreover, dropping Thomasville and recomputing the correlations between target coordinates and the coordinates in the four-dimensional rotated service space (as given in Table 4) did not increase the correlations to any significant degree because the deletion affected the variances as well as the covariances of the coordinates. Thus, despite its large deviation, the presence of this city in further analyses is not significantly masking relationships.

CHARACTERISTIC SERVICES

Cities' locations in the service space vary because they offer distinct services, and theoretically it is possible to scale the services themselves into this same space, with a service being located by the cluster of cities offering that service. With nearly 8,000 coded services, it was not possible to use scaling procedures to find the positions of services, because of size limitations in available programs. However, an ad hoc procedure was developed to roughly define services characteristic of different regions of the space by finding the services characterizing a pair of cities occupying that region. Since four meaningful dimensions were identified and each of these axes can be dichotomized into 'plus' and 'minus' segments, the space was partitioned grossly into 16 regions. A pair of cities was available in 12 of these regions, so the ad hoc procedure permits a rough specification of services characterizing most regions of the service space.

A service is considered characteristic of a region if three criteria are met: (1) both of the cities representing the region contain the service classification in their yellow pages; (2) the service classification is absent from the directories of at least two other cities in the sample; (3) the incidence of the service (number-of-dialings divided by county population) is unusually high for both cities — among the ten highest when all 35 cities are ranked from high to low in terms of the incidence of that service. Services characterizing different regions of the space under these criteria are listed in Figures 1 to 12.

Before examining the variations in these figures, a number of points need emphasis. First, a large number of elementary services, like grocers and gas stations, are not listed in the tables because they are present in all the cities. Thus all of the cities have many more services than are listed on a chart. Second, not all of the services that contributed to the scaling solution are listed here because a city may share a service with a city in an adjacent region rather than with a city in its same region. Such a service would have contributed to the scaling solution, but it would not be selected as characteristic of a region using the present procedure. Third, many of the cities may have completely idiosyncratic services that are not shared with any of the other cities, and these, too, are unlisted — indeed, we chose to examine pairs of cities to eliminate such instances. Finally, a few of the listings are not really characteristic

FIGURE 1
Characteristic services of
large cities with high-income adults; racially homogeneous:
Charlotte and Chapel Hill

Airline Companies
Air Travel Ticket Agencies
Apartments
Architects
Art Galleries and Dealers
Auto Dealers, Used Cars—Wholesale
Camps
Cement—Retail
Cheese—Wholesale
Christian Science Practitioners
Churches—Christian Science
City and Town Planners
Cleaners—Self-Service
Compressors, Air & Gas—Renting
Contractors, Equipment & Supplies
  —Renting
Copying and Duplicating Service
Electronic Equipment and Supplies
Engineers—Consulting
Engravers
Furniture—Children's
Hardware, Builder's
High Fidelity & Stereo Equipment
House Cleaning
Housewares, Retail

Importers
Jewelry Engravers
Labs—Research & Development
Leather Goods—Retail
Management Consultants
Marriage and Family Counselors
Notaries-Public
Pet Supplies and Foods—Retail
Phonograph Recording Service
Physicians & Surgeons—
  Group Practice
Pipe
Psychologists
Publishers—Periodicals
Real Estate Developers
Real Estate Management
Records and Tape Players—Sound
Schools—Nursery and Kindergarten
Screens, Doors and Windows
Spraying—Horticulture
Tailors—Ladies'
Travel Bureaus
Tree Service
Wines—Retail
Wrecking Contractors

FIGURE 2
Characteristic services of
large cities with high-income, older adults; racially homogeneous:
High Point and Gastonia

Airports
Bearings
Carpet Layers
Churches—Church of God
Churches—Wesleyan
Cotton
Drapery and Curtain Fabrics
Employment Contractors—
  Temporary Help
Filters—Air and Gas
Filters—Liquid
Furnaces—Repairing and Cleaning
Garbage Disposal Equipment—
  Household
Golf Courses—Miniature
High Fidelity & Stereo Equipment
Industrial Equipment and Supplies
Lawnmowers—Sharpening and
  Repair
Manufacturing Agents &
  Representatives
Material Handling Equipment
Mattresses
Mufflers & Exhaust Systems
  —Engines
Pest Control (Exterminating
  & Fumigating)
Plastic—Fabricating, Finishing
  & Decorating

Plastics—Molders
Plating
Scrap Metals
Shock Absorbers
Siding Materials
Silk Screen Processing
Springs—Distributors &
  Manufacturers
TV & Radio Supplies and Parts
Textile Machinery and Parts
Textile Manufacturers
Thread—Wholesale & Manufacturers
Travel Bureaus
Valves
Warehouses—Commodity
Waste—Cotton, Synthetic, Wool
Yarn—Wholesale & Manufacturers

FIGURE 3
Characteristic services of
large cities with high-income young adults; racially heterogeneous:
Wilmington and Durham

Acoustical Contractors
Advertising—Outdoor
Airport Transportation Service
Amusement Devices
Appraisers
Beds—Renting
Bibles
Building Materials
Burglar Alarm Systems
Churches—Seventh Day Adventist
Contractors—Telephone Line
Doors
Doors, Metal
Druggists, Wholesale
Dry Wall Contractor
Electric Motors
Elevators—Freight & Passenger
Engineer's Supplies
Filing Equipment—Systems &
   Supplies
Floor Laying—Refinishing &
   Resurfacing
Furniture Design & Custom Builders
Guns and Gunsmiths
Hardware, Builders'
High Fidelity & Stereo Equipment
House Cleaning
Kitchen Cabinets & Equipment
   Household
Labor Organizations
Labs—Research & Development
Letter Shop Service
Lingerie

Manicurist
Marine Equipment and Supplies
Muffler & Exhaust Systems—Engines
Painter's Equipment & Supplies
Photo Copying
Physicians & Surgeons—
   Dermatology
Physicians & Surgeons—
   Thoracic Surgery
Pizza
Printers—Continuous & Individual
   Form
Pumps—Repairing
Radio Telephone, CCC, Mobile
   Units
Rental Service Stores & Yards
Riggers
Roofers
Schools—Centralized Administration
Screens, Doors and Windows
Silverware
Sound Systems & Equipment
TV Stations & Broadcasting Co.
Tire Recapping
Uniforms
Water Heaters—Repairing
Water, Soft & Conditioning
   Equipment—Service & Supplies
Welding Equipment—Renting
Welding Equipment & Supplies
Window Cleaning
Windows—Metal
Wines—Wholesale
Wrecking Contractors

FIGURE 4
Characteristic services of
large cities with low-income young adults; racially homogeneous:
Hickory and Goldsboro

Adjusters
Advertising Agencies & Counselors
Advertising—Radio
Air Cargo Service
Air Conditioning—Room Units
Auctioneers
Auto Parts & Supplies—Wholesale
  & Manufacturers
Bakers—Wholesale
Batteries—Storage—Retail
Bearings
Beauty Schools
Beer and Ale—Wholesale
Billiard Parlors
Book Dealers—Retail
Boxes—Corrugated and Fiber
Carpet & Rug Cleaning Equipment
  —Rental
Churches—Methodist
Concrete Blocks and Shapes
Data Processing Service
Data Processing Systems—
  Equipment & Supplies
Electrical Heating
Electric Appliances—Major—
  Repairing
Engines—Diesel
Farm Equipment
Fence
Fire Extinguishers
Fisherman's Supplies
Floor Machines—Renting
Gas—Liquid Petroleum, Bottled &
  Bulk—Equipment & Supplies
Gates
House Cleaning
Insulation Contractors—Cold & Heat
Insurance—Health and Accident

Libraries—Public
Lighting Fixtures—Wholesale &
  Manufacturers
Material Handling Equipment
Mobile Homes and Trailers—Parks
Mobile Homes—Transporting
Nurserymen
Oil Burners—Servicing
Pest Control—Exterminating &
  Fumigating
Phonograph Records
Photographers—Commercial
Physicians & Surgeons—Urology
Plumbing Fixtures & Supplies—
  Wholesale & Manufacturers
Radio Service
Ranges and Stoves—Repairing
Refrigerating Equipment—
  Commercial
Refrigerators & Freezers—Service
Sandwiches—Wholesale
Sandwiches—Retail
Steel Distributors & Warehouses
Steel Fabricators
Storm Windows and Doors
Surveyors—Land
Tanks—Metal
TV & Radio—Service
TV & Radio—Supplies & Parts
Tree Service
Trucks Repairing Service
Trucks—Industrial
Warehouses—Merchandise
Washing Machines, Dryers & Ironers
  —Service
Water Well Drilling & Service
Woodworkers
Yarn—Retail
Yarn—Wholesale & Manufacturers

FIGURE 5
Characteristic services of
large cities with low-income young adults; racially heterogeneous:
Jacksonville and Fayetteville

Apartments
Appraisers
Auto Machine Shop Service
Auto Racing & Sports Car
  Equipment
Auto Radios & Stereo Systems
Awnings and Canopies
Bakers—Wholesale
Beer and Ale—Retail
Bookkeeping Service
Buses—Charter and Rental
Clothing Bought and Sold
Collection Agencies
Data Processing Systems—
  Equipment & Supplies
Draperies & Curtains—Retail &
  Custom Made
Electric Appliances, Major—Repair
Electric Equipment & Supplies—
  Wholesale
Electric Motors—Dealers & Repair
Electric Motors—Repairing
Encyclopedias
Exterminating & Fumigating
  (Pest Control)
Fence
Floor Machines
Furniture Renting and Leasing
Furniture—Used
Gas—Liquid Petroleum, Bottled
  & Bulk
Golf Courses—Miniature
Guns and Gunsmiths—Retail
Hair Goods
High Fidelity & Stereo Equipment
  —Dealers & Service

Ice Cream and Frozen Desserts—
  Manufacturers and Distributors
Investment Securities
Kennels—Equipment and Supplies
Laboratories—Dental
Mobile Homes—Equipment & Parts
Mobile Homes—Repairing & Service
Mobile Homes & Trailers—Parks
Mobile Homes—Transporting
Mufflers & Exhaust Systems—Engine
Musical Instruments—Dealers
Mutual Funds
Night Clubs
Notaries
Organs
Parking Stations and Garages
Pawnbrokers
Pet Shops
Phonograph Records
Phonographs—Coin-Operated
Photographers—Commercial
Physical Fitness
Plywood and Veneers
Real Estate Management
Recreation Centers
Reducing & Weight Control Service
Refreshment Stands
Refrigerating Equipment—
  Commercial
Roofing Contractors
Schools—Nursery & Kindergarten
Sewing Machines—Household
Slipcovers
TV & Radio Dealers—Retail
TV & Radio Service
TV Rental
Tourist Homes

FIGURE 5 (continued)

Trailer—Transporting
Tropical Fish
Typewriters
Washing Machines, Dryers & Ironers
Water Softening & Conditioning

Equipment—Service & Supplies
Welding Equipment & Supplies—
  Retail
Wheel Alignment, Frame & Axle
  Service—Auto

FIGURE 6
Characteristic services of
large cities with low-income older adults; racially heterogeneous:
Wilson and Rocky Mount

Cabinets
Children's & Infants' Wear—Wholesale & Manufacturers
Fruit & Vegetable Growers & Shipment
Gas, Liquid Petroleum, Bottled & Bulk—Equipment & Supplies
General Merchandise—Retail
Grain Dealers
Insurance—Hospitalization
Physicians & Surgeons—Radiology
Physicians & Surgeons—Urology
Rest Homes
Sandwiches—Retail
Timber and Timberland Companies
Tobacco Buyers
Tobacco Warehouses
Truck Repairing and Service
Truck Stops

FIGURE 7
Characteristic services of
small cities with high-income young adults; racially homogeneous:
Reidsville and Shelby

Artificial Flowers, Plants & Trees
Auto Air Conditioning Equipment
Bicycles—Dealers
Bottlers
Cemeteries
Dishwashing Machines
Farm Supplies
Fence
Formal Wear—Rental
General Merchandise—Retail
Glass—Auto, Plate, Window, etc.
Golf Courses—Public
Greenhouses
Hair Goods
Homes and Institutions
Hosiery—Wholesale &
  Manufacturers
Insurance—Hospitalization
Linoleum Dealers
Musical Instruments—Dealers
Pharmacies
Phonograph Records
Physicians & Surgeons—General

Road Service—Auto
Seeds and Bulbs
Sportswear—Retail
Stone—Crushed
Television Service
Towing—Auto
Water Well Drilling & Service

FIGURE 8
Characteristic services of
small cities with high-income older adults; racially homogeneous:
Concord and Lexington

Air Conditioning Equipment &
  Systems—Repair
Air Conditioning—Room Units
Auto Machine Shop Service
Auto Seat Covers, Tops &
  Upholstery
Batteries, Storage—Wholesale &
  Manufacturers
Billiard Parlors
Carpet & Rug Dealers—New
Chinaware—Retail
Churches—Lutheran
Churches—United Methodist
Concrete Contractors
Dancing Instruction
Draperies & Curtains—Retail &
  Custom Made
Electrical Appliances—Small
Electric Heating Equipment &
  Supplies
Fire Departments
Garbage Collection
Glass—Auto, Plate, Window, etc.
Homes and Institutions
Insulation Contractors—Cold & Heat
Kitchen Cabinets & Equipment—
  Household
Mail Order Houses
Meat Packers

Millwork
Nurserymen
Outboard Motors
Pest Control (Exterminating &
  Fumigating)
Physicians & Surgeons—Pediatrics
Plywood and Veneers
Poultry—Retail
Pumps
Radio Service
Savings and Loan Associations
Sewing Machines—Household
Swimming Pool Equipment &
  Supplies
Tile Ceramic Contractors
Tire Recapping, Retreading & Repair
TV Dealers—Retail
Television Service
Upholstery Fabrics
Wrecker Service—Auto

FIGURE 9
Characteristic services of
small cities with high-income older adults; racially heterogeneous:
Monroe and Statesville

Auto Electric Service
Awnings and Canopies
Bookkeeping Service
Churches—Methodist
Cotton Mills
Draperies & Curtains—Retail &
  Custom Made
Excavating Contractors
Feed—Wholesale & Manufacturers
Fence
Floor Laying, Refinishing &
  Resurfacing
Insurance—Health & Accident
Kerosene
Keys
Knit Goods—Wholesale &
  Manufacturers
Millwork
Mortgages
News Dealers
Nurserymen
Plywood and Veneers
Real Estate Developers
Refrigeration Service—Commercial,
  Service
Roofing Materials
Savings & Loan Associations
Seeds and Bulbs

Stone—Crushed
Storm Windows and Doors
Television Service
Tire Recapping, Retreading &
  Repairing
Towing—Auto
Transmission—Auto
Warehouses—Commodity
Water Well Drilling & Service
Wheel Alignment, Frame & Axle
  Service—Auto

FIGURE 10
Characteristic services of
small cities with low-income young adults; racially homogeneous:
Lenoir and Lumberton

Adding and Calculating Machinery
   & Supplies
Amusement Places
Artificial Flowers, Plants & Trees
Box Lunches
Clothing Bought and Sold
Draperies and Curtains—Retail &
   Custom Made
Electrical Appliances—Small
Farm Supplies
Fruits and Vegetables—Retail
Greenhouses
Hair Goods
Homes and Institutions
Kerosene
Organs
Photographers—Commercial
Physicians & Surgeons—Pediatric
Physicians & Surgeons—Surgery
Picture Frame—Dealers
Pumps—Repairing
Refrigeration Equipment—
   Commercial—Service
Road Service—Auto
Roofing Contractors

Soda Fountain Shops
TV & Radio—Service
Towing—Auto
Water Heaters—Dealers
Wheel Alignment, Frame & Axle
   Service

FIGURE 11
Characteristic services of
small cities with low-income adults; racially homogeneous:
Thomasville and Albemarle

Auto Seat Covers, Tops & Upholstery
Awnings and Canopies
Fire Departments
Furniture Manufacturers
Parks—Amusement
Pest Control—Exterminating & Fumigating
Plywood and Veneers
TV & Radio Service

FIGURE 12
Characteristic services of
small cities with low-income young adults; racially heterogeneous:
Roanoke Rapids and Henderson

Auto Parts & Supplies—Wholesale & Manufacturers
Barbecues
Bookkeeping Service
Bottlers
Clinics
Coal and Coke—Retail
Cotton Gins
Dairy Products—Retail
Druggists
Farm Supplies
Mail Order Houses
Nursing Homes
Rest Homes
Schools—Industrial, Technical, Trade

services so much as idiosyncratic codings of common services. For example, 'Pharmacists and Druggists' appear as characteristic services in some regions, but they probably would not have so appeared had they been coded in the same category (another example is provided by the categories 'Pest Control (Exterminating and Fumigating)' as opposed to 'Exterminating and Fumigating (Pest Control)'). Such variations are sufficiently uncommon to ignore for present purposes, with the understanding that they pose a kind of measurement error.

Absolute Number

A mere glance at the figures reveals that there are striking differences between the regions in their absolute numbers of characteristic services. This facet of the figures is summarized in Table 2, which presents the counts of characteristic services in each region. It is evident from the table that a city's position on the size dimension in the service space corresponds to its number of special services, but only if the city also is located on the 'youthful' side of the life-cycle dimension. Moreover, among these cities the effect of size seems most pronounced for cities on the lower end of the wealth dimension. These observations suggest that massing of poorer young adults generates the greatest numbers of characteristic services, and the massing of older adults, regardless of their wealth or racial balance, in itself has little effect on the development of characteristic services. Among cities on the older side of the life-cycle dimension, it is position on the wealth axis that corresponds with numbers of characteristic services. This is not because 'higher-income, older-adult' cities have a multitude of services but rather because the 'lower-income, older-adult' cities support very few special services.

The racial composition variable has relatively little relation to number of characteristic services. One might have supposed that racial heterogeneity would produce a greater range of services, and while there is a hint of such an effect, it is small and confined to 'larger, youthful' cities.

TABLE 2
Number of characteristic services in different sectors of the service space, with sectors identified by their demographic correlates

| | Predominantly white | | | |
| | Young adults | | Older adults | |
	High-income	**Low-income**	**High-income**	**Low-income**
Large	48	68	39	—
Small	29	27	41	8

	Racially mixed			
Large	60	71	—	16
Small	—	14	33	—

Types of Services

The services in Figures 1-12 can be divided roughly according to whether the major clients of the service are outside of the community, or are industries, firms, or professionals within the community, or are families or individuals engaged in private consumption. The first type — inter-community services — is a fairly small category in all of the figures, and the number of such services does not vary much from one figure to another. Probably this is because this category mainly embraces 'key industries' that are highly idiosyncratic for each city.

The second type — logistic support services — vary considerably in number from one region of the space to another, and the general rule seems to be that more such services occur in cities on the 'large' side of the size axis. There are two exceptions to the rule, however. Unexpectedly few logistic services occur for Charlotte and Chapel Hill, reflecting, perhaps, a special feature of young, large, middle-class communities and/or an artifactual effect produced by including a college town in this pair. Also, relatively few logistic services are found in Wilson and Rocky Mount, possibly reflecting a characteristic feature of large agrarian centers, since these are neighboring cities in the major agricultural area of the state, both surrounded by tenant-farmed tobacco and cotton fields.

Consumer-directed services are usefully divided further into services supporting property investments (especially homes and automobiles) and social-personal services oriented toward maintaining individuals' well-being, providing education, or supporting entertainment and leisure activities. Examination of the figures seems to indicate that the number of property services is directly related to the size dimension among cities on the youthful end of the life-cycle axis: the 'larger' cities have more property services, and this is largely independent of their position on the wealth or racial homogeneity dimensions. But this does not seem to be the case for cities on the older-adult end of the life-cycle dimension. Indeed, the relation with size, if any, is inverted among these cities, with 'larger' having fewer property services, and it is mainly position on the richer side of the wealth dimension that yields a larger number of property services in the older communities.

The number of social-personal services in a city correlates predominantly with position on the life-cycle dimension such that more of these services are found in cities with young adults. Additionally, a size correlation seems to exist in 'young, poor, and racially mixed' cities, such that the 'larger' of these cities (Jacksonville and Fayetteville) have more social-personal services that one might expect and the 'smaller' cities (Roanoke and Henderson) have fewer. (It is to be noted, however, that the two larger communities here are both military base cities.) Among 'older' communities, a moderate number of social-personal services is attained only for the 'small, wealthy, and racially homogeneous' pair (Concord and Lexington).

Racial Composition and Services

The above discussion has not yet revealed why the racial composition dimension appears as a component of the service space since in the above analyses this variable has contributed to interpretations only in a minor way via its involvement in some restricted interactions with other variables. Focusing attention on 'large, youthful' cities, where we have a complete set of comparisons on the racial homogeneity variable for both 'poorer' and 'richer' cities, and further focusing on services that characterize just racially homogeneous cities or just racially heterogeneous cities, leads to a tentative but plausible accounting of the racial axis. This dimension seems to be related to qualitative variations in services such that the racially heterogeneous communities have more of an 'Old South', 'blue-collar' character while the more homogeneously white communities have a 'New South', 'white-collar' flavor. For example, among the services specially characterizing racially heterogeneous cities are: Bibles; Burglar Alarm Systems; Churches — Seventh Day Adventist; Furniture — Used; Guns and Gunsmiths; Lingerie; Night Clubs; Pawnbrokers; Uniforms; Welding Equipment and Supplies. Among the services characterizing racially homogeneous cities are: Air Conditioning — Room Units; Art Galleries; Book Dealers — Retail; Churches — Christian Science; Carpet and Rug Cleaning Equipment — Rental; Fisherman's Supplies; Libraries — Public; Marriage Counselors; Tailors — Ladies'; Tree Service. Such comparisons suggest that the racial composition variable aligns with service offerings related to class but not comprehended merely by income distinctions. (The socioeconomic basis of this dimension is further supported by the fact that the cities' coordinates on the service space dimension correlate as well with percentage of unemployed in the county — $r = 0.56$ — as they do with percentage of non-white.) Thus, our hypothesis is that the racially heterogeneous cities, even those with a high average income, have not adopted New South, white-collar life-styles, possibly because wealth in such cities is so unevenly distributed and is concentrated in the hands of just a small portion of the population.

Distinctiveness of City Types

Qualitative variations in services contribute to the definitions of the other dimensions also, and the point is especially significant with regard to the size dimension. Increased size does not mean merely more services; it also means different services. In particular, the incidence of certain rural services and institutional forms drops in larger cities so that such services are less likely to appear as characteristic (e.g. Farm Supplies, Greenhouses, Kerosene, Feed — Wholesale and Manufacturers, Seeds and Bulbs, Water Well Drilling and Service, Homes and Institutions, Rest Homes, Nursing Homes).

Many qualitative variations in the service space are far more complex than simple contrasts along the major dimensions. For example, the services that give an 'Old South' character to racially heterogeneous communities are not identical in richer and poorer communities. And while small communities are more likely to provide rural services, there appear to be types of small cities (e.g. older, poorer, and white) that are not rural at all, while at least one type of large city (older, poorer, and racially heterogeneous) appears to be mainly an agrarian service center in this sample. Such findings suggest that a given type of population is associated with an idiosyncratic service profile, and presumably if a city changes demographically, regardless of direction, it tends to lose its original characteristic services and to develop new ones (unless the population becomes substantially older and smaller, in which case the city may simply lose services).

DISCUSSION

The results here generate some provocative hypotheses if urban service environments are viewed as systems by which certain kinds of socioeconomic transformations are made. For example, it would seem that money pumped into a city with young adults would circulate in the population longer (via the ubiquitous social-personal services) than would be the case in a city with older adults, where apparently money moves more directly into property and capital investments. Innovations in leisure and amenities might be expected to diffuse most rapidly in large, young cities, whereas innovations in property maintenance would diffuse more evenly in wealthy cities independent of age. Such hypotheses (and many more might be developed along the same lines) are of importance not merely to entrepreneurs but also, perhaps, to government administrators and their advisors, who are trying to direct the socioeconomic development of a region.

The results also seem to be relevant to programs intended to have specific consequences for the quality of urban life. For example, it would seem that to achieve maximum success, a program meant to improve social and cultural amenities should be directed at cities with large, young populations where new institutions have a natural chance of surviving. The fact that home maintenance is so focal a concern for older, higher-income populations confirms the importance of encouraging such persons to migrate to (or stay in) marginal areas of cities in order to preclude the need for redevelopment. The results here suggest that the consequences of demographic change for service environments might be predictable. For example, a city growing by a rapid influx of young adults presumably should display dramatic expansion in its social-personal services. Increased wealth in a small, older population should create an expansion in home maintenance services. Similarly, a population bulge produced by a period of increased births in a large, low-income city should generate more social-personal and private property services as the cohorts reach young adulthood, and then a decline in these as they age more. Ordinarily, declines in overall size would be expected to reduce special services, but results here suggest a possible partial exception: a declining population of older, higher-income, whites might actually gain in amenities (perhaps moving in the direction of a 'retirement community') even while losing logistic services.

The results are promising enough to encourage more work, and questions do remain. Would the same structures emerge in other sections of the United States? In other countries? How are the structures affected by historical shifts in available services? The results presented here are based on analyses of small cities: how do metropolises fit into the framework? These questions cannot be answered by the available data, but perhaps future studies will provide answers.

REFERENCES

Berry, B. J. L. (1972) 'Latent Structure of the American Urban System, International Comparisons,' pp. 11-60 in B. J. L. Berry (ed.), *City Classification Handbook*. New York: Wiley-Interscience.

Hadden, J. K. and E. F. Borgatta (1965) *American Cities: Their Social Characteristics*. Chicago: Rand McNally.

Hempel, C. G. (1952) *Fundamentals of Concept Formation in Empirical Science.* Chicago: University of Chicago Press.

Howard, William G. (1973) 'An Approach to a Functional Classification of Cities,' *The Southern Sociologist*, vol. 5 (Fall): 3-16.

Sokal, R. R. and P. H. A. Sneath (1963), *Principles of Numerical Taxonomy.* San Francisco: Freeman.

Southern Bell Telephone Company (1971) Headings for the Yellow Pages (February).

Young, F. W. (1972) 'A Model for Polynomial Conjoint Analysis Algorithms,' pp. 69-102 in Roger N. Shepard, A. K. Romney, and S. Nerlov (eds), *Multidimensional Scaling.* New York: Seminar Press.

Young, F. W. (1973) *POLYCON Users Manual, a FORTRAN-IV Program for Polynomial Conjoint Analysis.* Chapel Hill: The L. L. Thurstone Psychometric Laboratory, University of North Carolina, No. 118.

US Bureau of the Census (1970a) *Census of the Population and Housing: 1970,* Summary Tape.

US Bureau of the Census (1970b) *Census of Population: 1970*, General, Social and Economic Characteristics. Final Report PC(1)-C35 North Carolina. Tables 124, 120.

US Bureau of the Census (1970c) *Census of Population: 1970*, General Population Characteristics. Final Report PC(1)-B35 North Carolina. Tables 16, 35.

4

ALTERNATIVE CODING PROCEDURES AND THE FACTORIAL STRUCTURE OF ATTITUDE AND BELIEF SYSTEMS

Pablo Suárez
University of Uppsala, Sweden

THE PRACTICE OF METHODOLOGICAL SELF-CRITICISM

The various uses and limitations of opinionnaires for the study of attitude and belief systems have been the focus of much concern among sociologists and other practitioners of the social sciences. Since the days of — just to mention the forerunners of two radical traditions — Thurstone (1928) and LaPiere (1934) until now, much has been written on the subject of such controversies.

One main problem seems to be that, under the restrictions imposed by survey techniques, it is not possible either to detect feelings or attitudes directly, or to measure directly their intensity. Survey techniques force the researcher to make use of assumptions underlying inferred measurement. The fundamental assumption is that individuals express (cf., for a discussion of this and related terms, Kotarbinski, 1966:3-20) their attitudes and feelings (as well as their opinions, beliefs, images, ideas, thoughts, past experiences, hopes, judgments and expectations) by means of observable behavior, e.g. by means of words and phrases interpretable in the framework of a given language and a given socio-historical and cultural context (cf. Przeworski and Teune, 1970:91-112; for a contrasting view, see Deutscher, 1966).

This, of course, leads to a very controversial problem — the problem of the validity of inferred measurement. Since LaPiere's experiment on the possibilities of predicting actions on the basis of answers to questionnaires, there have been many attempts (e.g., Deutscher, 1966; Ray, 1976) to question the foregoing assumption (for a review, see Schuman and Johnson, 1976). At the core of the discussion is, on the one hand, the problem of whether or not individuals do express their real feelings, attitudes, etc., by means of their answers to questionnaires or in interviews. This is the classical problem of validity in the case of survey data. On the other hand, the question is raised whether it is possible to assume correspondence between actual behavior and the expressed attitudes, beliefs, etc. This is LaPiere's problem.

Recently, Lindsey (1977: 351-2) has argued that scales of 'socioeconomic status' measure ideological constructs rather than theoretical ones. Such scales are based upon 'the ideology of everyday perception' and not upon 'scientifically or theoretically constructed observation'. Socioeconomic status, as such, 'is ideological, since in everyday life, it hides the social relations of production from perception by the members of society.' Moreover, scales of socioeconomic status are constructed by way of 'an arbitrary combination of incommensurables.' Since 'no unique or objective way exists to transform a qualitative variable, such as occupation, into a quantitative variable,' socioeconomic status is measured on the basis of everyday perception, as 'an evaluation specific to a particular tradition, culture, society.' In addition, since the social structure is 'subjectively different depending upon where one is situated within it' status perceptions vary among the various social classes, groups and categories in which society is differentiated.

From a different perspective, Barton and Parsons (1977) have advanced some interesting considerations leading to a reappraisal of current notions in assessing attitude consistency. What is relevant to the discussion here is the attempt made by the authors to show the inadequacy of measures of consistency based upon item intercorrelations. The main problem with these measures, the authors argue, is that 'the correlation coefficient is affected not only by the structuring of beliefs but also by the heterogeneity of populations' (p. 161). Hence, average item intercorrelations or any other measure with the correlation coefficient at its base have an ambiguous interpretation concerning the degree of consistency in the patterning of attitudes. When calculated for any two variables whatsoever in an attitudinal heterogeneous sample (or population) constituted by various homogeneous sub-samples (groups) and in which the heterogeneity of the sample is basically a consequence of the homogeneity of the sub-samples, the value of the correlation coefficient is a function of the distance between the groups and of the relative variance within each group. In the extreme case, each sub-sample can be thought of as including only highly consistent individuals (i.e. either a high-high pattern or a low-low one) so that within-group variance on both variables is negligible, whereas between-group variance is as high as possible. Obviously, in such situation the value of the correlation coefficient between the two variables will be high for the entire sample, whereas the relationship between the variables within each sub-sample will be nearly orthogonal. The authors conclude that comparisons based upon item intercorrelations cannot but be misleading if the populations being subject to comparison are not equally heterogeneous.

The above lines of criticism lead to a questioning of what is actually being measured as contrasted to what is claimed to be measured — subjective evaluations or objective differentiations (Lindsey), or attitude consistency or sample heterogeneity (Barton and Parsons). This, once again, is a problem concerning the 'validity' of measurements. Additionally, Suárez (1980) has argued that reliability and validity assessments, by means of some usual procedures, are not independent of assumptions of attitude consistency — different definitions of consistency affect not only alternative forms' reliability estimates but factorial validity as well. Consequently, neither the reliability nor the validity of indices implying assumptions of attitude consistency can be assessed unambiguously by means of such procedures. Furthermore, both Suárez (1970, 1973) and, more recently, Turner (1979) have suggested, although arriving at rather different conclusions, some grounds for the criticism of the very notion of validity by pointing to the inconsistent or otherwise incongruous rationale underlying most validation procedures (see also Hirschi and Selvin, 1967: 193).

In this paper I will try to develop a different although related line of argumentation in connection with the problems faced when assessing the structure of attitude and/or belief systems by means of common procedures. My contention is that the factorial structure of such systems is dependent on the particular coding of the answers to the items included in the analyses. More specifically, alternative ways of coding residual answers, such as 'don't know', resulting from their ambiguous interpretation, may be shown to affect significantly the factor loadings and the configuration of the items in the factor space. The arbitrariness implied in the various ways of dealing with such answers results in no less arbitrary assessments of the structure of the attitudinal domain or the belief system under consideration.

Since decisions concerning coding procedures enter into the research process at the earliest stage of the analysis, and in some cases are defined beforehand in the design of the questionnaire, the resulting factorial structure is to a certain extent predetermined. The danger in this is that unchecked and often unreported assumptions underlying particular coding procedures may be at the core of some competitive 'theories' which basically claim the existence of a given number of factors supposedly 'discovered' according to scientific canons. Moreover, since the resulting factors are often interpreted as 'constructs,' the implications for the measurement of hypothesized 'latent' variables are obvious — depending on the coding procedure the estimated scores will be different and the interrelationships between such variables and other measures will vary accordingly. In addition, since the computer revolution has made it possible to 'play with the data,' the results might be manipulated so that, after testing all possible ways of coding, the one that best fits the 'theory' could be used when reporting the research. The above challenges common interpretations of factor analysis as not in need of any prior formulation of hypotheses (e.g. Cattell, 1952:21) or as a technique for the 'discovery' of concepts (e.g. Phillips, 1966: 171-4).

It should be stressed at this point that my concern here is with 'normal,' routine, uncritical research. For this reason in some of the illustrations presented below I have consciously decided to use a statistical-package-default-option type of analysis. Fortunately, not all social scientists fit into this pattern and few are prone to manipulate the results. However, it is not unusual to find papers and PhD disertations with gross misuses and abuses of statistical procedures and computer programs. In order to avoid embarrassment and sterile counter-argumentations, I have chosen to illustrate the analysis with data from a survey that I used in an attempt (Suárez, 1975) to measure fear towards communism as aroused by the 1970 pre-election propaganda in Chile, known as the 'terror campaign' (see, e.g., US Senate, 1975).

I am not sure whether this paper will stimulate methodological self-criticism, as is my primary intention, or, if on the contrary, will be another good reason, because of its weakness, for 'abandoning method' (Phillips, 1973). What is needed is to free ourselves from normal, textbook methodology — codified techniques and ready-to-be-used (what a temptation in a computerized world!) solutions for stereotyped handbook problems. However, the above is not meant to imply a rejection of methodical thinking or to advocate some 'method of no-method' à la Feyerabend (1970). On the contrary, I believe that what is needed is more method.

MEASURING FEAR:
AN EMPIRICAL ILLUSTRATION

The multidimensional patterning of fear towards communism was assumed to be the result of the multi-sided appeal of the 'terror campaign,' previous anti-communist socialization, and political cleavages within the population. However, the problem of studying the specific influence of the 1970 anti-communist propaganda as a fear-arousing campaign was faced by registering the various opinions the subjects ($N = 952$) manifested concerning the most agitated issues of the campaign. On the basis of a content analysis of the propaganda, the slogans used were classified into 12 groups. For each group one sentence was assigned as representative. These 12 sentences were written by the researchers and none was actually used during the campaign. Nevertheless, the content of the selected sentences corresponded largely to the various actual forms of anti-communist agitation. Moreover, the expressions used in the wording of the sentences were chosen in such a way as to come as close as possible to the actual wording of the slogans in the propaganda. The idea was to use a 'typical' sentence corresponding to each group of slogans.

During the interview the subjects were asked whether they agreed or not with each statement. To control the possible influence of the specific wording, half the sentences were written expressing an anti-communist attitude, opinion or image, whereas the other half expressed a pro-communist statement (parallel tests). To control the eventual bias introduced by the order in which the sentences were presented to the interviewee, the pro-communist and anti-communist sentences were intermixed so that an anti-communist sentence was followed by a pro-communist one, and vice-versa (odd-even method). Finally, to control the possible influence of the answer to the first sentence on the subsequent answers (owing to the very well-known tendency for individuals to show as much consistency as possible), half the sample was presented to the inverted list (split-ballot techique).

There is no reason to believe that the 12 selected items work redundantly and not complementarily. If the items were redundant, it would not be necessary — or even permissible — to include them into a composite index. Actually, however, the various issues in the propaganda seemingly had a differential influence in the population, whereas the order of their relative influence varies among different classes and social categories. The campaign was planned in such a way as to reach the sensibilities of practically all sectors within Chilean society. There was a slogan suitable for everyone. Considered as a whole, the propaganda carried a multi-directed message, characterized by a multi-sided appeal. However, the campaign was specifically oriented as well — it tried to maintain previously developed feelings of fear toward communism in particular social categories, i.e. women, 'middle-class,' 'white-collar,' and religious groups. The differential acceptability of the items suggests that the various forms of anti-communist agitation they express is related to different types of potential anti-communist receptivity, whereas the various issues included in the 'terror campaign' seem to be different aspects of a single multidimensional message.

Dichotomies

Bearing in mind the above considerations, it seemed to be suitable for the purposes of the research to develop an overall index measuring the multidimensional patterning of fear. In the early stages of the research we faced this problem in a rather traditional and intuitive way. Thus, on the basis of the answers to the 12 questions used in the questionnaire, the index was defined as: number of 'agreements' with *anti-communist* statements *minus* number of 'agreements' with *pro-communist* ones (FEAR1).

At first sight, nothing seems to be particularly wrong with this definition. A similar rationale is behind many indices as defined in the literature (cf. Hirschi and Selvin, 1967:207). However, the definition of the index is quite arbitrary.

First, it has been argued earlier that the wording of the questions could be affecting the answers of the subjects. This influence of the specific wording of questions upon answers has been explained, e.g., on the basis of the well-known tendency for people to 'agree' rather than to 'disagree.' It was for this reason that it was thought advisable to split the battery of questions into two halves. However, in the index defined above only 'agreements' either with anti-communist or with pro-communist statements are considered. What about 'disagreements'? One might, for example, argue that an index defined on the basis of 'agreement' with anti-communist statements and 'disagreements' with pro-communist ones 'taps better' the object to be measured.

A second aspect concerning the arbitrariness of indices of this type is related to the role of the residual answers (i.e. those answers that are neither 'agree' nor 'disagree', but 'don't know,' 'don't understand' or 'no answer'). In the definition the emphasis is set upon 'agreements' versus 'non-agreements,' so that the residual answers are included in the negative category. However, this is just one of several possible interpretations. Thus, for example, it could also be legitimate to ask whether centering the analysis in the number of 'disagreements' versus the number of 'not-disagreements' (i.e. the number of 'agree' plus the residual answers) is not more suitable for the theoretical interpretation of the measures.

In addition, a further source of ambiguity results from the assumptions of perfect attitude consistency underlying the definition of indices (cf. Suárez, 1980). At least two alternative assumptions are possible whenever there is a forced dichotomous coding of the answers, namely:

(1) $\{(ANT_{ji} = A) \leftrightarrow \sim(PRO_{ki} = A)\} \wedge \{(PRO_{ki} = A) \leftrightarrow \sim(ANT_{ji} = A)\}$
(2) $\{(ANT_{ji} = A) \leftrightarrow (PRO_{ki} = D)\} \wedge \{(PRO_{ki} = A) \leftrightarrow (ANT_{ji} = D)\}$

such that, given

(3) $ANT_j^*, PRO_k^* = \{A, D, R\}$

then:

(4) $\sim(ANT_{ji} = A) \leftrightarrow \{(ANT_{ji} = D) \vee (ANT_{ji} = R)\}$
(5) $\sim(PRO_{ki} = A) \leftrightarrow \{(PRO_{ki} = D) \vee (PRO_{ki} = R)\}$

where: ANT_{ji} = answer of individual i to anti-communist item ANT_j^*, PRO_{ki} = answer of individual i to pro-communist item PRO_k^*, and where A = 'agree', D = 'disagree', and R = residual answer, are the only three possible answers to the various items. (Logical Symbols: Λ = 'and', $\sim$ = 'not', V = 'or', $\leftrightarrow$ = 'if and only if'.)

The above discussion leads to the problem of validity. However, what is important for the discussion here is to realize the very arbitrariness of index construction whenever there is no theory on the basis of which it could be possible to fix the limits of interpretability of the measures empirically developed. As pointed out elsewhere (Suárez, 1980), in the absence of a guiding theory no possible decision can be taken between alternative definitions. The only way out in such conditions is to check for all possible interpretations on the grounds of empirical criteria. The lack of theory forces the definition of alternative measures. These alternative definitions are needed to handle the indeterminacy of the limits of interpretability that can be derived from simple and intuitive assumptions which, in the present case, result from the content analysis of the propaganda campaign. Such assumptions are too ambiguous and, consequently, are in need of further empirical checks and additional assumptions.

Accordingly, on the basis of all possible alternative dichotomous codings of the answers to the various items included in the index, four non-redundant measures may be defined as in Table 1. The indices resulting from the various ways of coding are difference-indices of the form $d = x - y$. However, it can be shown that these indices are redundant (i.e. explaining the same amount of variance) to additive-indices of the form $s = x' + y'$. Thus, for example, corresponding to the first index (FEAR1), one may define FEAR1* as the number of 'agreements' with anti-communist statements plus the number of 'disagreements' with pro-communist ones. The option here is between one-dimensional and two-dimensional coding. Obviously, the coefficient of determination, r_{jk}^2, for the two versions of each index will be 1.00. Nevertheless, if the items were to be factor-analyzed, the particular configuration of the items in the factor space will be different. It should be noted in this respect that one-dimensional coding is the common practice since it is recommended in most textbooks (e.g. Galtung, 1970:251).

TABLE 1
Difference-indices resulting from alternative interpretations
of residual answers by means of dichotomous coding

	ANSWERS TO ITEMS		FEAR1	FEAR2	FEAR3	FEAR4
ANTI-COMMUNIST ITEMS	AGREE	(A)	1	1	1	1
	RESIDUAL	(R)	0	1	0	1
	DISAGREE	(D)	0	0	0	0
PRO-COMMUNIST ITEMS	AGREE	(A)	1	1	1	1
	RESIDUAL	(R)	0	1	1	0
	DISAGREE	(D)	0	0	0	0

In the definition of the indices, no place was left for any 'neutral category.' The residual answers are coded in such manner that when the scores in the composite indices are computed the trichotomous raw-items are reduced to dichotomies; i.e., each item is defined as a two-point scale. In this respect, the logic underlying the various indices is the same. Notwithstanding, when considering how the residual answers are interpreted, the various versions of the index are shown to be grounded on a different rationale.

First, it can be shown that, underlying the definition of the first two difference-indices (FEAR1 and FEAR2), the first assumption concerning perfect response consistency is present. On the other hand, the last two versions (FEAR3 and FEAR4) are grounded on an interpretation of attitude consistency based on the second assumption.

Second, in the case of FEAR1 and FEAR3, the trichotomous raw-items corresponding to the answers to the anti-communist items are recoded so that a value of 1 is assigned to 'agree' (i.e. to A) whereas 0 stands for 'not-agree' (i.e. for D or R). The same is true in the case of FEAR1 and FEAR4 regarding the coding of answers to pro-communist items. Conversely, in the case of FEAR2 and FEAR4 the answers to the anti-communist items are coded so that 1 stands for 'not-disagree' (i.e. for A or R) and 0 for 'disagree' (i.e. for D). A similar reduction is present in the coding of the pro-communist items included in FEAR2 and FEAR3. Thus, underlying the construction of the indices there are two different interpretations concerning the residual answers. In one case, the rationale for interpretation may be expressed in terms of the following dictum: 'he who is not for me is against me'; i.e., the residual category is made equivalent to the negative one. In the second case, the interpretation that finds expression in the coding is: 'he who is not against me is for me'; i.e., the residual category is made equivalent to the positive one. However, the two interpretations of the residual answers thus far considered in the construction of the indices do not exhaust all possible alternatives (see Galtung, 1970:94-102, 250-1).

Trichotomies

A third possible interpretation of the residual answers is to consider these answers as a real 'neutral category,' which is thought to be definite, independent, and not reducible either to the negative or to the positive category but standing 'somewhere between' (e.g. Eysenck, 1975:324; Galtung, 1970:251; Wilson, 1973:51-2). Alternatively, one may claim that there is no empirical ground for assessing what the residual answers express and that they should be interpreted accordingly as 'missing data' (cf., e.g., Caffrey and Capel, 1968). In both cases the argument seems to be: 'he who is not for me is not necessarily against me nor is he necessarily for me either.' Nevertheless, the two interpretations differ in one significant respect, namely whether or not it is possible to assign a value within a trichotomy to the residual answers. From this stems the rationale for the definition of a new series of alternative versions of the basic index.

A first possibility is to code the answers so that the value $+1$ stands for 'agreement', -1 for 'disagreement', and 0 for the residual answers, here interpreted as the 'neutral category' (cf.

Galtung, 1970:251). On the other hand, one may either estimate the missing data or delete from the analysis cases and/or items with incomplete data (e.g. Cattell, 1978:515-17; Rummel, 1970:258-65; for a review of various procedures for treating missing data in multivariate analysis, see Kim and Curry, 1976).

For practical reasons, item deletion is seldom attractive (particularly when the number of items is low) since most items contain a rather significant proportion of missing data. As for estimation, the prospects are particularly obscure for the case of qualitative data since most of the methods suggested (inserting means, median values, multiple regression/correlation estimates instead of the 'blanks' or using some sort of iterative procedure based on the above values as first estimates) seem to be inadequate for this type of data. In other cases, even if the statistics used 'make sense' the assumptions concerning the distributions may not. Furthermore, when there is a limited number of possible values — as in a trichotomy — the error of the estimates may be as high as the error resulting from assigning values at random. For these and other reasons, with few exceptions, the common practice is to reduce the data matrix by deleting cases. In addition, 'pairwise' deletion is preferred to 'listwise' deletion, since the second procedure usually leads to a substantial reduction of the number of cases ('pairwise' deletion is available as the 'default option' in the most popular packages of statistical programs, namely, SPSS and OSIRIS).

Resulting from the above considerations, at least three additional difference-indices (FEAR5, FEAR6, and FEAR7) should be defined to check for the ambiguity of the coding procedures. The sets of codings corresponding to each alternative index are presented in Table 2. The first coding procedure (FEAR5) may be labeled 'simple bipolar coding' while the other two (FEAR6 and FEAR7) may be termed 'simple bipolar coding with deletion.' It should be noted that, as in the case of those indices based on dichotomous coding, it could be possible to define the indices by coding all items in one direction (either pro- or anti-communist). Of course, the information will be redundant although the configuration will be different.

Some remarks are pertinent at this point. First, deletion of missing data is tantamount to reducing the trichotomies to dichotomies, although residual answers are not collapsed either with the positive or with the negative category. Second, it seems that, normally,

TABLE 2

Difference-indices resulting from alternative interpretations of residual answers by means of trichotomous coding*

ANSWERS TO ITEMS		FEAR5	FEAR6[a]	FEAR7[b]
ANTI-COMMUNIST ITEMS AGREE	(A)	1	1	1
RESIDUAL	(R)	0	–	–
DISAGREE	(D)	-1	-1	-1
PRO-COMMUNIST ITEMS AGREE	(A)	1	1	1
RESIDUAL	(R)	0	–	–
DISAGREE	(D)	-1	-1	-1

*In the cases of FEAR6 and FEAR7 residual answers are not coded but deleted from the analysis: [a] pairwise deletion; [b] listwise deletion.

research tradition rather than theoretical assumptions is at the core of choice between trichotomous and dichotomous coding when comparing research in Europe and in the USA — European scholars seem to be more prone to the use of trichotomies than their counterparts in the United States (contrast, e.g., Eysenck, 1975; Galtung, 1970; and Wilson, 1973, with Cattell, 1978; and Rummel, 1970). Finally, it could be thought that a trichotomous interpretation has a higher degree of isomorphism with the structure of the data than a dichotomous one (cf. Galtung, 1970:251; Wilson, 1973:51-2). However, as Galtung also claims, 'the most important assumption is that clear answers are about equally distant from the middle' (1970:251); if this is not the case, 'the trichotomy should be reduced to a dichotomy.'

SOME PROBLEMS OF INTERPRETATION

Some cautions should be borne in mind. None of the indices can be thought of as actually measuring the impact of the 1970 'terror campaign' exclusively. This assertion leads once again to the problem of validity. The indices, insofar as they were built upon reactions to the issues agitated in that specific campaign, reflect its impact on the population. However, one must be aware of the fact that, before the 'terror campaign' of 1970, anti-communist propaganda had been, with more or less emphasis, a common denominator in Chilean politics. Thus, the indices can be better assumed to measure not only the impact of the specific campaign of 1970 but also the sedimentation in the minds of the people of previous anti-communist agitation.

None of the indices solves the problem faced in connection with the possibility of a unique interpretation of the residual answers. The basic problem here lies in the coding of the residual answers in the raw-items, in which the cognitive and evaluative components are mixed (cf. Galtung, 1970:94-102). The residual category includes three different types of answers: 'don't know,' 'don't understand,' and 'no-answer.' Whenever there is no empirical basis for further analysis of these answers and the cognitive level of the respondents cannot be assessed, each type of answer in the residual category could have more than one interpretation. Thus, for example, for some, 'don't know' may be an expression of *uncertainty* in the sense that the subject is prone neither to an open anti-communist attitude nor to an opposed one: he could be somewhere in the middle. In this sense, the subject's answer is of the kind that Galtung identifies as 'evaluative don't know.' For others, on the contrary, 'don't know' may be an expression of *evasion*: the subject doesn't want to give an answer and says 'don't know' only to cover his unwillingness to answer. This type of 'don't know' could be labeled 'evasive don't know.' It should be noted that 'evasive don't knows' are equivalent to a subset of the class of 'no answers': the case in which the individual chooses not to answer because he is not willing to answer. Finally, 'don't knows' can be interpreted as '*cognitive* don't knows': the individual answers 'don't know' because he really doesn't know. It should be noted again that in this case 'don't know' answers are equivalent to another subset of the class of 'no answers': the individual doesn't answer because he doesn't know. Similar analyses could be done for each one of the different types of answers included in the residual category. The important point, however, is that normally there is no empirical way to assess the different qualifications of the answers included in the category.

When interpreting the measurements it should be remembered that the scaling is arbitrary and that the transformation of the nominal raw-items into two-point interval-like scales leads to dubious assumptions when considered from the point of view of substantive theory. Thus, for example, it is assumed that between 'agreeing' with an anti-communist statement and 'not-agreeing' with it there is the same difference as between 'agreeing' and 'not-agreeing' with a pro-communist one (FEAR1). Similar or even stronger assumptions are present when considering other indices. The problems that arise from these assumptions are twofold. On the one hand, no attention is paid to the possible socio-psychological (and not only logical) different implications of 'agreeing' and 'disagreeing' as well as of 'not-agreeing' and 'not-disagreeing.' On the other hand, these assumptions can hardly be accepted if one considers, for example, that in the midst of strong anti-communist propaganda it could be expected to be psychologically 'easier' — in the social context of the interview — to agree (or, at least, not to disagree) with an anti-communist slogan rather than with a pro-communist one. Underlying the difficulty are the problems described in the literature as acquiescence, social desirability, and response set (e.g. Nunally, 1967:593-617; Peabody, 1966; Phillips, 1973:17-67). It could be argued that the problem can be easily solved by defining the various dichotomous or trichotomous variables so that different weights might be set for the various differences, thus taking into account the 'psychological distance.' However, it should be noted that, if the interval is not constant, the result will be a theoretically unwarranted weighting of the items.

An additional problem, closely related to the one discussed above, is that underlying the indices is the assumption that the answers to the various items are comparable. What is assumed is the commensurability of the items, a common assumption in index construction (e.g., Guttman, 1950:51-9) recently challenged by Lindsey (1977) on the grounds of Marx (1977:56). Moreover, although Galtung (1970:251) claims that one should not be concerned with the ambiguous interpretability of the resulting scores because 'it lies in the nature of any index,' one should be aware of its implications whenever Guttman-scalability cannot be assessed and commensurability is doubtful. If no differential weighting is introduced, one is forced to assume item interchangeability (cf. Lazarsfeld, 1968:609-17). If, on the contrary, items are weighted one should be aware that most weighting procedures are either arbitrary or lead to tautological reasoning or even to paradoxes. Thus, for example, if one weights an item higher because it seems to be 'harder,' the meaning of this qualification is rather ambiguous and will depend on the cultural as well as theoretical frame in which both the subjects and the researcher find themselves. It could be thought that the proportion of subjects agreeing (or, conversely, disagreeing) with a given item is a good estimator of its 'hardness.' However, this kind of argumentation leads to another assumption, namely, that it is necessary to substract (or, conversely, to add) from the various items that part that makes them different so that the items become 'equal.' Another approach could be to rank the items using 'judges' or 'experts' or population samples. In this case, the weighting will be based in 'the ideology of everyday perception.' It is also possible to argue that those items that correlate lower to the other items in the set should correspondingly be given a lower weight (e.g. McGranahan et al., 1972:132-4). However, the above is tantamount to saying that what the researcher should search for is perfect correlation between the items. If this is accepted, one should ask — at least in the case of simple additive indices, in which no assumptions are made concerning cummulativity as contrasted to the case of a perfect Guttman scale — why several items are necessary. On the other hand, no weighting is tantamount to assuming a priori the equivalence between the items — not weighting means that an equal weight is given to all items. This leads us again to the discussion concerning the rationale behind weighting.

The interpretation of dichotomies or trichotomies as interval-like two-point or three-point scales — necessary if one is to include the items in an additive or difference-index, since neither nominal nor ordinal variables can be added or substracted (Stevens, 1974) — is far beyond the possibility of empirical test. It has been argued (Guilford, 1954:345) that inspection of the normality of the distribution can be used as a criterion. However, no method is available to estimate unambiguously the distances between 'agreements', 'disagreements' and residual answers. Hence, the basic assumption for interval measurement remains unwarranted and as a matter of judgment.

Finally, neither the validity nor the reliability of indices of the type discussed here can be assessed by means of usual empirical procedures, since consistency assumptions underlay their definition (cf. Suárez, 1980). Therefore, the measures cannot be evaluated as to their content except by fiat unless a theory is developed on the basis of which it could be possible to derive the measures as well as the distances between the scores.

STRUCTURES

The basic assumption in factor analysis (e.g., Cattell, 1978; Gorsuch, 1974; Harman, 1967; Mulaik, 1972; Rummel, 1970) concerns the possibility of finding independent sources of variation in a given set of data. The goal of factor analysis is the decomposition of a set of observed variables as linear functions of another set of additive composites of the first one, called 'factors,' with known mathematical and statistical properties. Whenever the factors reproduce both the variables and their interrelations with a reduced loss of information, the system of factors can be thought of as a model of the system of variables. In this sense, it is claimed that factor analysis offers a mathematical and statistical model for the description of a set of variables. What is assumed is that the factor structure is isomorphous to the structure of the data and, by implication, with the structure of the real domain represented by the data (e.g., Ahmavaara and Markkanen, 1958; Rummel, 1967).

On these grounds, there have been many attempts to develop theories on the most diverse subjects supported with the results of factor analysis. Particularly, psychologists have striven to find out 'the vectors of mind' (e.g., Spearman, 1904; Thurstone, 1935; Burt, 1940; Thomson, 1948). Most of the development concerning the mathematical and statistical foundations of factor analysis is due to these efforts. Nevertheless, it was soon clear that reification of factors was doubtful since the results were not unique. The number and structure of the factors were shown to be dependent on particular techniques (e.g. two-factor, bifactor, centroid, principal-axes) used in the extraction of factors; on different approaches to orthogonal (e.g. Varimax, Quartimax or Equimax) or oblique (e.g. Biquartimin, Promax or Maxplane) rotation to 'simple structure'; on assumptions concerning communalities and variance components (e.g. principal components or common-factor analysis); and on criteria for deciding the number of factors (e.g. Guttman-Kaiser's eigenvalue-one criterion or Cattell's scree-test).

Notwithstanding the dependability of factor-analytical results, it is still a common practice among users of the method to interpret the factors as supporting one or another theory on 'the dimensions of nations,' 'the dimensions of politics,' 'the dimensions of conflict,' or the dimensions of whatever it may be (e.g. Eysenck, 1954, 1956, 1975; Gregg and Banks, 1965; Oster, 1979; Rokeach and Fruchter, 1956; Rummel, 1972; Tanter, 1966; Wilson, 1973). Much of the controversy between conflicting theories is focused on the number of 'dimensions discovered' in a given domain. However, as one author puts it, 'The difference is at least partly accountable for in terms of the different factor-analytic methods popular in Britain and the U.S.A.' (Ray, 1973).

To cope with the problem of the idiosyncracy of the results due to the specific techniques used, Rummel (1970:453) advocates some sort of standardization of the procedures employed if the results are to be comparable. Additionally, one may use some method of matrix transformation to rotate the factors found in one study to a least-squares fit to the factor matrix resulting from another, for example, by using Ahmavaara's (1954) transformation analysis or Schönemann and Carrol's (1970) rigid rotation (see also, Gorsuch, 1974:166-8; Levine, 1977:37-52; Rummel, 1970:449-71) to minimize exogenous influence. Whether transformation analysis or rigid rotation is used, the matrices are to some extent forced to convergence since the methods lead to a best fit (cf. Hurley and Cattell, 1962). In this sense, Jöreskog's confirmatory factor analysis (e.g., Jöreskog and Sörbom, 1978) may be a better alternative to matrix comparison than 'target analysis.' However, the fact remains that different procedures lead to different solutions so that the resulting factors are not unique and any attempt to reify them is misleading.

In addition to the technical procedures used, it is claimed that one may judge the invariance of factor-analytical results by due consideration of the units and the variables included in the analysis (e.g. Cattell, 1978:248-51; Gorsuch, 1974:249-57). Following Galtung (1970:437), one may also bring to consideration differences in data collection (for example, whether verbal or nonverbal data has been used) as well as concerning the set of possible values (e.g. number of cutting points or variations in their selection) in the variables.

It is the problem of 'replication on the value side,' as Galtung calls it, that has been particularly neglected in the theoretical interpretation of factor-analytical results. The number of values (for example, whether a dichotomy or a trichotomy is used) as well as the specific cuts chosen (e.g. owing to alternative coding procedures) may affect significantly the correlations between the variables (Galtung, 1970:444-9). From this follows directly that factorial results, no matter which solution is used, may be different depending on the coding procedures.

The extent to which alternative codings may affect the loadings of items on the resulting factors is illustrated by the figures presented in Table 3. Had we also included in the comparison the results for items coded in only one direction, the differences, owing to the appearance of one general factor, would have been even greater. However, since we are interested in illustrating the effect of alternative interpretations of the residual answers, the inclusion of such results would have confused the point to be stressed.

In working out the present analysis, we experienced at the computer several factor models (common, principal-components, alpha, image and canonical) and various rotated solutions (both orthogonal and oblique). Notwithstanding some minor differences, the results are similar. Nevertheless, I have deliberately chosen for this and the following illustrations the 'default-option' solution available in most statistical packages, namely principal-axes factoring with iteration of a correlation matrix (Pearson's r), R^2 as first communality estimates, Varimax rotation and Guttman-Kaiser's eigenvalue-one criterion for the number of factors (the program used is described in Nie et al., 1975:468-514). Following the usual practice, loadings were considered salient and allowing for interpretation when above or equal to 0.3 (cf. Gorsuch, 1974:186).

Although 'default-option' factor analysis may produce the most extreme results, in general the differences found are independent of the particular model, technique or rotation solution as well as of whether one-dimensional or two-dimensional coding is used. Consequently, the factorial structure of the attitudes and/or beliefs is not invariant under changing interpretations of the residual answers.

These results may be partly explained by changes in the distribution of the variables, the amount of information loss, and the selection bias resulting from alternative coding procedures. Particularly when the variables are highly skewed in opposite directions, the

TABLE 3
Varimax rotated matrices from seven common-factor analyses*

	DICHOTOMOUS CODING								TRICHOTOMOUS CODING					
	ASSUMPTION I				ASSUMPTION II				BIPOLAR CODING		PAIRWISE DELETION		LISTWISE DELETION	
	FEAR1		FEAR2		FEAR3		FEAR4		FEAR5		FEAR6		FEAR7	
ITEMS	F1	F2	F1	F2	F1	F2	F1	F2	F1	F2	F1	F2	F1	F2
ANT1		51		59		48		58		53		55		59
ANT2		42		56		45		54		53		54		54
ANT3		63		58		56		56		57		63		62
ANT4		67		66	−41	58	−40	60	−41	61	−43	65	−38	68
ANT5		64		68	−36	59	−34	61	−35	61	−37	67	−35	67
ANT6		43		42	−44		−31	33	−35		−37	32		47
PRO1	51		51		50		45		49		53		63	−32
PRO2	63		62		58		56	−30	58		62	−32	62	−37
PRO3	57		65		65		58		63		67		65	
PRO4	64		60		50	−39	59	−31	58	−35	64	−38	67	−41
PRO5	52		51		42	−33	44	−33	44	−31	46	−33	53	−35
PRO6	68		65		67		70		70		75		78	
% TV	19.5	17.1	19.7	18.7	21.1	16.4	20.3	18.5	21.5	14.6	24.5	20.5	25.7	23.1
% CV	53.3	46.7	51.3	48.7	56.3	43.7	52.3	47.7	59.6	40.4	54.4	45.6	52.7	47.3

* Only loadings ⩾ |0.30| are presented (decimal points omitted).
TV = total variance; CV = common variance.

estimated loadings may be substantially biased (cf. Olsson, 1978). Since the degree and direction of skewness may be affected by the codings, the correlation coefficients may be underestimated in some cases and overestimated in others, specially when Pearson's *r*, assuming normality, is used as a measure of association. Moreover, when classifying data, the amount of information lost is related to the similarity within each class as contrasted to the amount of dissimilarity between various classes. When dichotomizing the answers to the items by inclusion of residual answers in one or another category, the assumption of similarity is dubious so that the information loss may be substantial as compared to the case of trichotomous coding (cf., for the case of interval and ordinal data, Bryson and Phillips, 1974). Finally, under conditions of sub-sampling, as when deletion of missing data occurs, essentially different patterns may result from the same data, depending on the criteria for selection used (e.g., Gorsuch, 1974:305-10; Olsson, 1978). Particularly when the variables on which multivariate selection occurs are included in the analysis, the results may be misleading owing to the appearance of spurious factors. Under certain conditions, the restriction of range caused by selection may produce significant shifts of the position of the variables in the factor space so that the whole configuration may be different.

In addition, reduction of the number of categories may result in confirmation bias. Given a hypothesized relation between two variables, the probability that random distributions will confirm the hypothesis will be higher for a reduced set of values (Galtung, 1970:445). On the other hand, by changing the position of the cuts, not only the level but also the direction of the association measures may be affected (Galtung, 1970:448-9). By extension, both sources of variation will be present in factorial results based upon the same data but for which the coding has been performed according to different rationales.

Since usually no theory is behind the selected coding procedure, the results are based on unwarranted assumptions, and so are the 'theories' that imply some form of reification of the factors found.

CODING SYSTEMS

The coding procedures used in the transformation to interval-like scales of the nominal classifications of the answers to the various

TABLE 4
Coding procedures

ANSWERS TO ITEMS		DICHOTOMOUS CODING		TRICHOTOMOUS CODING	
		FORM A	FORM B	FORM C	FORM D
AGREE	(A)	1	1	1	1
RESIDUAL	(R)	0	1	0	-
DISAGREE	(D)	0	0	-1	-1

pro-communist and anti-communist items can be schematically summarized as in Table 4. However, the decomposition of a nominal variable or classificatory system with k categories into less than $k-1$ components does not allow for a full reproduction of the information contained in the parent variable. Neither less nor more than $k-1$ different vectors are needed to account for the distinctions within the full set of categories (e.g., Cohen and Cohen, 1975:172-3; Kerlinger and Pedhazur, 1973:117-18).

Five main coding systems have been discussed in the literature, namely dummy, ordinal, effect, orthogonal (or contrast), and random (or nonsense) coding. Since its introduction by Suits (1957), dummy coding has grown in popularity and it is widely used by sociologists in path and multiple regression analysis. Ordinal coding (Lyons, 1971), on the contrary, remains excluded from normal research. The same can be said in relation to the other three

TABLE 5
Coding systems

NOMINAL CATEGORY	DUMMY X_{11}	X_{21}	ORDINAL X_{12}	X_{22}	EFFECT X_{13}	X_{23}	ORTHOGONAL[a] X_{14}	X_{24}	ORTHOGONAL[b] X_{15}	X_{25}	RANDOM[c] X_{16}	X_{26}
A	1	0	1	1	1	0	1	0	n_B+n_C	0	r_1	r_1^2
B	0	1	0	1	0	1	$-\frac{1}{2}$	1	$-n_A$	n_C	r_2	r_2^2
C	0	0	0	0	-1	-1	$-\frac{1}{2}$	-1	$-n_A$	$-n_B$	r_3	r_3^2

a. Example of orthogonal coding with equal n's.
b. Example of orthogonal coding with unequal n's where $n_A \neq n_B \neq n_C$ represent the number of cases in category A, B, and C, respectively;
c. $r_1 \neq r_2 \neq r_3$ are any three real numbers, positive or negative, integral or fractional, assigned at random.

coding systems (for a representation of their properties and use in multiple regression analysis, see Cohen and Cohen, 1975:171-211; Kerlinger and Pedhazur, 1973:116-51). Table 5 illustrates the decomposition of a trichotomous nominal variable according to the various coding systems.

The operation called 'coding' consists in the assignment of arbitrary symbols to a set of objects to indicate membership in mutually exclusive and complementary subsets in a classification. Three conditions are satisfied by the coding systems considered here. First, the symbols are numbers, allowing for the resulting vectors to be used in numerical analysis. Second, each category is uniquely represented by one and only one vector among the set resulting from the decomposition, whereas all the information contained in the parent variable is accounted for by the full set of vectors. Third, no vector in the set representing the parent variable can be fully reproduced as a linear combination of the others. In addition, in the case of orthogonal contrast coding the vectors are uncorrelated (linearly independent), so that no redundant information is contained in the set.

Some conclusions can be drawn when comparing Tables 4 and 5. Whereas Form A is identical to X_{11} and X_{12}, Form B is the same as X_{22} and Form C is equivalent to X_{13}. Form A in conjunction with Form B fully represent the parent variable in accordance to ordinal coding, whereas each form is a partial representation of that variable. Consequently, the information contained in the various items is only partially accounted for by the alternative coding forms, except Form D. Since in the case of Form D the original trichotomy was reduced beforehand to a dichotomy by means of deletion of one of the categories as missing data, only one vector is needed to represent the information contained in the reduced parent variable. Of course, the original nominal classification is only partially reproduced.

The result of the above is that the information contained in the items included in the various indices is only partially entered in the factor analyses reported in Table 3. As a consequence, the number of factors, the loadings, the configuration of items in the factor space, and the communalities may be biased owing to unwarranted selection of the information contained in the original variables. The extent to which the results are significantly different can be judged on the basis of the figures presented in Table 6.

TABLE 6
Number of factors, total variance explained, and sum of eigenvalues, before and after iteration

CODING PROCEDURE	N OF FACTORS BEFORE	AFTER	TOTAL VARIANCE BEFORE	AFTER	SUM OF EIGENVALUES BEFORE	AFTER
1.0. Dichotomous coding						
1.1. Assumption I:						
(1) FEAR1	2	2	46.8	36.6	5.616	4.390
(2) FEAR2	2	2	48.4	38.4	5.812	4.612
1.2. Assumption II:						
(3) FEAR3	2	1	47.8	32.8	5.733	3.937
(4) FEAR4	2	1	48.8	33.6	5.854	4.032
2.0. Trichotomous cod						
2.1. Simple bipolar coding:						
(5) FEAR5	2	1	49.1	33.4	5.891	4.002
2.2. Pairwise deletion:						
(6) FEAR6	2	1	53.9	38.4	6.466	4.605
2.3. Listwise deletion:						
(7) FEAR7	2	1	57.4	42.9	6.888	5.153
3.0. Full coding						
3.1. Dummy coding	7	4	68.0	46.6	16.326	11.176
3.2. Ordinal coding	7	4	68.0	46.6	16.326	11.176
3.3. Effect coding	6	3	62.9	42.8	15.094	10.270
3.4. Random coding	3	2	44.6	33.5	10.714	8.031
3.5. Orthogonal coding	3	2	43.8	33.2	10.522	7.961

It should be noted that in most statistical packages the factors retained for further analysis when using the common-factor model are those that are estimated to be significant, according to some pre-established criterion, before the iterative process begins, i.e. on the bases of the first communality estimates. After iteration, the number of factors that fit the criterion may be different so that an additional source of ambiguity is to be considered when interpreting the final, rotated solution. The main point, however, is that, whether or not the decision concerning the number of factors is made before or after iteration, there are important differences when comparing the results both regarding the number of factors and the percent of variance explained. These differences are most significant when contrasting the various forms of partial coding with the case in which the full information contained in the original classifications is entered into the analysis.

Since in all but one of the coding systems the vectors representing the parent variables are correlated (i.e. partially redundant), and since these correlations are spurious, the interpretation of factorial results is not clear. In the case of orthogonal contrast coding, however, owing to the vectors being uncorrelated some important consequences may be drawn from the results.

The rationale for orthogonal coding may be roughly described as follows. Given a set of k groups or subsamples with unequal n's, a 'contrast' or comparison is defined as

$$(6) \quad C = a_1 n_1 + a_2 n_2 + \ldots + a_j n_j + \ldots + a_k n_k = 0$$

where: C = contrast or comparison; a_j = coefficient; n_j = number of cases in group j such that $\Sigma n_j = N$ = total number of cases in the sample (with equal n's the condition reduces to $\Sigma a_j = 0$). For $k = 3$ (as in the case of the items considered in the illustration), two comparisons are orthogonal if

$$(7) \quad n_1 a_{11} a_{21} + n_2 a_{12} a_{22} + n_3 a_{13} a_{23} = 0$$

where the first subscript for each coefficient refers to the number of the comparison and the second to the number of the group, subsample or category. On these grounds, the items were coded as indicated in Table 7. The first vector contrasts 'agreements' versus 'disagreements' while minimizing, as in the cases of simple bipolar trichotomies and effect coding, the influence of residual answers.

The second vector produces a comparison between residual and opinionated answers. As the figures in Table 8 indicate, this particular way of coding the answers leads to a three-factor solution when using 'default-option' factor analysis.

Two features must be borne in mind. First, when the full information contained in the items is brought into the analysis, all residual answers are clustered together irrespective of the content of the items, i.e. whether or not the 'don't knows,' etc., correspond to a pro-communist or an anti-communist statement. This may be interpreted as indicative of the existence of a group of 'know-nothings' in the population, something that is of interest in itself and not evidenced in the previous analyses presented in Table 3. Second, the factor associated with the residual answers (Factor 1) accounts for most of the common variance (45.4 percent) and for a relatively high proportion of the total variance (16.4 percent). Consequently, to omit this factor in an account of the 'dimensions of anti-communism' entails a gross simplification. This is further

TABLE 7
Orthogonal coding*

ANSWERS TO ITEMS		C_1	C_2
AGREE	(A)	n_D	$-n_R$
DISAGREE	(D)	$-n_A$	$-n_R$
RESIDUAL	(R)	0	$n_A + n_D$

* Note that this is only one possible set of contrast codes. n_k = number of cases in category k.

TABLE 8
Varimax rotated common-factor matrix for orthogonal codings*

ITEMS	FACTOR1	FACTOR2	FACTOR3	COMMUNALITY
ANT11		-.30	.52	.36
ANT12			.47	.22
ANT13			.57	.40
ANT14		-.44	.59	.55
ANT15		-.39	.59	.50
ANT16		-.36		.20
PRO11		.51		.30
PRO12		.61		.43
PRO13		.62		.39
PRO14		.60	-.30	.46
PRO15		.46		.29
PRO16		.71		.51
ANT21	.51			.26
ANT22	.46			.23
ANT23	.51			.27
ANT24	.60			.36
ANT25	.64			.41
ANT26	.62			.40
PRO21	.49			.24
PRO22	.59			.35
PRO23	.64			.43
PRO24	.52			.29
PRO25	.59			.35
PRO26	.59			.36
% TV	16.4	11.7	8.0	
% CV	45.4	32.5	22.1	

* Only loadings $\geq |0.30|$ are reported.

TABLE 9
Communalities

| ITEM | DICHOTOMOUS CODING | | | | TRICHOTOMOUS CODING | | | ORTHOGONAL |
| | ASSUMPTION I | | ASSUMPTION II | | BIPOLAR | PAIRWISE | LISTWISE | CONTRAST CODING |
	FEAR1	FEAR2	FEAR3	FEAR4	FEAR5	FEAR6	FEAR7	
ANT1	.30	.39	.30	.40	.35	.39	.43	.32
ANT2	.17	.31	.21	.30	.28	.29	.31	.23
ANT3	.40	.38	.37	.37	.39	.46	.44	.34
ANT4	.53	.51	.51	.52	.55	.61	.61	.46
ANT5	.46	.50	.48	.49	.50	.59	.57	.46
ANT6	.21	.18	.27	.21	.20	.24	.30	.30
PRO1	.29	.29	.29	.28	.29	.35	.51	.27
PRO2	.42	.43	.41	.41	.42	.48	.53	.39
PRO3	.33	.43	.45	.35	.40	.46	.45	.41
PRO4	.44	.42	.41	.44	.46	.55	.63	.38
PRO5	.30	.29	.29	.31	.29	.33	.40	.33
PRO6	.48	.43	.47	.52	.51	.58	.65	.44

stressed when considering the total amount of variance explained by the factors retained as significant, as indicated by the sum of their eigenvalues (see Table 6, above).

Finally, since the vectors representing each item are uncorrelated, it could be argued that their communalities correspond to independent portions of the variance of the parent nominal variable, and as such they might be added and divided by the number of orthogonal vectors to estimate the communality of the item's full variance. In Table 9 these estimations are contrasted to the communalities resulting from the factor analyses of the partial information of the items as presented earlier (see Table 3 above). As figures indicate, there are substantial differences regarding communalities owing to variations in the way of interpreting residual answers as expressed in the various coding procedures even if the column for orthogonal coding is excluded from the comparison. Thus, for example, the range for PRO_6 is from 0.43 to 0.65: a variant of about 50 percent! The main point, however, is that, when the full information contained in the items is allowed to enter in the analysis, the estimated communalities are not affected by any selection bias, change in the distributions, or information loss resulting from arbitrary collapsing of categories, deletion of residual answers, and/or partial representation of variables.

If the above argument is correct, many consequences might be drawn regarding, for example, normal uses of factor analysis in the assessment of validity and reliability. Nevertheless, the above should be considered with caution since much experimentation is needed concerning the use of orthogonal coding in factor analysis. These first results and the analysis thereof do not do more than to open the door to further research.

SUMMARY AND CONCLUDING COMMENTS

In this paper I have been concerned with some sources of ambiguity in common interpretations of factorial results as warranting evidence for the assessment of the structure of attitude and/or belief systems. I have argued that composite indices are dependent on the procedures used in the coding of the answers to the items included in the indices. Particularly, I have discussed the effect of various ways of dealing with residual answers on the resulting composites. Furthermore, I have illustrated how alternative codings may affect the patterning of the items in the factor space and the extent to which differences are of importance for the theoretical reconstruction of the real structure. Finally, I have tried to show that common approaches to coding of items in factor-analytical studies lead to a partial representation of the items so that the results may be misleading since not all the information is entered into the analysis.

Some main conclusions should be stressed. First, coding is not a trivial operation but it entails assumptions that should be made explicit since various alternatives are possible. Second, whenever coding assumptions cannot be derived from a theory, as is usually the case, testing for invariance over alternative coding procedures is required to avoid too precipitate conclusions regarding the structure of a given attitudinal domain on the basis of factorial results. Third, factor analysis of items as coded for computation of final scores in additive or difference-indices do not allow for reproduction of the full information accounted for by the items since these are only partially represented by the codings. Finally and most important, factors should be de-reified. Dimensional theories based on factorial results are to be cautiously examined since solutions are not unique but depend, inter alia, on particular procedures used in the coding of raw-data. Factors are not 'discovered' but are constructed, on the basis of a set of assumptions. Factors allow for the representation of a set of variables by means of a model, which only under very restrictive conditions may be developed into a theory.

REFERENCES

Ahmavaara, Y. (1954) 'Transformation Analysis of Factorial Data,' *Annales Academiae Scientiarum Fennicae*, vol. 88:1-150.

Ahmavaara, Y. and T. Markkanen (1958) *The Unified Factor Model*. Helsinki: Finnish Foundation for Alcohol Studies.

Barton, A. H. and R. W. Parsons (1977) 'Measuring Belief System Structure,' *Public Opinion Quarterly*, vol. 41:159-80.

Bryson, K. R. and D. P. Phillips (1974) 'Method for Classifying Interval-scale Data and Ordinal-scale Data,' pp. 171-90 in D. R. Heise (ed.), *Sociological Methodology 1975*. San Francisco: Jossey-Bass.

Burt, C. (1940) *The Factors of the Mind*. London: University of London Press.

Caffrey, B. and W. C. Capel (1968) 'The Predictive Value of Neutral Positions in Opinion and Attitude Research,' *Journal of Psychology*, vol. 69:145-54.

Cattell, R. B. (1952) *Factor Analysis*. New York: Harper.

Cattell, R. B. (1978) *The Scientific Use of Factor Analysis in Behavioral and Life Sciences*. New York: Plenum Press.

Cohen, J. and P. Cohen (1975) *Applied Multiple Regression/Correlation Analysis for the Behavioral Sciences*. Hillsdale: Lawrence Erlbaum Associates.

Deutscher, I. (1966) 'Words and Deeds: Social Science and Social Policy,' *Social Problems*, vol. 13:235-54.

Eysenck, H. J. (1954) *The Psychology of Politics*. London: Routledge and Kegan Paul.

Eysenck, H. J. (1956) 'The Psychology of Politics and the Personality Similarities between Fascists and Communists,' *Psychological Bulletin*, vol. 53:431-8.

Eysenck, H. J. (1975) 'The Structure of Social Attitudes,' *British Journal of Social and Clinical Psychology*, vol. 14:323-31.

Feyerabend, P. K. (1970) 'Against Method: Outline of an Anarchistic Theory of Knowledge,' *Minnesota Studies in the Philosophy of Science*, vol. 4:17-130.

Galtung, J. (1970) *Theory and Methods of Social Research*. Oslo: Scandinavian University Books.

Gorsuch, R. L. (1974) *Factor Analysis*. Philadelphia: Saunders.

Gregg, P. M. and A. S. Banks (1965) 'Dimensions of Political Systems: Factor Analysis of a Cross-Polity Survey,' *American Political Science Review*, vol. 59:602-14.

Guilford, J. P. (1954) *Psychometric Methods*. London: McGraw-Hill.

Guttman, L. (1950) 'The Problem of Attitude and Opinion Measurement,' pp. 46-59 in S. A. Stouffer et al. (eds), *Measurement and Prediction*. Princeton: Princeton University Press.

Harman, H. H. (1967) *Modern Factor Analysis*. Chicago: University of Chicago Press.

Hirschi, T. and H. C. Selvin (1967) *Delinquency Research. An Appraisal of Analytic Methods*. New York: Free Press.

Hurley, J. R. and R. B. Cattell (1962) 'The Procrustes Program: Producing Direct Rotation to Test a Hypothesized Factor Structure,' *Behavioral Science*, vol. 7:165-78.

Jöreskog, K. G. and D. Sörbom (1978) *LISREL IV — User's Guide. Analysis of Linear Structural Relationships by the Method of Maximum Likelihood*. Chicago: National Educational Resources.

Kerlinger, F. N. and E. J. Pedhazur (1973) *Multiple Regression Analysis in Behavioral Research*. New York: Holt, Rinehart and Winston.

Kim, J. and J. Curry (1977) 'The Treatment of Missing Data in Multivariate Analysis', *Sociological Methods and Research*, vol. 6:215-40.

Kotarbinski, T. (1966) *Gnosiology. The Scientific Approach to the Theory of Knowledge*. Oxford: Pergamon Press.

La Piere, R. T. (1934) 'Attitudes versus Actions,' *Social Forces*, vol. 13:230-7.

Lazarsfeld, P. F. (1968) 'Evidence and Inference in Social Research,' pp. 608-34 in M. Brodbeck (ed.), *Readings in the Philosophy of the Social Sciences*. New York: Macmillan.

Levine, M. S. (1977) *Canonical Analysis and Factor Comparison*. Beverly Hills: Sage.

Lindsey, J. K. (1977) 'Variables and Scaling — A Reply,' *Quality and Quantity*, vol. 11:351-3.

Lyons, M. (1971) 'Techniques for Using Ordinal Measures in Regression and Path Analysis,' pp. 147-71 in H. L. Costner (ed.), *Sociological Methodology*. San Francisco: Jossey-Bass.

Marx, K. (1977) *Capital*, vol. 1. London: Lawrence and Wishart.

McGranahan, D. V. et al. (1972) *Contents and Measurement of Socioeconomic Development*. New York: Praeger

Mulaik, S. A. (1972) *The Foundations of Factor Analysis*. New York: McGraw-Hill.

Nie, N. H., C. H. Hull, J. G. Jenkins, K. Steinbrenner and D. H. Bent (1975) *SPSS. Statistical Package for the Social Sciences*. New York: McGraw-Hill.

Nunnally, J. C. (1967) *Psychometric Theory*. New York: McGraw-Hill.

Olsson, U. (1978) *Some Data Analytic Problems in Models with Latent Variables*. Uppsala: University of Uppsala.

Oster, G. (1979) 'A Factor Analytic Test of the Theory of Dual Economy,' *Review of Economics and Statistics*, vol. 61, 1:33-9.

Peabody, D. (1966) 'Authoritarianism Scales and Response Bias,' *Psychological Bulletin*, vol. 65:11-23.

Phillips, B. S. (1966) *Social Research. Strategy and Tactics*. New York: Macmillan.

Phillips, D. L. (1973) *Abandoning Method*. San Francisco: Jossey-Bass.

Przeworski, A. and H. Teune (1970) *The Logic of Comparative Social Inquiry*. New York: John Wiley.

Ray, J. J. (1973) 'Conservatism, Authoritarianism, and Related Variables: A Review and Empirical Study,' pp. 17-35 in G. D. Wilson (ed.), *The Psychology of Conservatism*. London: Academic Press.

Ray, J. J. (1976) 'Do Authoritarians Hold Authoritarian Attitudes?' *Human Relations*, vol. 29:307-25.

Rokeach, M. and B. Fruchter (1956) 'A Factorial Study of Dogmatism and Related Concepts,' *Journal of Abnormal and Social Psychology*, vol. 53: 356-60.

Rummel, R. J. (1967) 'Understanding Factor Analysis,' *Journal of Conflict Resolution*, vol. 11:444-80.

Rummel, R. J. (1970) *Applied Factor Analysis*. Evanston: Northwestern University Press.

Rummel, R. J. (1972) *The Dimensions of Nations*. Beverly Hills: Sage.

Schönemann, P. H. and R. M. Carrol (1970) 'Fitting One Matrix to Another under Choice of a Central Dilatation and Rigid Motion,' *Psychometrika*, vol. 35:245-55.

Schuman, H. and M. P. Johnson (1976) 'Attitudes and Behavior,' *Annual Review of Sociology*, vol. 2:161-207.

Spearman, C. (1904) 'General Intelligence, Objectively Determined and Measured,' *American Journal of Psychology*, vol. 15:201-93.

Stevens, S. S. (1974) 'Measurement,' pp. 22-41 in G. M. Maranell (ed.), *Scaling: A Scource-book for Behavioral Scientists*. Chicago: Aldine.

Suárez, P. (1970) *Las Dimensiones de la Sociedad. Introducción a la Metasociología*. Santiago: University of Chile Press.

Suárez, P. (1973) 'El Problema de los Referentes Empiricos,' Santiago: University of Chile (mimeo).

Suárez, P. (1975) 'Understanding Fascism: Some Data on the 'Terror Campaign' of 1970 in Chile,' Uppsala: Department of Sociology, Uppsala University. Paper presented at the IX Nordiska Sociologkongressen, 15-18 August 1976, Lund, Sweden.

Suárez, P. (1980) 'Attitude Consistency and Validity-Reliability Assumptions: An Exercise in Methodological Self-criticism,' *Quality and Quantity*, vol. 14: 415-29. Paper presented at the Ninth World Congress of Sociology, 14-19 August 1978, Uppsala, Sweden.

Suits, D. B. (1957) 'Use of Dummy Variables in Regression Equations,' *Journal of the American Statistical Assocation*, vol. 52:548-51.

Tanter, R. (1966) 'Dimensions of Conflict Behavior Within and Between Nations, 1958-69,' *Journal of Conflict Resolution*, vol. 10:1-20.

Thomson, G. H. (1948) *The Factorial Analysis of Human Abilities*. London: University of London Press.

Thurstone, L. L. (1928) 'Attitudes Can Be Measured,' *American Journal of Sociology*, vol. 33:529-54.

Thurstone, L. L. (1935) *The Vectors of Mind*. Chicago: University of Chicago Press.

Turner, S. P. (1979) 'The Concept of Face Validity,' *Quality and Quantity*, vol. 13:85-90.

US Senate (1975) *Covert Action in Chile, 1963-1973*. Washington: US Government Printing Office.

Wilson, G. D. (1973) 'The Factor Structure of the C-Scale,' pp. 71-92 in G. D. Wilson (ed.), *The Psychology of Conservatism*. London: Academic Press.

5

MEASUREMENT ISSUES IN MENTAL HEALTH NEEDS ASSESSMENT

Charles E. Holzer III
Yale University

Lynn Robbins
University of Florida

INTRODUCTION

The purpose of this paper is to examine the methodological basis for estimating community levels of mental health from aggregate social and demographic characteristics. This is accomplished through an examination of two competing models: one based on social area analysis and the other based on a strategy that we will call demographic risk assessment. Both approaches make use of aggregate demographic data such as are available in the US Census. The models differ, however, in that social area analysis takes primarily a geographical orientation and focuses on areas such as the census tract as its unit of analysis; whereas demographic risk assessment concentrates on individual levels of risk, as estimated through membership in demographic sub-populations defined by factors such as age, sex, and race. This paper identifies and tests

Authors' Note. This research was supported in part by NIMH Grant MH15900, John J. Schwab, Principal Investigator, and by NIMH Grant MH24740, George J. Warheit, Principal Investigator. Survey data for Polk and Jefferson Counties were made available by Roger A. Bell. MHDPS materials were made available by Harold F. Goldsmith, Beatrice M. Rosen, and Charles D. Windle. Special thanks are given to David Jackson for his encouragement and many suggestions.

basic assumptions of both models and provides an empirical comparison of their predictive powers.

The interest in these two methods is derived from their increasing use in the assessment of need for mental health services. Together they constitute what is termed the social indicators approach to needs assessment, a concept originally developed by Bauer (1966) in his call for a national system of social accounts. Many have hoped that estimates of need based on census data will provide an impartial and low-cost guide for the allocation of increasingly scarce mental health program dollars.

BACKGROUND

Demographic Risk Assessment

Demographic risk assessment has its origins in the epidemiological techniques of rate analysis, rate standardization (Malzberg, 1959), and ridit analysis (Langner and Michael, 1963: Bross and Feldman, 1956). In demographic risk assessment, rates supplied by a reference population are applied to the demographic profile of a population for which estimates are desired.

The demographic risk assessment procedure takes the following form. First, a criterion data base is obtained. This might consist of data obtained from sample surveys or from a case register of treated illness. The mental health criterion may be the fact of treatment, the presence of a specific diagnosis, or a high score on a standardized measure of mental health. Second, a set of relevant predictor variables is isolated. The predictors must be related to the mental health criterion variable and must be known in the population for which estimates are to be obtained. Age, sex, race, income, and marital status are important predictors, although other variables might also be considered. Third, each variable selected is categorized into a moderate number of levels, and a complete cross-tabulation of all the variables is formed. For each of the cells defined by the cross-tabulation, the specific proportion of individuals meeting the criterion of risk is determined.

In order to make an estimate of need for a specified population, a cross-tabulation matching that of the original reference population must be constructed with the population count within each cell obtained from census data or some similar source. This count is multiplied by the cell-specific rate obtained from the reference population to estimate the number of individuals within each cell needing service. Estimates of the total level of need are derived by summation of the cell estimates, with the proportion of total need obtained by dividing the estimated total need by the matching population total.

Demographic risk assessment rests on the assumption that rates within demographic sub-categories are the same in the population being estimated as in the criterion population. It is reasonable, therefore, to identify the circumstances that will meet this assumption, given that the utility of the demographic risk assessment method depends on the rates being as widely applicable as possible.

The psychiatric literature provides mixed evidence concerning the generality of rates. There is much evidence identifying certain variables that are strong and consistent predictors of psychological disorder, particularly those related to social status (cf. Dohrenwend and Dohrenwend, 1969). Life event and stress variables have also been consistently related to disorder. Nonetheless, the specific rates reported vary widely from study to study, reflecting methodological as well as substantive differences. The presence of a strong relationship with the predictor variable does not insure that the specific rates will be consistent across populations.

Epidemiological studies suggest that there may be regional differences as well as localized ecological variations in the rates of psychiatric disorder. Culture plays an important factor in mental health, with cultural differences identified in some but not all types of mental illness (Murphy, 1976). Schwab et al. (1974) have reported urban-rural differences in scores on a symptom measure. Also suggesting local differences in rates is the finding of Faris and Dunham (1939) that rates of treated illness were greater for whites living in black areas and for blacks living in white areas of the city. Similar results were obtained by Klee et al. (1967). Because these studies did not provide control for the relevant individual characteristics or factors controlling access to treatment facilities, more extensive tests of the generality of the rates within demographic sub-populations are needed. If such factors were established as major sources of variation, different rates would be needed for each new context. In essence, a typology of contexts would have to be established and included as one of the dimensions of the rate-setting cross-tabulation.

Applications of the Model

Two different applications of the risk assessment model are found in the needs assessment literature. First, Marden (n.d.) has proposed that survey data collected by Cahalan (Cahalan et al., 1969) be used to project rates of alcoholism to other populations. To accomplish this estimation, Marden defined a demographic matrix based on age, occupation, and sex, and made estimates using a procedure like that described above.

Marden's paper demonstrates one of the major limitations of using the risk assessment method with a survey-based criterion measure; i.e., a complete cross-tabulation creates a large number of cells, even when the number of predictor variables is limited. Unless the survey data base is extremely large, the number of sample points that can be used to estimate any given cell is likely to be very small. In order to obtain reasonable estimates Marden was forced to average the rates in some of the adjoining cells of his table. Although averaging facilitates estimation of the rates for the criterion population, it also reduces the predictive power of the method when applied to another population. One potential solution to this estimation problem is the smoothing of rates across adjacent cells through the use of procedures for modeling cross-tabulations, for example maximum likelihood or generalized least squares log-linear models. This would stabilize the estimates without losing all the information generated by the demographic matrix.

MHDPS — High-Risk Subgroups

A second form of demographic risk assessment attempts to avoid the above limitation of Marden's approach. Instead of using a complete cross-tabulation of the demographic variables, Goldsmith et al. (1975) and Rosen et al. (1975) have focused one part of their analyses on specific sub-populations for which exceptionally high levels of need and high rates of disorder are expected. Their strategy makes use of data selected from the US Census, which have been combined into an integrated package called the Mental Health Demographic Profile System (MHDPS) (1975). The 'high-risk groups' identified by the MHDPS relate directly to the stressful situations discussed in clinical literature: thus, these categories of high-risk groups provide a greater sense of relevance than many of the individual demographic variables. What Goldsmith et al. sacrifice to add these additional variables is completeness of cross-classification. Only the highest-risk cell of what would have been a complex cross-tabulation is used in the estimation. Nonetheless, the basic strategy for using that cell remains the same. The individuals in the high-risk cell are assumed to need treatment.

The MHDPS high-risk group strategy has one central limitation. One cannot add the numbers found in each high-risk group without obtaining a biased estimate of total need because the groups are not mutually exclusive, nor do they provide complete coverage. No precise estimate of the degree of overlap among these groups is available, although one might be obtained from the public-use sample of the US Census.

Discussion

Overall, the demographic risk assessment approach to projecting need for mental health services appears to be on firm ground, but several issues need further study. First, the degree of variation in risk within each demographic category must be demonstrated to be stable in similar social environments. Second, more work is needed to demonstrate the degree to which social environment influences rates of disorder. Finally, more extensive study is needed to discover the optimal combination of demographic variables to be used with this method. The high-risk groups provide some guidance in this direction, but the problem inherent in their nonexclusivity and lack of complete coverage must be resolved.

Social Area Analysis

The second general strategy for estimating the need for mental health services is based on social area analysis. This strategy analyzes aggregate characteristics of geographical areas and makes a direct prediction of total levels of need for the area, rather than building the total estimate of need from the cells of a demographic tabulation as in demographic risk assessment. This strategy may use any geographic unit of analysis but, conventionally, census tracts are the unit of analysis.

The origins of social area analysis are found in the work of Park and Burgess and their theories of social ecology. A more recent focus of social area analysis has been the work of Shevky and Williams (1949) and Shevky and Bell (1955). They identified three major dimensions of variability among urban census tracts: social rank, urbanization, and segregation. Social rank is a general index of social status taking into account education and occupation levels. Urbanization emphasizes fertility, women in the labor force, and the presence of single-family dwellings. This dimension was later renamed family status. The third dimension, segregation, indicates the disproportionate presence of blacks and ethnic groups defined by national origin. Shevky and Bell demonstrated an empirical basis for these dimensions through a factor analysis of census tracts for Los Angeles. This use of factor analysis was to become a major element of social area.

Although Shevky and Bell demonstrated their model for Los Angeles, its generality could be established only through its application to other cities. Tryon (1955) conducted a cluster analysis of the census tracts of San Francisco and obtained a set of dimensions conceptually similar to that of Shevky and Bell. Van Ardsol, Camilleri and Schmid (1958) made a more direct test of the dimensions through examination of the dimensions in ten large American cities. The dimensions were found in eight of the cities, but were not replicated in two north-south border cities, both having high correlations between social rank and fertility. The authors suggest that 'the range of family forms in these cities, as described by the fertility measure, has not become disassociated from social rank' (Van Arsdol et al., 1958). They imply that the size or age of cities may determine the stage of development at which the three Shevky-Bell dimensions become fully applicable. (See also Borgatta and Hadden, 1977).

Social Area Analysis and Mental Health

Even if the consistency of a set of social area dimensions is assumed, there remains a question of how effective they are in estimating levels of mental health. The most general evidence for this applicability is found in the mental health epidemiological literature. The three Shevky-Bell dimensions correspond directly to individual characteristics of great importance in the etiology and the course of mental illness. Social rank corresponds to social class and to social status, both of which have been identified in numerous studies as strongly related to reported symptomatology and to treated illness (see Hollingshead and Redlich, 1958: Srole et al., 1962: and Dohrenwend and Dohrenwend, 1969).

Marital status, one element of urbanization, has been related to mental illness (Gove and Tudor, 1973: Warheit et al., 1976). Race and ethnicity also have been related to mental illness (Dohrenwend and Dohrenwend, 1969: Warheit et al., 1973; Rosen et al., 1977). Therefore variables like those in the MHDPS are demonstrably related to mental health at the individual level, but their relationships at the aggregate level are less well documented.

Working at the aggregate level, Faris and Dunham (1939) demonstrated a strong relationship between rates of psychiatric hospitalization and the characteristics of the urban census tracts from which the patients were admitted.

One of the few studies that directly relates the social area dimensions to mental health is that of Bloom, who correlated treatment rates with data from the US Census and local sources. Bloom (1968; 1975) applied a cluster analysis to 35 variables from 34 tracts of Pueblo, Colorado. This provided three sets of cluster scores describing over 80 percent of the variance among tracts on the items examined. The strongest correlation with the overall rates of disorder was found for Social Disequilibrium, $r = 0.64$ (1960) and $r = 0.76$ (1970). Interestingly, this cluster incorporated many locally collected variables that are not available in the US Census. Other correlations were $r = 0.40$ (1970) for Socioeconomic Affluence and $r = -0.38$ (1960) for Young Marrieds. Although Bloom's study demonstrates a relationship between the social area dimensions and mental health, the strongest relationship was found for social disequilibrium, which is not one of the Shevky-Bell dimensions.

MHDPS — Social Area Analysis

Goldsmith and his associates at the National Institute of Mental Health have provided extensive analyses of social indicator variables, further developing the Shevky-Bell dimensions. They have approached social area analysis in two ways. First, they have taken a 'typological approach,' which presumes a set of social area dimensions based largely on those of Shevky and Bell, and a second approach, which uses factor analysis to identify new dimensions of the census variables considered.

The typological approach (Goldsmith et al., 1975) starts with the three Shevky-Bell dimensions of social rank, segregation (ethnic composition), and family status. To those are added familism (size of household), family life-cycle, housing type, housing quality and community instability, in addition to the high-risk sub-populations. Type and level of need are then inferred from the characteristics of the area.

In their second approach to social area analysis, Goldsmith and his associates have used principal factor analysis to uncover major dimensions of variability among the variables in the MHDPS. One analysis was conducted for 1,499 CMHC catchment areas using 108 of the 161 variables in the MHDPS. The major factors obtained were: (1) social rank; (2) urbanization; (3) family life-cycle; (4) poor and overcrowded housing; and (5) migration. These factors are regarded as indicators of 'potential needs for services' owing to their similarity to the demographic variables associated with elevated risk in epidemiological studies.

In a related set of results, Rosen et al. (1975) report analyses of the entire set of 161 MHDPS items for samples consisting of both the national CMHC catchment areas and the census tracts of a single county.

These factor analyses highlight the difficulty of introducing sub-population-specific information into an aggregate level analysis. The MHDPS contains a number of variables that refer specifically to characteristics of the white or black sub-populations and not to the entire aggregate. These race-specific variables become unstable or even undefined for areas that are either exclusively white or exclusively black, resulting in missing values within the correlation base.

Rosen's analysis raises an additional issue regarding the level of aggregation to be used in analyses. Robinson (1950) has shown that ecological correlations may be grossly discrepant from the individual relationships that produce them, depending on the homogeneity of the units in the ecological correlation. See also studies by Firebaugh (1978) and Moorman (1979). These effects influence the relationship between factor analyses at different levels of aggregation and further influence the application of individual level epidemiological results to aggregate level factor scores.

Comparison of the Two Methods

A comparison of the demographic risk assessment and social area analysis approaches must recognize that, although both start from the same database, the US Census, they make different applications of it. The basic risk assessment approach retains a smaller number of items but creates a complete cross-classification from each set of variables considered. The basic thrust of social area analysis is much different. It focuses almost exclusively on the geographic unit and, therefore, constructs variables that reflect attributes of the geographic unit.

Because these variables are seen as assessing the need 'of the geographical unit,' there is a tendency to focus on characteristics that relate to the highest levels of need or the highest-risk subgroups without adequately representing characteristics of the remainder of the population. These excluded categories of people have specific levels of risk for mental health problems, even though they may constitute an attribute of the geographical area that is poorly or even negatively associated with the overall risk of that aggregate.

In the analyses that follow we will examine the assumptions and predictive power of the demographic risk assessment and the social area analysis models.

METHODS

The Setting

This study uses data from two counties in Florida and one county in Kentucky to test the methodologies described above. Alachua County, Florida, is a Standard Metropolitan Statistical Area which in 1970 had a population of 104,764. Geographically, the county is dominated by a central city of 64,510 (1970) with the remaining eight towns each having a population under 3,000. The zoning and planned development of the central city is reflected in the ecological distribution of its various sub-populations.

Polk County, Florida, has recently experienced great and unplanned growth which has been distributed across the county. The total population of the county was 228,026 in 1970, with one city of 42,803, two towns between 10,000 and 20,000 and 14 incorporated places under 10,000. Only one city had census tracts assigned; therefore a portion of the aggregate data is reported for minor civil divisions (MCDs) rather than for tracts.

The third county, Jefferson County, Kentucky, is situated on the Ohio River in north-west Kentucky. Louisville, with a population of 361,477 in 1970, is the principal city. The remainder of the county's population of 695,055 reside in the suburban areas adjacent to the city. Unlike the Florida counties, Jefferson County is an industrialized urban county.

Data Sources

Mental Health Demographic Profile System and Census Data

The data from the Mental Health Demographic Profile System were provided directly by NIMH in the form of an intermediate data tape. Rosen et al. (1975) have provided a general description of the system, its variables, and its uses.

A second source of demographic data for tracts and MCDs is the Special Fifth Count of the US Census of Population and Housing.

Survey Data

The epidemiological field survey of Alachua County was conducted in 1970 as part of NIMH Grant MH15900. A systematic probability sample of households was obtained from utility listings and supplemented by area sampling where utility hookups were lacking. Individuals aged 18 years or older were selected to be interviewed through use of the method described by Kish (1965:398). The overall level of nonresponse was 16.07 percent with a refusal rate of 8.06 percent. A total of 1,645 completed interviews was obtained.

The Polk County survey was conducted by Roger Bell, then of Winter Haven Hospital and Mental Health Center. The Polk County survey used the same sampling procedures as the Alachua County survey and a revised interview instrument. The total nonresponse for Polk was 12 percent with a refusal rate of 7.6 percent; a total of 2,029 interviews was obtained.

The Jefferson County survey was conducted during 1975 and 1976 by Roger Bell through the University of Louisville Department of Psychiatry. Its methodology was based on the Alachua and Polk surveys. A total of 1,078 interviews was obtained, distributed over 109 census tracts. Because the number of individuals within many of the tracts was small, the aggregate analyses are based on the 58 tracts with sample sizes greater than five.

The Leighton HOS Measure

The mental health measure selected for use in this paper is the Health Opinion Survey (HOS), which was developed originally by Macmillan (1957) and revised by A. Leighton (Leighton et al., 1963). This measure was developed as a general screening instrument to identify those likely to be judged by a psychiatrist as needing treatment. It has been used extensively in field studies and its validity has been tested in a number of settings. It is our conclusion, based on a review of content, previous research, and our own studies, that the HOS is an acceptable screening measure for use in needs assessment. We are, however, aware of its limitations and thus recommend the use of other measures when estimates of more specific components of mental health are desired.

RESULTS

The analyses presented here attempt to test the major assumptions of the two estimation techniques described above, i.e. social area analysis and demographic risk assessment.

Social Area Analysis

Test of Assumptions

We addressed the assumptions of the Shevky-Bell model by means of the confirmatory factor methods of Jöreskog (1971) and Jöreskog and Sörbom (1978). Their method permits elements of a factor model to be constrained to theoretically derived values, thus making possible a direct test of models, such as that of Shevky and Bell.

TABLE 1
Confirmatory factor analysis of social, area dimensions: items and loadings for restricted model

Alachua County tracts ($N = 19$)	Polk County tracts/MCDs ($N = 42$)	Jefferson County tracts ($N = 58$)	MHDPS items
Factor 1: Social rank			
-0.61	-0.64	-0.82	Income of families and unrelated individuals
0.94	0.89	0.78	Families in poverty
1.00	0.99	0.98	Low occupational status, males
-0.89	-0.79	-0.94	High occupational status, males
-0.87	-0.87	-0.91	School years completed
0.92	0.91	0.90	Overcrowding
-0.73	-0.78	-0.56	Standard housing
Factor 2: Segregation			
0.89	0.38	0.59	Household population, Negro
-0.65	0.28	-0.07	Other non-white
-0.79	-0.51	-0.92	Foreign stock
Factor 3: Family status			
1.31*	0.54	0.67	Husband- wife household
0.16	-0.93	-0.87	Age of household heads
0.41	0.65	0.44	Youth dependency ratio
-0.19	-1.02*	-1.03*	Aged dependency ratio
0.60	0.73	0.37	Single-dwelling units
Significance of the model			
405	363	620	χ^2 value ($df = 87$) for restricted model
249	180	319	χ^2 value ($df = 63$) for unrestricted model
156	183	301	χ^2 value ($df = 24$) for difference
$p < 0.001$	$p < 0.001$	$p < 0.001$	Significance level
Correlations among factors			
-1.01*	1.12*	0.92	Correlations of Factors 1 & 2
0.49	0.80	0.21	Correlations of Factors 2 & 3
-0.54	0.07	-0.16	Correlations of Factors 1 & 3

* Some unusual values are obtained due to the iterative nature of the solution.

Restricted model. A first test of the social area analysis model asks whether the approximate Shevky-Bell model with three factors — social rank, segregation, and family status — provides a reasonable fit to a representative set of 15 MHDPS items. Table 1 identifies seven items that closely fit the definition of social rank and therefore were permitted arbitrary loadings on that factor, while their remaining loadings were fixed at zero. Three segregation items were identified and permitted nonzero loadings on the second factor, and five items were permitted nonzero loadings on the third factor, family status. Each factor was forced to have a unit variance so the model would be identified, but the correlations among factors were left free to provide an oblique or correlated-factors solution. The residual covariance matrix was forced to be diagonal.

Unrestricted Model. As a test alternative to the above model, an unrestricted factor model was constructed having the factor loadings constrained to provide three orthogonal factors, but with arbitrary rotations. For the model to be identified, one loading of the second factor and two from the third factor were forced to zero.

Comparison. The above comparison was made separately for each of the three counties, with the results presented in Table 1. In each instance the unrestricted three-factor model provides significantly better fit than the restricted model. One should also note that the three-factor model itself has a significant lack of fit compared with a generalized alternative. Jöreskog (1971) notes that a variety of elements other than factor structure can produce lack of fit. Although the factor structures obtained are similar to those of Shevky-Bell, the above test indicates that the Shevky-Bell model may be inappropriate for the specified items in the counties examined. These results suggest the Shevky-Bell dimensions should not be used uncritically for all types of areas.

Simultaneous Factor Analysis. A second test of the social area dimensions asks whether the factor structures vary among the three counties. In this test, both restricted and unrestricted models were considered as above, but one additional constraint was added, requiring the factor loadings to be equal among the counties. Additionally, the set of three covariance matrices was rescaled so that their pooled covariance matrix would have ones on the diagonal; i.e., it is a correlation matrix (see Jöreskog, 1971).

The solution obtained for the restricted (Shevky-Bell) model provides a fit of $\chi^2 = 1,537$, d.f. (degrees of freedom) = 291, with the factor structures of the counties constrained to be equal. The fit obtained without the equality constraint is $\chi^2 = 1,389$, d.f. = 261. The difference in the fit of the two models provides a test of the equality constraint. That difference is $\chi^2 = 148$, d.f. = 30, $p < 0.001$, which identifies significant differences among the factor structures of the counties. Smaller but significant differences among the counties were also identified using the unrestricted model. The unrestricted model without the constraint of equality provides a $\chi^2 = 749$, d.f. = 189. Addition of the equality constraint raised the χ^2 to 968, d.f. = 219. The difference of $\chi^2 = 220$, d.f. = 30, is significant at the $p < 0.001$ level.

The above results indicate that constraining factor structures to be equal among the counties leads to a significantly worse fit for both restricted and unrestricted models. The difference produced by the equality constraint is somewhat greater for the restricted model, suggesting that some of the improvement in fit provided in the unrestricted model was parallel among the counties. More work is needed in the direction of finding factor structures that would do a better job of fitting a range of counties.

Factor Scores. In order to complete the analysis of social areas it was necessary to have a common set of factors and factor scores for the three counties. To obtain this set of factors, the tracts /MCDs from the three counties were refactored as a set and factor scores were generated. For this analysis, a principal factor (PRIN) procedure was used (Barr et al., 1979), followed by Varimax rotation. (Similar results were obtained when a maximum likelihood procedure was used.) The scores obtained from this analysis are called factor scores in the general sense of the term, although they might more properly be called standardized component scores, owing to the use of principal component analysis. The set of factor loadings obtained is presented in Table 2. As can be seen, these factors are similar, although not identical, to the Shevky-Bell dimensions. The first factor is clearly interpretable as social rank, although the percentage of blacks in the population loads heavily on that factor rather than creating a separate factor for segregation. The second factor has high positive loadings for median age and aged dependency and thus is interpreted as family life-cycle. The third factor loads heavily on the presence of single-family dwellings and husband-wife families, thus corresponding to family status or familism.

TABLE 2
**Varimax rotated factor loadings for principal factor analysis
of 119 tracts and MCDs from three counties**

Factor 1	Factor 2	Factor 3	MHDPS items
Factor 1: Social rank			
-0.93	0.12	-0.15	Low occupational status, males
-0.93	-0.11	-0.16	Overcrowding
0.89	-0.20	-0.07	High occupational status, males
0.87	-0.29	0.00	School years completed
0.83	0.22	-0.15	Foreign stock
-0.78	0.09	-0.47	Families in poverty
-0.68	-0.03	-0.29	Household population, Negro
0.60	-0.25	0.53	Income of families
-0.57	-0.50	0.33	Youth dependency ratio
0.55	-0.12	0.22	Standard housing
Factor 2: Life-cycle			
-0.06	0.94	-0.19	Aged dependency ratio
-0.11	0.93	0.08	Age of household heads
Factor 3: Single-family households			
0.22	-0.16	0.82	Single-dwelling units
0.37	-0.37	0.77	Husband-wife household
0.15	-0.19	-0.53	Other non-white

Relationship Between Mental Health
and Social Area Analysis

This section examines the relationship between mental health and social area analysis at the census tract level of aggregation. It is shown that many of the individual MHDPS items, and all three sets of factor scores, are significantly correlated with tract level HOS means in at least one of the counties. Also, a regression analysis is used to test whether the above relationships are the same in all three counties.

Correlations. Table 3 presents zero-order correlations between selected MHDPS items and tract level means of HOS scores. Many strong correlations are observed, with two patterns visible in the correlations. First, the strongest correlations are found for items related to social rank. Second, there are large differences in the magnitude of the correlations among the three counties considered. Overall, stronger correlations are found for Alachua County than for Jefferson or Polk Counties. The two strongest correlations in the table are 'Low occupational status, males' ($r = 0.80***$) and 'Families in poverty' ($r = 0.79***$), both in Alachua County. Asterisks indicate levels of significance as noted in Table 3.

Simple correlations between factor scores and means HOS scores also are presented in Table 4. Factor 1, Social rank, yields high correlations with Alachua County having the highest ($r = 0.67***$) and the other two counties being considerably lower ($r = 0.34*$ and $r = 0.39***$).

Factor 2, Family life-cycle, provided the strongest correlation for Alachua county ($r = 0.70***$) but was not significant elsewhere. Finally, Factor 3, Single-family households, has a significant relationship to mental health in Jefferson County ($r = 0.39**$), a small correlation in Polk County ($r = 0.21$) and no relationship in Alachua County ($r = 0.01$). The correlations obtained with all tracts and MCDs pooled are $r = 0.39***$ for Factor 1, $r = 0.15$ for Factor 2, and $r = 0.29**$ for Factor 3.

TABLE 3
Correlations between health opinion survey means and 23 mental health demographic profile system variables

Alachua County tracts (N = 19)	Polk County tracts/MCDs (N = 42)	Jefferson County tracts (N = 58)	MHDPS items
Social rank			
0.80***	0.28	0.43***	Low occupational status, males
0.79***	0.35*	0.41**	Families in poverty
-0.66**	-0.36*	-0.42***	High occupational status, males
-0.63**	-0.41	-0.51***	School years completed
-0.59**	-0.29	-0.52***	Income of families and unrelated individuals
Urbanization: family status			
0.75***	-0.14	0.31*	Aged dependency ratio
0.62**	-0.03	0.21	Age of household heads
-0.48*	-0.11	-0.47***	Husband-wife households
0.09	0.17	-0.09	Youth dependency ratio
Urbanization: housing			
-0.71***	-0.26	-0.40**	Standard housing
0.70***	0.39*	0.39**	Overcrowding
-0.22	-0.02	0.32*	Recent movers
-0.22	-0.09	0.11	High-rise apartments
-0.18	0.14	-0.44***	Single-dwelling units
Segregation: ethnicity			
0.75***	0.25	0.18	Household population, Negro
-0.54*	-0.19	-0.27*	Foreign stock
-0.28	0.32*	0.09	Other non-white

* $p < 0.05$
** $p < 0.01$
*** $p < 0.001$

TABLE 4
Correlations between mean HOS scores for tracts
from three counties and factor scores from 15 MHDPS items

	Alachua tract $N=19$	Polk tracts/ MCDs $N=42$	Jefferson tract $N=58$	Combined tract and MCDs $N=119$
Factor 1 (Social rank)	-0.67**	-0.34*	-0.39**	-0.39***
Factor 2 (Life-cycle)	0.70***	-0.16	0.26	0.15
Factor 3 (Families)	-0.01	-0.22	-0.39**	-0.29**

*** $p < 0.001$
** $p < 0.01$
* $p < 0.05$

TABLE 5
Regression estimates of HOS mean scores for tracts
from factor scores and county designations

Regression parameter	Metric beta	Std error of estimate	t	Sig.*
Factor 1: Social rank	-0.720	0.143	-5.03	0.001
Factor 2: Life-cycle	0.360	0.152	2.37	0.019
Factor 3: Single-family household	-0.459	0.148	-3.09	0.003
Polk (Dummy)**	-0.938	0.481	-1.95	0.054
Jefferson (Dummy)**	0.047	0.449	0.10	0.917
(Intercept)	27.525	0.392	70.13	0.0001

* Overall significance $F(5,113) = 10.42$ $p < 0.001$
  $R^2 = 0.31$
** Alachua County provided the reference base for these dummy variables.

Regression. Table 5 presents a regression analysis predicting mental health levels for census tracts/MCDs from factor scores obtained in the previous section. Mean HOS scores for the census tracts/MCDs of each county form the dependent variable. The independent variables include the three factors corresponding to social rank, life-cycle and single-family households. Additionally, a county effect is included in the model through the use of two dummy variables, one for Polk and one for Jefferson County, with Alachua County used as a base reference.

Overall, this regression was significant, explaining 31 percent ($R^2 = 0.31$) of the variance of HOS score means among tracts. Each of the three factors contributed significantly to the model, with the greatest contribution coming from Factor 1, social rank. The coefficients for county indicate that Jefferson and Alachua Counties have almost the same level and that Polk County has scores of 0.938 points below the Alachua County level when the factor differences are controlled. This difference gives only a $p < 0.054$ probability that Polk and Alachua County scores are at the same true level when the social area factors are controlled.

In order to test whether the effects of the factor scores are the same among the counties, interaction terms were formed between both of the county dummy variables and all three factor scores. These six terms, when added to the model above, raised the percentage of variance explained from 31.6 percent to only 34.3 percent, which is too small an increase to be significant. The individual coefficients for the interaction terms were also small, indicating that the regression lines for the three counties are nearly parallel.

If the regression slopes are parallel, an explanation is needed for the wide range of correlations between mental health and the factor scores in the three counties. This difference must be found in the means and variances of the variables in the different counties. To test these differences, Table 6 presents a comparison of the counties on each factor. Because the factor scores were not standardized separately for each county, they reveal county differences. Significant differences in level were observed for both Factor 2 and Factor 3. Alachua County tracts are atypical in that they have higher average social rank (Factor 1), are younger in life-cycle (Factor 2), and have fewer complete families (Factor 3). Polk County tracts, in contrast, have lower average social rank (Factor 1), are older in life-cycle (Factor 2) and have more complete families. Polk County also has an unusually small variation among tracts on social rank

TABLE 6
Comparison of means for HOS and MHDPS factor scores among counties, using the tract or MCD as the unit of analysis

	Alachua County ($N=19$) Mean (s.d.)	Polk County ($N=42$) Mean (s.d.)	Jefferson County ($N=58$) Mean (s.d.)	$F(2,118)$	Sig.
HOS	27.26	26.71	27.6	3.17	$p<0.05$
	(1.19)	(1.11)	(2.25)		
Factor 1	0.384	-0.079	-0.068	1.69	NS
(Social rank)	(1.221)	(0.671)	(1.103)		
Factor 2	-0.778	0.278	0.053	8.39	$p<0.001$
(Life-cycle)	(0.740)	(0.925)	(1.010)		
Factor 3	-0.677	0.177	0.093	5.68	$p<0.01$
(Families)	(1.376)	(0.534)	(1.040)		

and familism. Jefferson County is intermediate in the character of its tracts except for a much larger variance in HOS score means, lower social rank and more complete families. The low variation among tracts is sufficient to explain the low correlations observed between HOS scores and characteristics of the tracts/MCDs. Further examination of the tracts in Polk County also suggests a greater heterogeneity within the MCDs used in place of tracts in the untracted sections of Polk County.

Demographic Risk Assessment

The second part of the analysis focuses on demographic risk assessment as an alternative to social area analysis. The risk assessment approach provides a marked contrast to social area analysis in its focus on the individual as the unit of analysis and its usual treatment of mental health as a dichotomy between cases and non-cases. The analyses that follow address the primary assumptions of the method: risk levels for mental health vary among demographic categories, but do not vary across geographic location. These assumptions are examined for two risk models, one based exclusively on education and another based on a cross-tabulation of

TABLE 7
Risk levels for demographic subgroups: percentages of individuals scoring 33 and above on the HOS index within three counties

Education completed	Alachua N	%	Polk N	%	Jefferson N	%	Combined N	%
0-8th grade	304	33.9	528	24.4	173	34.7	1007	29.0
Some high school	246	25.2	422	17.8	193	24.9	861	21.5
High school graduate	319	12.9	587	9.0	346	15.9	1252	11.9
Some college	422	12.3	265	7.9	191	11.0	878	10.7
College graduate	140	5.0	104	5.8	169	5.3	413	5.3

Age by race by sex		N	%	N	%	N	%	N	%
White males:	18-24	157	9.6	110	3.6	52	5.8	319	6.9
	25-44	229	3.9	221	10.4	145	9.0	595	7.6
	45-59	108	13.0	173	17.9	63	22.2	344	17.1
	60+	80	18.8	238	31.9	76	9.2	394	24.9
White females:	18-24	160	15.0	128	9.4	74	18.9	362	13.8
	25-44	252	14.7	285	13.3	207	15.9	744	14.5
	45-59	142	26.8	227	17.2	118	31.4	487	23.4
	60+	136	23.5	367	20.2	124	28.2	627	22.5
Black males:	18-24	27	14.8	12	16.7	8	0.0	47	12.8
	25-44	54	7.4	33	3.0	19	0.0	105	4.7
	45-59	29	31.0	23	4.3	14	14.3	66	18.2
	60+	43	44.2	31	25.8	25	28.0	99	34.3
Black females:	18-24	35	20.0	26	11.5	20	5.0	81	13.6
	25-44	70	21.4	64	18.8	64	14.1	198	18.2
	45-59	51	27.5	35	31.4	30	40.0	116	31.9
	60+	56	32.1	34	8.8	32	18.8	122	22.1

age by sex by race. Finally, the implications of that estimation technique for tract level analyses are examined by correlating risk estimates for census tracts with the tract level HOS means used in the previous section.

Test of Assumptions

Education. The percentages of survey respondents scoring 33 or above on the HOS measure for each of five educational categories are reported in Table 7 for the three counties separately and for the counties combined. The major differences among cells correspond to educational level, with much smaller differences among the counties. The education and county effects were analyzed using a procedure developed by Grizzle et al. (1969) and implemented as FUNCAT by SAS (Barr et al. 1979). FUNCAT provides a linear generalized least ⌐quares model of logits (logs of probability ratios). Two specific models were considered. In the first model, both education and county were treated as categorical main effects, with no interaction term present. In that model both effects were significant, although education accounted for much greater variation ($\chi^2 = 202.3$, d.f. $= 4$, $p<0.0001$). In the second model, education was treated as a quantitative effect so that a county by education interaction term could be tested. Education remained the strongest effect ($\chi^2 = 192.2$, d.f. $= 1$, $p<0.0001$) and county retained significance ($\chi^2 = 18.1$, d.f. $= 2$, $p<0.0001$), although the interaction term was not significant ($\chi^2 = 0.23$, d.f. $= 2$, $p<0.89$). Therefore, we conclude that county differences, although present, are small relative to the education effect and do not influence the relationship of education to mental health.

Age by Sex by Race. The second part of Table 7 presents percentages of respondents scoring 33 or above on the HOS measure, for age by sex by race by county. This table was also modeled using the FUNCAT procedure with main effects included for county, race, sex and age, and two-way interaction terms provided for each pair of main effects. No triple interaction terms were considered. Again, two models were run, the first one treating age as categorical and the second as quantitative. In the first model the main effects were signfiicant for age ($\chi^2 = 63.4$, d.f. $= 3$, $p<0.0001$), race ($\chi^2 = 8.2$, d.f. $= 1$, $p<0.01$), and sex ($\chi^2 = 3.93$, d.f. $= 1$,

$p<0.05$), but not for county ($\chi^2 = 2.56$, d.f. = 2, $p<0.27$). Of the interaction terms considered, Race* Age ($\chi^2 = 18.1$, d.f. = 3, $p<0.0001$) and County* Race ($\chi^2 = 13.19$, d.f. = 2, $p<0.056$) produced a strong trend. These effects were approximately the same when age was treated as a quantitative effect and therefore are not reported separately. From these results we conclude that county is a minor effect relative to the three demographic categorizations. The small effect of county in both of the demographic cross-tabulations suggests that rates may be reasonably stable across region once demographic effects are controlled.

Estimation of Mental Health Levels for Tracts

Because the demographic risk assessment approach is based on the individual as the unit of analysis, it is not limited to any particular geographic unit for use in estimation. Thus it can be applied directly to the characteristics of an entire county or catchment area. Nonetheless, it is useful to see how demographic risk assessment compares with social area analysis as a predictor of need at the tract/MCD level of analysis. Therefore, overall estimates of risk were calculated for each tract/MCD within Alachua and Polk counties. Using the procedure outlined for demographic risk assessment, the proportions of individuals scoring high (33 or above) within each education category and within each cell of the age by race by sex table were applied to the population counts for the corresponding cells for each census tract. This yielded estimated counts of people scoring high for each cell. These cell estimates were summed to obtain an estimate of those scoring high for the tract. Division by the tract population count provided a proportion of need for each tract or MCD. These estimates were correlated with the observed mean HOS scores for each tract. Means are used as the criterion in order to be comparable with the social area analyses, and thus the tract/MCD is the unit of analysis. Correlations were formed for nineteen tracts in Alachua County. The estimates obtained from the education risk table produced a correlation of $r = 0.65$ ($p<0.01$) for Alachua County, of $r = 0.27$ (NS) for Polk County, and $r = 0.35$ ($p<0.01$) for the two combined. The estimates based on race by sex by age produced correlations of $r = 0.82$ ($p<0.001$) for Alachua County, $r = 0.27$ (NS) for Polk County and $r = 0.39$ ($p<0.01$) for the combined counties. These are comparable in magnitude to the correlations obtained from the first or second social area factor scores.

TABLE 8
Percentage of respondents with scores of 33 and higher for selected MHDPS high-risk populations

Demographic category	Alachua N	Alachua %	Polk N	Polk %	Jefferson N	Jefferson %	Sig.
Total	1,645	16.72	2,029	14.59	1,078	17.90	*
Disabled population unable to work	58	68.97	57	52.63	38	73.68	
Working mothers with children under 18	418	14.35	177	9.60	79	16.46	
Working mothers of preschool children	N/A	N/A	56	12.50	43	16.28	
Aged persons living alone	79	26.58	176	14.77	89	30.34	**
Aged persons in poverty	62	37.10	175	22.86	7	57.14	*
Large households with income under $7,000	76	22.37	80	27.50	2	N/A	

* $p < 0.05$
** $p < 0.01$

SUMMARY AND CONCLUSIONS

Two alternative models for estimating need for mental health services have been presented. The models differ both in procedure and in basic assumptions. The social area analysis model assumes the census tract as its basic unit of analysis and also assumes that most of the variability among tracts can be described by the three dimensions: social rank, family status/urbanization, and segregation. A three-factor model based on these dimensions was tested by means of confirmatory factor analysis and was found not to fit the data as well as an unrestricted three-factor model. The unrestricted model did however resemble the Shevky-Bell model, particularly in terms of social rank and family dimensions. The segregation dimension was lost as part of social rank.

A test of whether a single-factor structure is adequate to describe the three different counties in this analysis demonstrated that neither a restricted nor an unrestricted model could fit all three counties as well as three separate models. If, as these data suggest, the Shevky-Bell three-factor model is not universally applicable, the conditions of its applicability must be determined, and alternative models must be developed for those alternative circumstances. In order to test the power of a social area model to predict need for mental health services, a principal factor analysis was used to produce factor scores which were related to tract means on a mental health scale. The factor scores were related to mental health and had similar regression slopes in all three counties. Nonetheless, the amount of variance explained in each county varied widely as a result of different distributions of both mental health scores and the characteristics of the social areas. We conclude that social area analysis can be used to estimate mental health need but that its effectiveness will be limited by the characteristics of the region involved.

The demographic risk assessment assumes the individual as its basic unit of analysis and further assumes that rates within demographic cells are independent of location. That assumption was tested for two sets of demographic controls: education, and a race by sex by age classification. Comparisons among three counties for both demographic controls revealed that the demographic effects were much stronger than the county effects. Therefore, we tentatively accept the assumption that risk levels are the same across location, although further tests should be conducted using more diverse types of areas. Specifically, comparisons should be made within counties, particularly between different types of tracts identified by social area analysis.

Finally, the ability of the risk assessment model to predict mental health need at the tract level was evaluated by correlating aggregate estimates of need for the tract with mean scores on the HOS measure. The correlations obtained for demographic risk assessment were comparable in magnitude to those obtained for the social area factors.

IMPLICATIONS FOR FURTHER RESEARCH

In this paper, demographic risk assessment and social area analysis have been portrayed as competing methodologies. They differ both in form and in their basic assumptions. Yet, they start from a common data base to accomplish a common purpose. Therefore it is reasonable to ask whether elements of the two models can be combined into a more powerful integrated approach. Seeking the answer to that question will be the subject of continued research.

REFERENCES

Barr, A. J., J. H. Goodnight, J. P. Sall and J. T. Helwig (1979) *A User's Guide to SAS*. Raleigh, North Carolina: SAS Institute Inc.

Bauer, R. A. (ed.) (1966) *Social Indicators*. Cambridge: MIT Press.

Bloom, B. L. (1970) 'Changing Patterns of Hospitalization for Disorders,' *Public Health Reports*, vol. 85:81-7.

Bloom, B. L. (1975) *Changing Patterns of Psychiatric Care*. New York: Human Sciences Press.

Borgatta, E. F. and J. K. Hadden (1977) 'The Analysis of Social Areas: A Critical Review and Some Empirical Data,' in J. B. Ferreira and S. S. In Jha (eds), *The Outlook Tower*, Bombay, India: Popular Prakashan Private Limited.

Bross, I. E. J. and R. Feldman (1956) *Ridit Analysis of Automotive Crash Injuries. Division of Automotive Crash Injury Research*. Ithaca: Department of Public Health and Preventive Medicine, Cornell University Medical College.

Cahalan, D. and I. H. Cisin (1968) 'American Drinking Practices: Summary of Findings from a National Probability Sample: I. Extent of Drinking by Population Subgroups,' *Quarterly Journal of Studies on Alcohol*, vol. 29:130-51.

Cahalan, D. , I. H. Cisin, and H. M. Crissley (1969) *American Drinking Practices*. New Brunswick: Rutgers University Center of Alcohol Studies.

Dohrenwend, B. P. and B. S. Dohrenwend (1969) *Social Status and Psychological Disorder: A Causal Inquiry*. New York: John Wiley.

Donabedian, A. (1973) *Aspects of Medical Care Administration*. Cambridge, Massachusetts: Harvard University Press.

Faris, R. E. L. and H. W. Dunham (1939) *Mental Disorders in Urban Areas*. Chicago: University of Chicago Press.

Firebaugh, G. (1978) 'A Rule for Inferring Individual-level Relationships from Aggregate Data,' *American Sociological Review*, vol. 43:557-72.

Goldsmith, H. F., E. L. Unger, B. M. Rosen, J. P. Shambaugh and C. D. Windle (1975) *Approach to Doing Social Area Analysis*, DHEW Publication No. (ADM) 76-262. Washington, DC: US Government Printing Office.

Goldsmith, H. F., J. P. Shambaugh, C. D. Windle and B. M. Rosen (1976) *Demographic Structure of Mental Health Catchment Areas: Principal Component Factor Analysis with Varimax Rotation of 18 Factors*, MHDPS Working Paper No. 35. Adelphi, Maryland: National Institute of Mental Health.

Gove, W. R. and J. F. Tudor (1973) 'Adult Sex Roles and Mental Illness,' *American Journal of Sociology*, vol. 78:812-35.

Jöreskog, K. G. (1971) 'Simultaneous Factor Analysis in Several Populations,' *Psychometrika*, vol. 36:400-26.

Jöreskog, K. G. and D. Sörbom (1978) *A General Computer Program for Estimation of Linear Structural Equation Systems by Maximum Likelihood Methods: LISREL IV User's Guide*. Uppsala, Sweden: University of Uppsala.

Kish, L. (1965) *Survey Sampling*. New York: John Wiley.

Klee, G. D., E. Spiro, A. K. Bahn and K. Gorwitz (1967) 'An Ecological Analysis of Diagnosed Mental Illness in Baltimore,' in R. R. Monroe, G. D. Klee and E. E. Brody (eds), *Research Reports #22*. Washington, DC: American Psychiatric Association.

Langner, T. S. and S. T. Michael (1963) *Life Stress and Mental Health*. Glencoe, Ill: Free Press.

Leighton, D. C., J. S. Harding, D. B. Macklin, A. M. Macmillan and A. H. Leighton (1963) *The Character of Danger: The Stirling County Study of Psychiatric Disorder and Sociocultural Environment*, vol. III. New York: Basic Books.

Macmillan, A. M. (1957) 'The Health Opinion Survey: Technique for Estimating Prevalence of Psychoneurotic and Related Types of Disorder in Communities,' Monograph Supplement 7, *Psychological Reports*, vol. 3:325-39.

Malzberg, B. (1959) 'Mental Disease Among Negroes: An Analysis of First Admissions in New York State, 1949-51,' *Mental Hygiene*, vol. 43.

Marden, P. G. (n.d.) *A Procedure for Estimating the Potential Clientele of Alcoholism Service Programs*. Washington, DC: Division of Special Treatment and Rehabilitation Programs, National Institute on Alcohol Abuse and Alcoholism.

Moorman J. E. (1979) 'Aggregation Bias, An Empirical Demonstration,' *Sociological Methods and Research*, vol. 8:69-94.

Murphy, J. M. (1976) 'Psychiatric Labeling in Cross-Cultural Perspective,' *Science*, vol. 191:1019-28.

Robinson, W. S. (1950) 'Ecological Correlations and the Behavior of Individuals,' *American Sociological Review*, vol. 15:351-7.

Rosen, B. M., L. Lawrence, H. F. Goldsmith, C. D. Windle and J. P. Shambaugh (1975) *Mental Health Demographic Profile System Description: Purpose, Contents and Sampler of Uses*, DHEW Publication No. (ADM) 76-263. Washington, DC: US Government Printing Office.

Rosen, B. M., H. F. Goldsmith and R. W. Redick (1977), *Demographic and Social Indicators from the US Census of Population and Housing: Uses for Mental Health Planning in Small Areas*. Rockville, Maryland: Applied Biometrics Research Branch, Division of Biometry and Epidemiology, National Institute of Mental Health, ADAMHA.

Shevky, E. and W. Bell (1955) *Social Area Analysis: Theory, Illustrative Application, and Computational Procedures*. Stanford: Stanford University Press.

Shevky, E. and M. Williams (1949) *The Social Areas of Los Angeles*. Berkeley: University of California.

Srole, L., T. Langner, S. M. Michael, M. Opler and T. Rennie (1962) *Mental Health in the Metropolis: The Midtown Manhattan Study*, vol. I. New York: McGraw-Hill.

Van Arsdol, M. D., Jr., S. F. Camilleri and C. F. Schmid (1958) 'The Generality of Urban Social Area Indexes,' *American Sociological Review*, vol. 23:277-84.

Warheit, G. J., C. E. Holzer and J. J. Schwab (1973) 'An Analysis of Social Class and Racial Differences in Depressive Symptomatology: A Community Study,' *Journal of Health and Social Behavior*, vol. 14:291-9.

Warheit, G. J., L. Robbins, E. Swanson, N. H. McGinnis and J. J. Schwab (1975) *A Review of Selected Research on the Relationship of Sociodemographic Factors to Mental Disorders and Treatment Outcomes 1968-1974*. Gainesville: Department of Psychiatry, University of Florida.

Warheit, G. J., R. A. Bell and J. J. Schwab (1977) *Planning for Change: Needs Assessment Approaches*. Rockville, Maryland: DHEW, Drug Abuse and Mental Health Administration.

II

FACTOR ANALYSIS AND CAUSAL MODELS

6

THE USE OF LISREL IN SOCIOLOGICAL MODEL BUILDING

Dag Sörbom
Karl G. Jöreskog
University of Uppsala, Sweden

INTRODUCTION

In this paper we give an expository account of the uses of LISREL in sociological model-building. LISREL is a general statistical model for analysis of LInear Structural RELationships among quantitative variables. It was introduced by Jöreskog (1973) but a more up-to-date description of it is given by Jöreskog (1977). An accompanying computer program, LISREL IV, has recently been released in a new version (Jöreskog and Sörbom, 1978).

The computer program fits and tests various models for linear structural relationships among quantitative variables. The variables in the system of structural equations may be observed measurements or unobserved constructs or latent variables. The latent variables may each have one or more observable and possibly fallible indicators. Both dependent or endogenous and independent

---

Authors' Note. This paper was presented at the Ninth World Congress of Sociology in Uppsala, Sweden, 14-19 August 1978. Research reported herein was supported by the Bank of Sweden Tercentenary Foundation under the project entitled 'Structural Equation Models in the Social Sciences,' Karl G. Jöreskog, project director.

179

or exogenous variables may be subject to measurement errors, and these errors may be correlated both within and between these sets of observed variables. The program estimates the unknown coefficients of the structural equations and the covariance matrices of the residuals and the measurement errors, provided all are identified. Standard errors of all estimated quantities are provided as well as chi-square tests of the fit of the model and of structural hypotheses within models. The program can handle a wide range of models useful especially in the social and behavioral sciences, e.g. regression models, path analysis models, recursive and interdependent econometric models, factor analysis and covariance structure models. The program can also analyze samples from several populations simultaneously; for example, one can test the hypotheses of equality of covariance matrices, equality of correlation matrices, equality of regressions, equality of factor patterns, etc. In general, some or all of the parameters can be constrained to be equal in all populations. The program uses run-time, dynamic storage allocation and can handle any size problem up to machine capacity. The program is controlled by easily prepared free-format key word parameter cards. The case of fixed independent variables is handled automatically.

The following section describes the LISREL model in general terms. The rest of the paper is devoted to illustrating various uses of LISREL by an elaborate analysis of a small set of data on subjective class identification. The data were previously analyzed by Kluegel, Singleton and Starnes (1977).

THE LISREL MODEL

In its most general form the LISREL model assumes that one specifies a causal structure among a set of latent variables or hypothetical constructs, some of which are designated as dependent and others as independent variables. These latent variables may not be directly observed but there is a set of observed variables that are related to the latent variables. Thus, the latent variables appear as underlying causes of the observed variables. However, latent variables can also be treated as caused by observed variables or as intervening variables in a causal chain.

The LISREL model consists of two parts: the measurement model and the structural equation model. The measurement model specifies how the latent variables or hypothetical constructs are measured in terms of the observed variables and is used to describe the measurement properties (validities and reliabilities) of the observed variables. The structural equation model specifies the causal relationships among the latent variables and is used to describe the causal effects and the amount of unexplained variance.

Schematically the LISREL Model can be described by the diagram in Figure 1. In this figure, circles denote sets of unobserved or latent variables. Thus in the model there are two sets of unobserved variables, the dependent variables η and the independent variables ξ, the latter being thought of as a cause of η in the system of linear structural relations:

(1) $B\eta = \Gamma\xi + \zeta$

where B and Γ are parameter matrices of direct causal effects and ζ a vector of structural disturbance terms or residuals. The

FIGURE 1
The general LISREL model

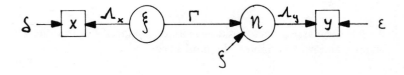

parameters in *B* are included in order to allow for relations also among the dependent η-variables. In Figure 1, observed variables are enclosed in squares. The measurement models are

(2) $y = \Lambda_y \eta + \varepsilon$
     $x = \Lambda_x \xi + \delta$

where Λ_y and Λ_x are matrices of regression coefficients and ε and δ are errors, usually errors of measurements, associated with y and x, respectively. It is assumed that ζ and δ are uncorrelated with ξ, ε is uncorrelated with η and that ζ, ε and δ are uncorrelated.

The elements of the parameter matrices Λ_y, Λ_x, *B* and Γ may be fixed parameters with a priori known values, free parameters which are unknown and to be estimated from data, or constrained parameters which are also unknown but specified to be equal to other parameters in the model.

THE LISREL IV PROGRAM

The LISREL IV computer program is intended to be used for the analysis of models of the kind described by Figure 1 and equations (1) and (2). The program is structured in such a way that one can handle all kinds of reasonable submodels in a simple manner. For example, by specifying that there are no *y* and η variables, the model becomes

(3) $x = \Lambda_x \xi + \delta$

which is the classical factor analysis model. By specifying that there are no *x* and no ξ variables, the model reduces to

(4) $y = \Lambda_y \eta + \varepsilon$
     $B\eta = \zeta$

With this model we also have an ordinary factor analysis model, but in this case we can handle relations among the factors by specifying a structure of the *B*-matrix. For example, by specifying a *B* that generates an autoregressive structure one can handle simplex models; see e.g. Jöreskog and Sörbom (1977).

By specifying that there are no x variables and that B is an identity matrix, we get

(5) $\quad \eta = \Gamma \xi + \zeta$

$\quad\quad y = \Lambda_y \eta + \varepsilon$

or equivalently

$\quad\quad y = \Lambda_y (\Gamma \xi + \zeta) + \varepsilon$

which is a second-order factor analysis model equivalent to the ACOVS model (Jöreskog, 1974). In a similar manner we can get a model for interdependent systems by specifying that the Λ_y and Λ_x matrices are identity matrices and that δ and ε are zero, i.e. the model

(6) $\quad By = \Gamma x + \zeta$

In addition to the above features of handling submodels, the program can also handle several groups of data simultaneously. For example, these groups may be data from different nations, states or regions, culturally or socioeconomically different groups, groups of individuals selected on the basis of some known or unknown selection variable, groups receiving different treatments, etc. In fact, they may be any set of mutually exclusive groups of individuals or observational units that are clearly defined. By the model in equation (3) and data from a number of different groups we can have the SIFASP model (Jöreskog, 1971a).

A LISREL model is fully defined by the specification of the structure of the following eight matrices:

$$\Lambda_y, \ \Lambda_x, \ B, \ \Gamma, \ \Phi, \ \Psi, \ \theta_\varepsilon \text{ and } \theta_\delta$$

where the first four matrices have been explained before and the last four matrices are the covariance matrices of ξ, ζ, ε, and δ, respectively. Also, the matrices Φ, Ψ, θ_ε and θ_δ may contain fixed, free or constrained elements as before. If there are several groups, these matrices must be specified for each group. However, any number of elements, including whole matrices, may be specified to be the same for all groups.

The main output for the LISREL IV program consists of the

estimates of the parameters and their estimated standard errors as well as a measure of the extent to which the estimated model can be used to describe the input data. For large samples this measure is distributed as a χ^2 variable. At the option of the user there is a wide variety of other outputs that can be obtained.

SUBJECTIVE CLASS IDENTIFICATION

The rest of this paper will be devoted to an analysis of a set of data emanating from a paper by Kluegel et al. (1977). To cite from this paper,

> Recent research (cf. Hodge and Treiman, 1968; Jackman and Jackman, 1973) on the relationship between objective and subjective placements in the system of social inequality has focussed almost entirely upon theoretical issues.The empirical finding that this relationship is far from perfect has tended to be treated as a social fact, and the methodological problems inherent in tests of the relationship have been largely ignored. This is surprising, especially since these same studies have employed research measures which may only crudely approximate the relevant theoretical constructs. [p. 599]

The data in Kluegel et al. (1977) consist of 12 variables taken from the 1969 Gary Area Project of the Institute for Social Research at Indiana University. A sample of 800 adults was analyzed and the sample was divided into two groups, one with 432 whites and one with 368 blacks. For present illustrative purposes we have selected seven variables, three measuring objective status and four measuring subjective status. The objective status measures were: (a) education — indicated by five categories ranging from less than ninth grade to college graduate; (b) occupation — indicated by the two-digit Duncan SEI score; (c) income — indicated by the total yearly family income before taxes in 1967, coded in units of $2,000 and ranging from under $2,000 to $16,000 or more. All subjective class indicators were structured questions asking respondents to place themselves in one of four class categories: lower, working, middle, or upper. One indicator was a standard, general class identification item; the other four asked respondents to indicate which social class they felt their occupation, income, way of life, and influence were most like. The criteria, in terms of which class self-placements were made, correspond directly to the Weberian dimensions of economic class (occupation and income), status (life-style),

TABLE 1
Correlations, means and standard deviations for indicators
of objective class and subjective class.
Correlations for whites below diagonal and for
blacks above diagonal
N (whites) = 432; N (blacks) = 368

Variables	x_1	x_2	x_3	x_4	x_5	x_6	x_7	Mean (s.d.)
x_1 education		404	268	216	233	211	207	1.274 (1.106)
x_2 occupation	495		220	277	183	270	157	23.467 (16.224)
x_3 income	398	292		268	424	325	282	4.041 (2.097)
x_4 s.c. occupation	218	282	184		550	574	482	1.288 (0.747)
x_5 s.c. income	299	166	383	386		647	517	1.129 (0.814)
x_6 s.c. life-style	272	161	321	396	553		647	1.235 (0.786)
x_7 s.c. influence	269	169	191	382	456	534		1.318 (0.859)
Mean (s.d.)	1.655 (1.203)	36.698 (21.277)	5.040 (2.198)	1.543 (0.640)	1.548 (0.670)	1.542 (0.623)	1.601 (0.647)	

and power (influence) (Kluegel et al. 1977:601). In our re-analysis we shall not make use of the standard general class identification item. The variance-covariance matrices for the two groups are given in Table 1.

The purpose of the paper of Kluegel et al. (1977) was twofold: (1) to investigate the internal validity for the subjective measures, and (2) to investigate the external validity of the subjective measures, i.e., to what extent the subjective items measure the same thing as the objective measures.

THE MEASUREMENT MODELS

Our first task is to see whether the four selected subjective class indicators could be used as indicators of a single-factor, subjective class, i.e., whether or not one factor is sufficient to account for the observed correlations among the four measures. The model could be depicted as in Figure 2, where x_1, x_2, x_3, and x_4 correspond to x_4, x_5, x_6, and x_7 in Table 1. One way to specify the model in terms of the parameters in the general LISREL model would be to say that there are no y, η, ε, and ζ variables, and to say that

$$\Lambda_x = \begin{bmatrix} 1 \\ \lambda_2 \\ \lambda_3 \\ \lambda_4 \end{bmatrix}, \ \Phi = [\varphi] \text{ and } \theta_\delta = \text{diag} \ (\sigma^2_{\delta_1}, \ \sigma^2_{\delta_2}, \ \sigma^2_{\delta_3}, \ \sigma^2_{\delta_4}).$$

Then the model for the four observed x-variables is

$$\begin{aligned}
&x_1 = \xi + \delta_1 \\
(7) \quad &x_2 = \lambda_2 \xi + \delta_2 \\
&x_3 = \lambda_3 \xi + \delta_3 \\
&x_4 = \lambda_4 \xi + \delta_4
\end{aligned}$$

FIGURE 2
Model for the subjective class measures

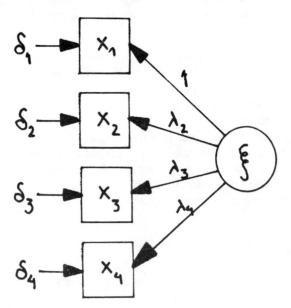

It should be noted that we have to fix the scale of the unobserved ξ-variable in some way, and in (7) we have done this by specifying $\lambda_1 = 1$. If this is not done, the λs and the variance of ξ will be undetermined, since we can multiply ξ by a constant and divide all elements in Λ_x by the same constant, and this would not affect the observable x-variables at all.

Analyzing the subjective measures for the whites and the blacks separately results in χ^2 measures with 2 degrees of freedom equal to 2.02 and 5.56, respectively. None of these χ^2 measures are significant at the 5 percent level, so we can retain this model. To see whether the measurements are operating similarly in the two groups we next analyze the data for the two groups simultaneously by specifying $\Lambda^{(1)} = \Lambda^{(2)}$. In the following we will denote the groups by superindices. The simultaneous analysis results in a χ^2 with 7 degrees of freedom equal to 8.74, which is not significant. Thus, we can not reject the hypothesis that the same measurement model applies to both groups. With the model we are saying that the measures are congeneric (see Jöreskog, 1971b) and that the slopes in the regression of each of the four observed variables on the factor are the same in the two groups. However, the variance of the factor, φ, and the error variances in θ_δ may differ among the groups in these regressions. We could test these assumptions also. A simultaneous analysis with the restrictions $\theta_\delta^{(1)} = \theta_\delta^{(2)}$ added, results in a χ^2 with 11 degrees of freedom equal to 26.22, and thus, by a χ^2 equal to $17.48 (= 26.22 - 8.74)$ with $4 (= 11 - 7)$ degrees of freedom we can reject the hypothesis that the error variances are equal over the groups. In a similar manner we can reject the hypothesis of equal factor variances by a χ^2 with 1 degree of freedom equal to $29.31 (= 38.05 - 8.74)$, since an analysis with the restriction $\Phi^{(1)} = \Phi^{(2)}$ results in a χ^2 with 8 degrees of freedom equal to 38.05. Hence there is some evidence that the factor has a different variance in the two groups and also that the error variances of the four subjective class measures are unequal in the two groups.

An alternative way to describe the differences among the two groups would be to say that the groups differ in variability in the observed variables, but that otherwise the whole factor model is invariant over groups. This means that the standard deviations are allowed to differ between the groups but the correlation matrix is the same and the latter is consistent with the congeneric measurement model above or, which is equivalent, with the one common factor model. Another way to express this is to say that the two

FIGURE 3
Model for an invariant subjective class factor

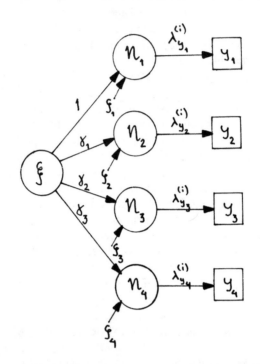

covariance matrices differ only by scale factors in the variables. The LISREL formulation of this model is shown in Figure 3. Here y_1, y_2, y_3, and y_4 correspond to the observed subjective class measures x_4, x_5, x_6, and x_7 of Table 1. The four η-variables η_1, η_2, η_3, and η_4 differ only from y_1, y_2, y_3, and y_4 by a scale factor. The subjective class factor is still denoted ξ and the factor loadings are now 1, γ_2, γ_3, and γ_4. These and the variance of ξ are estimated and are assumed to be the same for both groups. The scale factors $\lambda_{y_1}^{(1)}$, $\lambda_{y_2}^{(1)}$, $\lambda_{y_3}^{(1)}$, $\lambda_{y_4}^{(1)}$ are all equal to one but $\lambda_{y_1}^{(2)}$, $\lambda_{y_2}^{(2)}$, $\lambda_{y_3}^{(2)}$, and $\lambda_{y_4}^{(2)}$ are estimated as free parameters.

The χ^2 for the model in Figure 3 is 21.87 with 8 degrees of freedom. This value is significant and thus the model is not very good in describing the data. When this happens we can ask the program to provide the first-order derivatives of the function being minimized and with these derivatives we can detect possible misspecifications of the model. By looking for the derivative with

FIGURE 4
Model for two factors

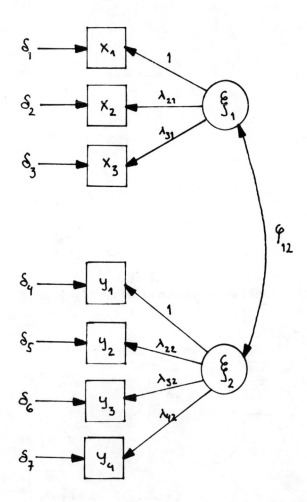

FIGURE 5
Model for a subjective factor caused by an objective factor

FIGURE 6
LISREL formulation of the model in Figure 5

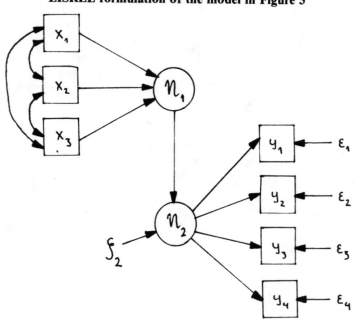

the largest absolute value, we can find that particular restriction which, if relaxed, will result in the largest decrease in χ^2. An inspection of the derivatives for the model in Figure 3 indicates that the restrictions $\Phi^{(1)} = \Phi^{(2)}$, on the variance of ξ, might not be tenable; i.e., the variance of the factor may differ over groups. An analysis of the data with this restriction relaxed gives a χ^2 with 7 degrees of freedom equal to 10.66, and thus by a χ^2 with 1 degree of freedom equal to 11.21 ($= 21.87 - 10.66$) we can conclude that the variances of the factor are unequal. This last model has a fairly good fit and can therefore be used to describe the data. The probability level for the χ^2 with 7 degrees of freedom is 0.15.

We now have the two models in Figures 2 and 3 which both can be used to describe the data fairly well, and we are free to choose among them. The choice is merely a matter of taste. For illustrative purposes we will retain both of them in the following.

We could now proceed as in Figure 4 to include the objective measures, and then the correlation between the two factors, the objective and subjective social class, would be our measure of external validity for our subjective measures. However, mainly for illustrative purposes, we will use a different approach. Suppose that the objective measures determine social class rather than being just indicators of social class. Then the model should be as in Figure 5, where the latent variables are denoted η_1 and η_2 rather than ξ_1 and ξ_2 since they are now dependent variables. In this model the objective factor, $\eta_1 =$ social class, is a linear combination of the objective measures. To make the model an explicit LISREL Model we have to specify it as in Figure 6, since in LISREL the only arrows going *to* a latent variable are the arrows going from ξ to η. The three ξ-variables in Figure 6 are simply identical to the corresponding x-variables; i.e., we take $\Lambda_x = I$ and $\theta_\delta = 0$. In Figure 6 we have fixed γ_1 to be equal to 1, since otherwise the model would not be identified. This merely fixes the scale for η_1. It should also be noted that the model for the objective measures in Figure 6 is not identified if separated from the subjective measures, because in this model there are eight parameters, six for the variances and covariances among the ξ variables and the two γ parameters, but there are only six observed variances and covariances for the three objective class measures. However, the model for the objective class measures in Figure 4, where x_1, x_2, and x_3 are indicators rather than causes of social class, is just identified.

Taking the white group as an exploration sample to investigate the validity of the model in Figure 6, we find that this is not sufficient to describe our data: the χ^2 with 11 degrees of freedom equals 40.16. An inspection of the first-order derivatives suggests that there should be a direct influence from the objective occupation measure to the subjective occupation measure. This can be interpreted as a tendency for people to answer the subjective occupation item differently depending on their actual occupation. The χ^2 for the model with this arrow added equals 24.81, and we can conclude that the influence is significant by a χ^2 with 1 degree of freedom equal to 15.35 ($= 40.16 - 24.81$). Investigation of the derivatives for this latter model reveals that there also might be a direct influence to the subjective life-style measure from the objective occupation measure. However, the estimates of this model show that the coefficient for the path from objective occupation to life-style equals 0.001 with a standard error of 0.001, and thus, the path is not significant. The derivatives also indicate that there may be a direct influence from the objective income measure to the subjective income item. The inclusion of this path gives a significant decrease in χ^2, from 24.81 to 12.22, and the overall fit $\chi^2 = 12.22$ with 9 degrees of freedom of this last model is acceptable.

By using the data for the black group we can confirm the model. An analysis results in a χ^2 with 9 degrees of freedom equal to 15.45, and we can not reject the model at the 5 percent level for this group either.

Before analyzing the two groups simultaneously with the model above we will illustrate the use of the LISREL program for testing equality of covariance and correlation matrices over groups. To test the hypothesis that the covariance matrices of the objective measures are the same for the white and the black group we specify the model in Figure 7. Here $\Lambda_x = I$ and $\theta_\delta = 0$ for both groups. Then, according to (2), $x \equiv \xi$ and the equality of the covariance matrices can be tested by specifying $\Phi_1 = \Phi_2$. The χ^2 for this test is 31.10 with 6 degrees of freedom. To test the hypothesis of equal correlations we specify the model in Figure 8 and test the hypothesis $\Phi^{(1)} = \Phi^{(2)}$, with the diagonal elements of Φ set equal to 1. The standard deviations of the observed measures are contained in the diagonal matrix Λ_x. The χ^2 for the model in Figure 8 equals 5.82 with 3 degrees of freedom, and we can not reject the hypothesis that the correlations among the objective measures are the same for the two groups. Thus, the objective measures differ only in variances over groups.

FIGURE 7
Model for equal covariance matrices

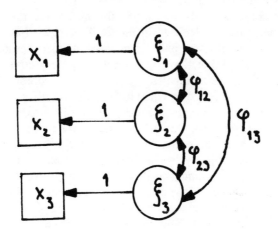

FIGURE 8
Model for equal correlation matrices

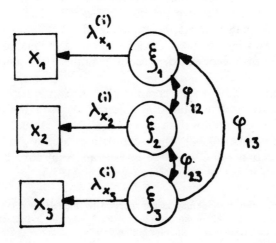

The estimates of the parameters Λ_x show that the white group is more homogeneous thant the black group in the sense that $\lambda_{x_j}^{(1)} < \lambda_{x_j}^{(2)}$ for $j = 1, 2, 3$.

We are now ready to specify the model for the two groups simultaneously as depicted in Figure 9. Here we have added two dummy η-variables η_3 and η_4, in order to incorporate the direct paths from ξ_2 (objective occupation) to y_1 (subjective occupation) and ξ_3 (objective income) to y_2 (subjective income). The dummy variables η_3 and η_4 are set equal to ξ_2 and ξ_3 by letting $\gamma_{32} = 1$, $\gamma_{43} = 1$, $\zeta_3 = 0$, and $\zeta_4 = 0$ so that $\lambda_{y_{13}}$ and $\lambda_{y_{24}}$ are the direct paths. In Figure 9 we assume that the Λ_y matrix is invariant over groups, since we have concluded that the regression slopes of the observed subjective measures on subjective social class are invariant over groups. The Λ_x matrices are assumed to differ, however, since we have found that the variances of the objective measures differ among groups. Also, we let the regression slope of η_2 (true subjective class) on η_1 (true objective class) and the error, ζ_2, to be different among groups. However, all parameters defining the true variables are invariant over groups, so these variables, and thus their regressions, are comparable over groups.

The χ^2 for the simultaneous model equals 39.19 with 28 degrees of freedom, so the model fit is acceptable, at least at the 5 percent level. The estimates and their standard errors are listed in Table 2.

A test of interest would be whether the true regression slope, β_{21}, is the same in the two groups. This can be tested by specifying $\beta_{21}^{(1)} = \beta_{21}^{(2)}$ and estimate the model again. The χ^2 for this model is 45.62 with 29 degrees of freedom, so with a χ^2 equal to 6.43 with 1 degree of freedom we can reject the hypothesis of equal true regression slopes.

From Table 2 we can compute the correlation between the true subjective class and the true objective class for the two groups. For the white groups this correlation equals 0.401 and for the black group it equals 0.449. These correlations are low, indicating that the external validity for the investigated subjective items is low, which is in agreement with Kluegel et al. (1977):

> While prior research may have underestimated the relationship by virtue of ig-noring unreliabilities and employing a single indicator, it appears unlikely that increased reliability via multiple indicators will produce a high observed correla-tion between objective and subjective class. By and large, it remains for theory and substantive research to explain the large residual. [p. 610]

TABLE 2
Maximum likelihood estimates for the model in Figure 9
(Standard errors of estimates in parentheses)

Parameter	Whites				Blacks	
λy_{22}	1.236	(0.089)				
λy_{32}			1.460	(0.094)		
λy_{42}			1.329	(0.092)		
λy_{13}			0.097	(0.021)		
λy_{24}			0.117	(0.022)		
λx_{11}	1.177	(0.039)			1.136	(0.040)
λx_{22}	20.977	(0.693)			16.506	(0.588)
λx_{33}	2.177	(0.073)			2.121	(0.076)
β_{21}	-0.054	(0.014)			-0.085	(0.022)
γ_{12}			0.542	(0.318)		
γ_{13}			1.663	(0.519)		
ψ_{21}			0.455	(0.028)		
ψ_{31}			0.340	(0.031)		
ψ_{32}			0.260	(0.033)		
ψ_{22}	0.092	(0.013)			0.178	(0.024)
$\theta_{\varepsilon 11}$	0.281	(0.021)			0.299	(0.025)
$\theta_{\varepsilon 22}$	0.225	(0.019)			0.272	(0.025)
$\theta_{\varepsilon 33}$	0.150	(0.017)			0.154	(0.022)
$\theta_{\varepsilon 44}$	0.224	(0.019)			0.348	(0.031)
$\sigma^2_{\eta_1}$	6.152				6.152	
$\sigma^2_{\eta_1 \eta_2}$	0.330				0.526	
$\sigma^2_{\eta_2}$	0.110				0.223	

FIGURE 9
Final model

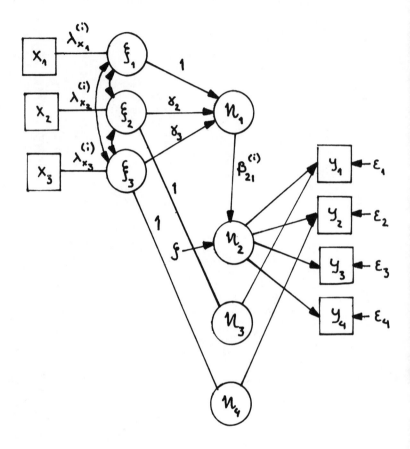

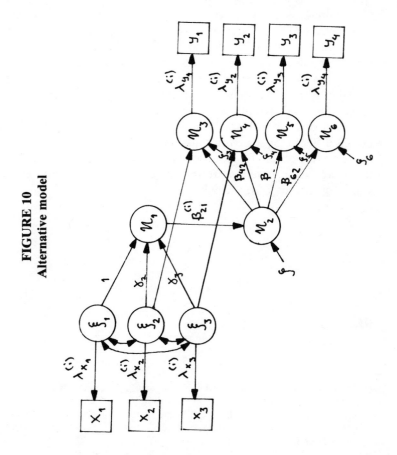

FIGURE 10
Alternative model

In Figure 3 we suggested an alternative to the model for the subjective measures, saying that the factor model was invariant over groups. To incorporate this model into the full model we can specify a model as in Figure 10. The model fit is as good as the fit for the previous model, χ^2 with 28 degrees of freedom equals 40.69, and is discussed here mainly for illustrative purposes. We see in Figure 10 that there is no need to have observed variables for each latent variables; e.g., η_1 is defined only by the ξ variables and η_2 is a common factor of the latent variables η_3, η_4, η_5, and η_6. The model in Figure 10 is quite complex, being a mixture of canonical correlations and second-order factor analysis. However, the interpretation of its parameters is intuitive and straightforward. The groups differ in the structural equation for the regression of subjective class on objective class. However, the relations that define these two latent variables are invariant, except for differences in scales for the observed variables.

REFERENCES

Hodge, R. W. and D. J. Treiman (1968) 'Class Identification in the United States,' *American Journal of Sociology*, vol. 73: 535-47.

Jackman, R. R. and R. W. Jackman (1973) 'An Interpretation of the Relation Between Objective and Subjective Social Status,' *American Sociological Review*, vol. 38: 569-83.

Jöreskog, K. G. (1971a) 'Simultaneous Factor Analysis in Several Populations,' *Psychometrika*, vol. 36: 409-26.

Jöreskog, K. G. (1971b) 'Statistical Analysis of Sets of Congeneric Tests,' *Psychometrika*, vol. 36: 109-33.

Jöreskog, K. G. (1973) 'A General Method for Estimating a Linear Structural Equation System,' pp. 85-112, in A. S. Goldberger and O. D. Duncan (eds), *Structural Equation Models in the Social Sciences*. New York: Seminar Press.

Jöreskog, K. G. (1974) 'Analyzing Psychological Data by Structural Analysis of Covariance Matrices,' pp. 1-56, in R. C. Atkinson, D. H. Krantz, R. D. Luce and P. Suppes (eds), *Contemporary Developments in Mathematical Psychology*, vol. II. San Francisco: Freeman.

Jöreskog, K. G. (1977) 'Structural Equation Models in the Social Sciences: Specification, Estimation and Testing,' pp. 265-87 in P. R. Krishnaiah (ed.), *Application of Statistics*. Amsterdam: North-Holland.

Jöreskog, K. G. and D. Sörbom (1977) 'Statistical Models and Methods for Analysis of Longitudinal Data,' pp. 285-325, in D. J. Aigner and A. S. Goldberger (eds), *Latent Variables in Socioeconomic Models*. Amsterdam: North-Holland.

Jöreskog, K. G., and D. Sörbom (1978) *LISREL IV: Analysis of Linear Structural Relationships by the Method of Maximum Likelihood*. Chicago: International Educational Services.

Kluegel, J. R., R. Singleton Jr and C. E. Starnes (1977) 'Subjective Class Identification: A Multiple Indicator Approach,' *American Sociological Review*, vol. 42:599-611.

7

FACTOR ANALYSIS OF DICHOTOMOUS VARIABLES: AMERICAN ATTITUDES TOWARD ABORTION

Bengt Muthén
University of Uppsala, Sweden

I. INTRODUCTION

The aim of this paper is to illustrate the usefulness of newly developed statistical techniques for the factor analysis of dichotomous variables; see e.g. Bock and Lieberman (1970), Christoffersson (1975), Muthén (1978), Muthén and Christoffersson (1979). The presentation will be relatively non-technical, placing emphasis on the data analysis. Data on American abortion attitudes will be analyzed. The analysis will be carried out in some detail, although no attempt at completeness will be made. In Section 2 the data are described. In Section 3 the models and purpose of analysis are outlined, and in Sections 4, 5, and 6 the data analysis is carried out.

II. THE DATA

The data have been collected within the General Social Surveys

---

Author's Note. This research was supported by the Bank of Sweden Tercentenary Foundation under project, 'Structural Equation Models in the Social Sciences,'' project director Karl G. Jöreskog.

I acknowledge the good assistance from Bengt Dahlqvist regarding the computer runs.

1972-78 of the National Opinion Research Center at the University of Chicago; Davis et al. (1978). This paper analyzes data on abortion attitudes arising from the responses to the following questions:

> Please tell me whether or not you think it should be possible for a pregnant woman to obtain a legal abortion if...
> A. If there is a strong chance of serious defect in the baby?
> B. If she is married and does not want any more children?
> C. If the woman's own health is seriously endangered by the pregnancy?
> D. If the family has a very low income and cannot afford any more children?
> E. If she became pregnant as a result of rape?
> F. If she is not married and does not want to marry the man?

The following mnemonics will be used. A — DEFECT, B — NOMORE, C — HEALTH, D — POOR, E — RAPE, F — SINGLE. The response alternatives were Yes, No, Don't Know. The number of Don't Know responses were less than 6.5 percent (typically considɾ ably less) of the total sample for each item and year, and are noι included in the analysis. The above questions were asked within interviews lasting about one hour and conducted during February, March and April. Each survey (each year) is an independently drawn sample of about 1,500 English-speaking persons 18 years of age or more, living in non-institutional arrangements within the continental United States. For the purpose of this paper, simple random sampling will be assumed for each year; the sampling design is however more complex, see Davis et al. (1978: 171-5).

It is also of interest to relate the responses to the above six abortion items to various background variables. The following variables were chosen:

1 year of survey 1972-74;
2 religious preference of respondent (only Protestants and Catholics are included in the analysis);
3 respondent's education (three categories are used: less than high school education, high school only, more than high school education).

III. THE FACTOR ANALYSIS MODEL

Let u_i ($i = 1, 2, \ldots, p$) be a dichotomous variable (item) and let ξ be a latent variable thought to influence each u_i. Let the response alternatives of each u_i be 1 and 0. For the abortion data, the u_i's would correspond to the six abortion items and ξ would correspond to a hypothetical construct such as a general attitude toward abortion, which can be more or less 'liberal.'

There are two alternative and equivalent ways to describe the relation between the u_i's and ξ. In the classical formulation of latent trait theory we have the normal ogive model (see e.g. Lord and Novick, 1968):

$$P\,(u_i = 1|\xi) = \Phi[a_i(\xi - b_i)]$$
$$(1)\quad P\,(u_i = 0|\xi) = 1 - P(u_i = 1|\xi)$$

where $\Phi[\cdot]$ is the standard normal distribution function. Thus, the conditional probability is modelled as an S-shaped curve, increasing or decreasing monotonically with ξ. In addition it is assumed that for given ξ the responses to the items are independent. This reflects the notion of ξ as a factor, explaining the interrelations between the u_i's.

The alternative formulation is more closely related to the ordinary factor analysis model for quantitative variables. Underlying each u_i it is assumed a latent response variable ξ_i^*, such that

$$(2)\quad u_i = \begin{cases} 1, & \text{if } \xi_i^* \geqslant \tau_i \\ 1, & \text{otherwise} \end{cases}$$

where the τ_i's are viewed as threshold parameters. The latent response variables are related to the factor ξ via the linear regression

$$(3)\quad \xi_i^* = \lambda_i \xi + \varepsilon_i$$

where the parameter λ_i will be called a factor loading and ε_i is an error, independent of ξ and with zero mean. If each ξ_i^* were in fact observed (and not only u_i), (3) would describe an ordinary single-factor model.

Taking the errors in (3) to be normal and independent, the two formulations are equivalent with

$$(4)\quad a_i = \Psi_i^{-\frac{1}{2}} \cdot \lambda_i$$
$$(5)\quad b_i = \tau_i / \lambda_i$$

where Ψ_{ii} is the variance of ε_i. In both formulations the unconditional probability of a certain response is obtained adding the specification of a certain distribution for ξ.

In this paper we will use the factor analytic formulation; see also Christoffersson (1975) and Muthén (1978). In the general multiple-factor case, (3) generalizes to

(6) $\xi^* = \Lambda \xi + \varepsilon.$

In (6), ξ^* $(p \times 1)$ is the vector of latent response variables, Λ $(p \times k)$ is a matrix of factor loadings, $\xi(k \times 1)$ is a vector of factor scores with zero expectation, and $\varepsilon(p \times 1)$ is a vector of errors, independent of ξ and with zero expectation. We assume multinormality for ξ and ε. Each ξ_i^*, u_i pair is related as in (2), via the $p \times 1$ vector of thresholds τ. Under the assumptions,

(7) $V(\xi^*) = \Lambda \Phi \Lambda' + \Psi$

where Φ $(k \times k)$ is the covariance matrix of ξ and Ψ is the covariance matrix of ε. In general we assume uncorrelated errors so that Ψ will be diagonal, but this is not necessary. We note that (7) has the same structure as the covariance matrix for the observed (quantitative) variables of an ordinary factor analysis model. From the above assumptions we may deduce the probability of any combination of response to the p items (any response pattern).

The purpose of the analysis is the same as in ordinary factor analysis. We may want to perform an exploratory analysis in order to find the number of factors yielding a good fit. The factor loadings give information on which factors are measured well by which items. We may also want to restrict the model further and test a certain structure on Λ and/or Φ. For instance, we may want to restrict some loadings to zero corresponding to a hypothesis that certain sets of items measure only one factor. These two types of analyses will be illustrated in Section 4.

The estimation is carried out using generalized least-squares and information from the first- and second-order proportions. Asymptotically, the resulting estimates are normally distributed. Large-sample standard errors are obtained as well as a large-sample chi-square test of overall fit of the model. The computations are performed by the computer program LADI-A (Muthén and Dahlqvist, 1980). For technical details see Muthén (1978).

Often it is also of interest to compare different groups of individuals, for instance groups defined by different survey years. In Muthén and Christoffersson (1979) a method is developed to handle this situation. It is assumed that the same set of items has been administered to all the groups. The measurement characteristics of the items are described by the parameters of τ and Λ. It is assumed that τ and Λ are group-invariant, and that differences in response probabilities depend on group-specific factor means, factor variances/covariances and error variances/covariances. Let $g(g = 1, 2, \ldots, G)$ be the group index. The model is:

(8) $\quad u_i^{(g)} = \begin{cases} 1, \text{ if } \xi_i^{*(g)} \geqslant \tau_i \\ 0, \text{ otherwise} \end{cases}$

(9) $\quad \xi^{*(g)} = \Lambda \xi^{(g)} + \varepsilon^{(g)}$

$$E(\xi^{(g)}) = \nu^{(g)}, \quad V(\xi^{(g)}) = \Phi^{(g)}, \quad V(\varepsilon^{(g)}) = \Psi^{(g)}.$$

The errors have zero means and are independent of $\xi^{(g)}$ in all groups. Multinormality of $\xi^{*(g)}$ is assumed in all groups.

The special case of a single factor illustrates the invariance assumptions. Assuming diagonal $\Psi^{(g)}$, the factor model is the same as the normal ogive model. In the latter formulation, consider group-invariant S-shaped curves (item-characteristic curves) for all items. Given a certain factor score the probability of a certain response is assumed to be the same in all groups. However, the likelihood of obtaining that particular factor score may differ between groups. In the factor analysis formulation invariant item-characteristic curves correspond to invariance of τ, Λ, and Ψ (Ψ diagonal). See also (4) and (5). (The variance of Ψ in addition to τ and Λ may be tested.) The relation to the normal ogive model indicates that we may also think of the error variances as describing (possibly group-invariant) measurement characteristic of the items.

With the method of Muthén and Christoffersson (1979) one may also test the various invariance hypotheses of main interest, namely regarding $\nu^{(g)}$ and $\Phi^{(g)}$. This will be illustrated in Sections 5 and 6. Again, the computations are carried out by the LADI-A program (Muthén and Dahlquist, 1980).

IV. SINGLE-GROUP ANALYSES

As a first step of our analysis, we will explore the number of factors for each survey year. Does a single factor explain the data sufficiently well, or is the item content more heterogeneous, so that several factors are required?

The number of factors is tested by a chi-square measure of fit. One and two factors were tested. With three factors a just-identified model is obtained so that no chi-square test is available. In Table 1 the test results are given. As can be seen, a single factor is clearly insufficient for each of the seven years. For all years there is also a large drop in chi-square when going from one to two factors, indicating that a two-factor model is more suitable. For 1973, 1974, 1975, and 1976 the two-factor model gives a good overall fit, but for the remaining years some modification of the model seems necessary. We will return to this issue shortly.

The two-factor solution may be rotated as in ordinary factor analysis. We will use the Promax method (see e.g. Lawley and Maxwell, 1971), allowing for correlated factors. The estimates for 1972, 1975, and 1978 are given in Table 2 (the results for other years are in close resemblance). The yes-answers have been coded 1. This means that the estimated probability of a yes-answer to item i is given by the area of a standard normal distribution exceeding the estimated value of τ_i (this holds for zero factor means). Thus, a negative τ-value implies that more than 50 percent answer yes to that particular item. For all three years, HEALTH, RAPE and DEFECT are the three most highly approved items (80-90 percent).

In the present coding, a positive loading corresponds to an increasing probability of a yes-answer for increasing value of the factor score. The three loading matrices exhibit a similar and easily interpretable pattern (see (10) below). The first factor is measured by items where the arguments in favor of abortion are of a 'medical' nature (HEALTH, DEFECT). The second factor is measured by items where the arguments are of 'social' nature (NOMORE, POOR, SINGLE). The factors will be named Medical and Social. Alternatively, we may think of the factors as representing traditional versus more modern justifications for abortion. The RAPE item is of an intermediate type, being related to both factors.

TABLE 1
Tests of the number of factors for each survey year

Year	Number of cases Interviewed	Number of cases Analyzed*	1 factor (9 d.f.) χ^2	1 factor (9 d.f.) p-level	2 factors (4 d.f.) χ^2	2 factors (4 d.f.) p-level
1972	1,613	1,319	68.24	0.000	11.75	0.019
1973	1,504	1,349	50.34	0.000	3.22	0.522
1974	1,484	1,288	58.18	0.000	6.47	0.167
1975	1,490	1,286	64.50	0.000	3.62	0.460
1976	1,499	1,330	52.28	0.000	3.77	0.439
1977	1,530	1,353	75.81	0.000	15.62	0.004
1978	1,532	1,360	77.31	0.000	8.34	0.080

* Number of cases with Yes/No answer registered for all six items

TABLE 2
1972, 1975, and 1978 estimates of the two-factor model
(Promax-rotated)

Item	1972 Thresh-old	1972 Loadings	1972 Error var.	1975 Thresh-old	1975 Loadings	1975 Error var.	1978 Thresh-old	1978 Loadings	1978 Error var.
DEFECT	-0.79	0.79	0.20 0.11	-0.98	0.90	0.08 0.08	-0.92	0.73	0.28 0.12
NOMORE	0.16	0.04	0.94 0.05	0.02	0.02	0.96 0.05	0.19	0.05	0.94 0.06
HEALTH	-1.07	0.96	0.00 0.08	-1.30	0.91	0.03 0.14	-1.29	1.05	-0.06 -0.01
POOR	-0.04	0.17	0.83 0.07	-0.14	0.12	0.87 0.08	0.02	0.03	0.93 0.10
RAPE	-0.80	0.63	0.38 0.12	-0.98	0.51	0.50 0.15	-0.95	0.60	0.37 0.19
SINGLE	0.08	0.17	0.81 0.11	-0.02	0.14	0.85 0.09	0.17	0.12	0.87 0.10

	Factor correlation	
0.71	0.69	0.69

The pattern of the loading matrices suggests a simple measurement structure:

$$(10) \quad \Lambda = \begin{bmatrix} x & 0 \\ 0 & x \\ x & 0 \\ 0 & x \\ x & x \\ 0 & x \end{bmatrix}$$

where x's represent non-zero loadings. The results of testing the structure of (10) are given in Table 3 below. Since the hypothesis of (10) has been generated from data, the probability levels stated should not be regarded in a strict sense, but rather as descriptive measures of fit. For 1973, 1974, and 1975 the fit is good. For the remaining years the model will be relaxed somewhat. To guide the modification of the model, it is useful to study the derivatives of the parameters fixed to zero (c.f. Sörbom, 1975). Freeing parameters corresponding to large derivative values (absolute values) often gives a large reduction in chi-square. Possible candidates are the zero elements of Λ and the zero off-diagonal elements of Ψ. Freeing an error covariance term in Ψ was found to give a large reduction in chi-square for 1972, 1976, 1977, and 1978, as shown in Table 4. For all years a reasonable fit is obtained. In three of the cases the error covariance for the RAPE item and SINGLE item is involved (Ψ_{65}). The estimates are all positive. Without the correlated errors, the model underestimates the correlation between the latent response variables for RAPE and

TABLE 3
Tests of a simple measurement structure

	1972	1973	1974	1975	1976	1977	1978
χ^2 (7 d.f.)	17.69	10.66	7.95	8.04	20.36	18.60	17.30
p-level	0.017	0.150	0.370	0.330	0.005	0.008	0.019

TABLE 4
Tests of a simple structure allowing for correlated errors:
1972, 1976, 1977, 1978

	1972	1976	1977	1978
Free error covariance term	Ψ_{65}	Ψ_{42}	Ψ_{65}	Ψ_{65}
χ^2 (6 d.f.)	6.32	8.90	7.99	9.40
p-level	0.388	0.182	0.239	0.154

SINGLE. When answering no to RAPE there seems to be a tendency to give a consistent answer to SINGLE. The error covariance for 1976 may be given a similar interpretation.

V. SIMULTANEOUS ANALYSIS OF THE 1972, 1973, 1974 SURVEYS

An interesting further step of analysis is to study the development of the factors over time. This may be done in a simultaneous analysis of different groups corresponding to different survey years, in the way described in Section 3. We will limit the study to the years 1972, 1973, and 1974. The time period chosen is of particular interest since abortion for any reason was legalized in January 1973. Before this, abortion was legal in certain states and for certain medical reasons.

Thus, we have three groups for which we assume invariance of τ and Λ, where Λ has the structure of (10). For 1972 we allow the errors for RAPE and SINGLE to be correlated as before. For this model a χ^2 of 30.76 with 26 degrees of freedom (d.f. ($p = 0.237$) was obtained. Adding the assumption of invariant error variances resulted in a χ^2 of 40.58 with 38 d.f. ($p = 0.357$). The difference gives a χ^2 of 9.82 with 12 d.f., and we will therefore retain the model of invariant error variances. The estimates are given in Table 5.

The factor means are of special interest. For both factors, 1972 is taken as a reference group standardized to zero mean. Increasing factor mean value corresponds to a more 'liberal' view. We note that for both factors the mean values increase with time. However, the standard errors of the medical factor's means are large and a

TABLE 5
Estimates from the simultaneous analysis of
1972, 1973, 1974*

Item	Threshold	Loadings				Error variance
DEFECT	-0.78 (0.04)	1.01	(0.01)	0.00**	(—)	0.08
NOMORE	0.15 (0.03)	0.00**	(—)	1.00***	(—)	0.07
HEALTH	-1.08 (0.04)	1.00***	(—)	0.00**	(—)	0.09
POOR	-0.03 (0.03)	0.00**	(—)	1.00	(0.01)	0.07
RAPE	-0.81 (0.04)	0.65	(0.05)	0.34	(0.05)	0.17
SINGLE	0.08 (0.03)	0.00**	(—)	0.99	(0.01)	0.09

	1972		1973	1974
Medical factor mean	0.00***	(—)	0.06 (0.10)	0.13 (0.10)
Social factor mean	0.00***	(—)	0.12 (0.05)	0.14 (0.04)
Medical factor variance	0.91	(0.02)	0.58 (0.12)	0.65 (0.14)
Social factor variance	0.93	(0.01)	1.18 (0.18)	0.85 (0.13)
Factor covariance	0.77	(0.02)	0.69 (0.10)	0.59 (0.09)
Error covariance (ψ_{65})	0.07	(0.02)	—	—

   * Standard errors are given in parentheses next to the estimates
  ** Parameter fixed according to hypothesis
 *** Parameter fixed to eliminate scale indeterminacy

TABLE 6
Estimates from the simultaneous analysis of groups classified by religion and education, 1978*

Item	Threshold	Loading		Error variance
NOMORE	0.63 (0.07)	1.00**	(—)	0.08
POOR	0.37 (0.07)	0.95	(0.04)	0.18
SINGLE	0.60 (0.07)	0.93	(0.57)	0.20

Group		Number of cases analyzed***	Social factor mean		Social factor variance
PROT	LHS	316	0.00**	(—)	0.93 (1.11)
	HS	315	0.24	(0.12)	1.75 (1.00)
	MHS	267	0.75	(0.15)	2.83 (1.01)
CATH	LHS	94	-0.11	(0.16)	2.87 (1.00)
	HS	142	-0.11	(0.16)	2.87 (1.00)
	MHS	125	-0.11	(0.16)	2.87 (1.00)

 * Standard errors are given in parentheses next to the estimate

 ** Parameter fixed to eliminate scale indeterminacy

 *** Individuals with complete data for the three abortion items, religious preference and education test of time-invariant medical factor means should be performed. This resulted in an overall fit of 42.20 with 40 d.f. ($p = 0.376$). The difference in χ^2 is 1.62 with 2 d.f. There is no evidence that the level of the medical factor has increased at all. Legalizing abortion for any reason in 1973 seems to be connected with a change of the social factor level only. Despite the new law the approval rate of the 'medical items' DEFECT and HEALTH remain at the estimated level of about 80-85 percent.

From Table 5 we note that the variance of the medical factor has decreased after 1972, so that the opinion seems to have become more homogeneous with respect to these types of arguments. This does not seem to be the case for the social factor.

VI. SIMULTANEOUS ANALYSIS OF GROUPS WITH DIFFERENT RELIGION AND EDUCATION

A further study of the least approved items NOMORE, POOR, and SINGLE is of interest. These items will be viewed as measuring the social factor, although this changes the definition of the factor somewhat since also the RAPE item was found to reflect this factor. The factor will be related to the background variables, respondent's religious preference and respondent's education, for the survey of 1978. For religion there are two categories used; Protestants (PROT) and Catholics (CATH). For education three categories are used: less than high school education (LHS), high school education only (HS), and more than high school education (MHS). The cross-classification gives six groups of individuals for which a simultaneous analysis will be performed.

In this case some more specific hypotheses are of interest. Respondents with high education may be expected to have a more liberal view on abortion (see e.g. Blake, 1971). However, since the Catholic church bans abortion, the relation between abortion attitude and education may not be the same for Protestants and Catholics. Indeed, for Catholics there may be no relation at all.

Again, invariant τ and Λ is assumed, and also invariant error variances (uncorrelated errors). For this baseline model the χ^2 measure of fit is 16.85 with 20 d.f. ($p = 0.663$). There is certainly room for a more restricted model. We may test if Protestants and Catholics show the same relationship with education. This amounts to testing invariance over religion of the factor means and the factor variances; that is, six restrictions are added to the baseline model. The overall test of fit has the value of 44.78 with 26 d.f. ($p = 0.012$), so that a significant worsening of fit is obtained. Instead, the hypothesis of no relation to education for Catholics can be tried. This restricts the factor means and variances for Catholics to be equal over the three educational levels. The overall χ^2 test value is 23.95 with 24 d.f. ($p = 0.464$), indicating a good fit. There is no evidence that Catholics with different educational levels differ with respect to the social factor. The estimates for this model are given in Table 6. We note that the factor mean for Catholics is actually not significantly different from zero (relating the standardized value to critical values of the normal distribution). A factor mean of zero corresponds to the level of Protestants with less than high school education. For Protestants, on the other hand, there is a strong positive relation between the attitude and education.

REFERENCES

Blake, J. (1971) 'Abortion and Public Opinion: The 1960-1970 Decade,' *Science*, vol. 171:540-9.

Bock, R. D. and M. Lieberman (1970) 'Fitting a Response Model for *n* Dichotomously Scored Items,' *Psychometrika*, vol. 35:179-97.

Christoffersson, A. (1975) 'Factor Analysis of Dichotomized Variables,' *Psychometrika*, vol. 40:5-32.

Davis, J. A., T. W. Smith and C. B. Stephenson (1978) *General Social Surveys, 1972-1978: Cumulative Codebook*. Chicago: National Opinion Research Center.

Lawley, D. N. and A. E. Maxwell (1971) *Factor Analysis as a Statistical Method* (2nd ed.). London: Butterworths.

Lord, F. and H. Novick (1968) *Statistical Theories of Mental Test Scores*. Reading, Mass.: Addison-Wesley.

Muthén, B. (1978) 'Contributions to Factor Analysis of Dichotomous Variables', *Psychometrika*, vol. 43:551-60.

Muthén, B. and A. Christoffersson (1979) 'Simultaneous Factor Analysis of Dichotomous Variables in Several Groups,' Department of Statistics, University of Uppsala. Forthcoming in *Psychometrika*.

Muthén, B. and B. Dahlqvist (1980) 'LADI-A. Latent analysis of dichotomous indicators — version A', *User's Guide*, Department of Statistics, University of Uppsala.

Sörbom, D. (1975) 'Detection of Correlated Errors in Longitudinal Data,' *British Journal of Mathematical and Statistical Psychology*, vol. 28:138-51.

8

NEW DEVELOPMENTS IN
LATENT STRUCTURE ANALYSIS

Clifford C. Clogg
Pennsylvania State University

I. INTRODUCTION

This paper surveys new developments in latent structure analysis, a statistical method somewhat related to factor analysis but different from it in important ways. This method has a rich tradition in social research beginning with the studies in item analysis occasioned by World War II. Lazarsfeld's creative genius was largely responsible for the conceptual underpinning of the method (cf. Lazarsfeld, 1950). An influential text by Lazarsfeld and Henry (1968) codifies many of the important generalizations of the latent structure model, and is still necessary reading for anyone who desires a firm understanding of the method. Latent structure analysis can be considered as a straightforward generalization of

Author's Note. A previous version of this paper was presented to the Ninth World Congress of Sociology, ISA Research Committee 33, Session 2, 'Issues and Approaches to Measurement,' Uppsala, Sweden, 14-18 August 1978. Some of the data utilized in this paper were made available by the Inter-University Consortium for Political and Social Research. The data for the Spring 1975 General Social Survey, National Data Program for the Social Sciences, were originally collected by James Davis, then of the National Opinion Research Center, University of Chicago, and were distributed by Roper Public Opinion Research Center, Williams College. Neither the original collector of the data nor the consortium bear any responsobility for the analyses presented here. For helpful comments, the writer is indebted to Lutz Erbring, Leo A. Goodman, Neil W. Henry, David M. Jackson, and Steven A. Tuch.

the elaboration methodology which became the organizing principle of modern survey research (cf. Rosenberg, 1968), as can be demonstrated in the following logic. Often in social research an association among observable qualitative (nominal or ordinal) variables can be 'explained' when controlling for one or more other qualitative variables considered as 'test factors.' This means that the relationship among the original variables would be one of mutual independence in each of the conditional tables obtained at each level of the 'test factor.' If the test factor (or test factors) is (are) also observable, then the logic is that of a standard elaboration. If the test factor is unobservable or latent, then the situation is precisely that of latent structure analysis. The objective of latent structure analysis is to characterize the latent variable that does explain the observed association of interest, and this is done by (1) estimating the relative frequency distribution of the latent variable, (2) estimating the relative frequencies of the observed variables for each category of the latent variable, and (3) inferring from (1) and (2) the substantive meaning of the latent variable for the research question at hand.

As conceptually elegant as the latent structure approach will appear, application of it was from the first burdened with computational and statistical difficulties. For example, the determinantal method popularly used in estimating model parameters (cf. Madansky, 1960; Lazarsfeld and Henry, 1968, Chapter 4; Press, 1972; Fielding, 1977) often produced estimates of probabilities that were not permissible, e.g., estimates that were outside the range [0, 1] or even complex. The LASY computer program based on the determinantal method could for a given set of dichotomous items produce several different sets of parameter estimates for the same data, and conventional rules of thumb rather than rigorous statistical procedures often guided the choice among rival estimates. Efficient maximum likelihood methods were developed for some special cases (McHugh, 1956; 1958), as were certain methods to determine the identifiability of model parameters. But these methods were of very limited practical utility, and to our knowledge were seldom used. These difficulties implied that latent structure methods were largely inaccessible to the majority of empirical social researchers. The complete absence of a convincing substantive analysis of social data using latent structure techniques in professional sociological journals is ample testimony to this claim. In spite of the acknowledgement by Coleman (1964) and others (e.g. Wiggins, 1973; Lazarsfeld and Henry, 1968) of the tremendous potential of the latent structure technique as a general language for the expression of social theory, this potential has been virtually untapped. However, recent improvements in numerical algorithms and computational machinery have made latent structure methods practical for the empirical social researcher. This paper is intended to serve as a brief overview of these new developments, and to provide compelling evidence of the veracity of our claim.

In most respects our survey is based on the innovative contributions recently put forth by Goodman (1974a, b, c; 1975; 1976) and Haberman (1974, 1976, 1977, 1978). Numerical results in this paper were all obtained from a general computer program for maximum likelihood latent structure analysis (MLLSA) which is available from the writer (Clogg, 1977). The algorithm used for estimation is based on the iterative proportional scaling of parameter estimates (Goodman, 1974a), and when properly applied as in the MLLSA program it avoids the difficulties associated with some other methods and some other algorithms. A tremendous range of unrestricted or restricted models can be estimated, and polytomous data can be considered. MLLSA also allows the routine examination of the identifiability of model parameters, and provides many simplifying options for the user. We believe that this program, or ones similar to it, will enable latent structure methods to enjoy the serious empirical application that they so richly deserve.

In Section 2 we formally define the latent structure model, and describe various restrictions that can be imposed on model parameters with the MLLSA program. These restrictions suffice to define many special kinds of restricted latent structures, and a suggestive list of some of these models is offered. In Section 3 we briefly describe the algorithm used in MLLSA, and show how it guarantees permissible parameter estimates when it is correctly programmed for the computer. The rescaling of parameters prior to each cycle of iteration, necessary for the use of this algorithm, has been neglected in some applications (cf. Formann, 1978; Goodman, 1978). We also comment on why this algorithm is easier to apply than some other algorithms. In Section 4 we discuss two alternative methods for determining the identifiability of model parameters, and we apply both methods to re-analyze an unidentifiable model. Section 5 considers the problem of predicting latent class membership from observed response patterns, and presents a simple index of the quality of the prediction. Sections 6, 7, and 8 present latent structure models appropriate for a variety of substantive topics which up until now have not been approached from the latent structure point of view. Rather than defining these new models in a rigorous and general fashion, we instead present empirical applications which should suggest the proper extensions to more general situations. In Section 6 a 'multiple-indicator, multiple-cause' model is applied to Lazarsfeld's panel data on voting intentions. This model is related to but different from the range of models considered in Goodman (1974b), and illustrates the close resemblance of certain restricted latent structure models to some of the corresponding models considered by Jöreskog (1973). Section 7 presents latent structure models for ordinal indicators (viz. Likert-type data). Ordinal indicators of underlying attributes are ubiquitous in social research, and the models presented here exploit the ordinality of item categories without assuming intervalness. Finally in Section 8 latent structure methods are applied to the analysis of social mobility processes. A particular 'quasi-latent structure' model which was actually proposed by Goodman (1974b) in a much different context is shown to provide a compelling summarization of the mobility table. In each of the substantive applications the special merit of the latent structure approach is emphasized.

Consider a three-way cross-classification of the observable variables A, B, and C, and let π_{ijk} denote the probability that an individual will be observed in response pattern (i, j, k), for $i = 1, \ldots, I$; $j = 1, \ldots, J$; $k = 1, \ldots, K$. We suppose that there exists a single latent variable X with T classes so that the following relationships hold:

$$(1) \quad \pi_{ijk} = \sum_{t=1}^{T} \pi_{ijkt}^{ABCX}$$

where

$$(2) \quad \pi_{ijkt}^{ABCX} = \pi_t^X \pi_{it}^{\bar{A}X} \pi_{jt}^{\bar{B}X} \pi_{kt}^{\bar{C}X}$$

Equation (1) expresses the assumption that the observable cross-classification is obtained by collapsing over the categories of the X

variable. The observable proportions π_{ijk} contain only indirect information concerning X; or, equivalently, the X variable is indirectly observed in the ABC table. The X variable is 'mixed up' in or incompletely specified with the π_{ijk}. (See Chen and Fienberg, 1976, for related material concerning 'mixed-up' frequencies.) Implicit in equation (1) is the additional important assumption that the T classes exhaust the population. In equation (2) the assumption is expressed that X 'explains' the association among A, B, and C. Here π_t^X refers to the probability that an individual will be a member of the tth class of X; $\pi_{it}^{\bar{A}X}$ refers to the conditional probability that an individual in the tth latent class will be observed in the ith class of A; and $\pi_{jt}^{\bar{B}X}$, $\pi_{kt}^{\bar{C}X}$ denote similar kinds of conditional probabilities. Applying the law of conditional probability, we can see that equation (2) states that A, B, and C are conditionally independent, given the levels of X. If X were logically antecedent to A, B, and C, then this would correspond to the elaboration concept of X 'explaining' the A-B-C association. Such an interpretation would be appropriate, e.g., if A, B, and C were fallible indicators of X.

Note that variables A, B, and/or C could themselves be *joint* variables composed of two or more other observed variables. To illustrate, suppose that B and C were considered as a joint variable, say BC. Then equation (2) could in some contexts be replaced by the relationship

$$(3) \quad \pi_{ijkt}^{ABCX} = \pi_t^X \, \pi_{it}^{\bar{A}X} \, \pi_{jkt}^{\bar{B}\bar{C}X} \, .$$

Here X would be said to explain the association between A and the joint variable BC, but *mutual dependence* between B and C would still be a part of the model. (For related details, see Harper, 1972.) Using the technique just illustrated a wide variety of additional latent structures can be tested using methods adopted for the situation of (1) – (2). Note further that the variable X may itself be composed of two or more latent variables. A latent variable with four classes can, for example, be considered as a four-fold cross-classification of two dichotomies. These results will be used in Section 6 to develop the multiple-indicator, multiple-cause model.

Because the latent structure parameters on the right-hand side of (2) are probabilities, they will be non-negative and satisfy the restrictions

$$(4) \quad \sum_t \pi_t^X = \sum_{i=1}^{I} \pi_{it}^{\bar{A}X} = \sum_{j=1}^{J} \pi_{jt}^{\bar{B}X} = \sum_{k=1}^{K} \pi_{kt}^{\bar{C}X} = 1.$$

Sample estimates of these parameters should be non-negative and should also satisfy similar restrictions. Some methods of estimation (e.g. the determinantal method used in the LASY computer program) do not produce estimates that are guaranteed to satisfy these restrictions. This difficulty has been responsible, in part, for the development of alternative procedures. We shall comment further on the implications of equation (4) for computation in the next section.

In the sampling situation it is, of course, important to estimate the model parameters from the data. MLLSA can do so directly for the unrestricted model. (The unrestricted model is one where the model parameters satisfy the restrictions of (4), but no other restrictions.) In other contexts it will be of interest to estimate the parameters when they are subject to various restrictions in addition to those of (4). The types of restrictions that can presently be considered with MLLSA are of the following types:

1. restrictions of parameters to fixed constants; e.g., $\pi_1^X = 0.5$, or $\pi_{11}^{AX} = 1.0$;

2. equality restrictions on the latent class proportions; e.g., $\pi_1^X = \pi_2^X$;

3. equality restrictions on the conditional probabilities; e.g.,

$$\pi_{11}^{AX} = \pi_{12}^{AX}, \text{ or } \pi_{11}^{AX} + \pi_{21}^{BX}, \text{ or } \pi_{11}^{AX} + \pi_{22}^{BX}$$

4. restrictions mixing types 1-3.

(See Goodman, 1974a; Clogg, 1977). These restrictions suffice to define a tremendous range of models. MLLSA can be used, for example, to define restricted latent structures which are equivalent to the following models:

1. Lazarsfeld's latent distance model (Lazarsfeld and Henry, 1968);

2. restricted latent distance models (cf. Hays and Borgatta, 1954);

3. Goodman's modified latent distance model (Goodman, 1974c):

4. Proctor's probabilistic model of Guttman scaling (Proctor, 1970; 1971);

5. the new Goodman scale model based on the quasi-independence concept (Goodman, 1975);

6. certain quasi-independence models which arise, e.g., in the study of social mobility (Goodman, 1969, 1972; Pullum, 1975);

7. multiple-indicator, multiple-cause models appropriate for discrete data (see our Section 6);

8. many path models depicting the relationships among observable and unobservable qualitative variables (Goodman, 1974b; Jöreskog, 1973);

9. quasi-latent structure models (Goodman, 1974b; see our Section 8);

and many other models directly or indirectly related to these. Some specific kinds of restricted latent structures will be dealt with later herein. The latent structure method can be seen to be very general in character, and many log-linear models that have appeared in various substantive and theoretical contexts can be interpreted as special types of restricted latent structures.

III. MAXIMUM LIKELIHOOD ESTIMATION BY ITERATIVE PROPORTIONAL SCALING OF PARAMETERS

A variety of algorithms are currently available which provide solutions to the latent structure model. These include Haberman's program based on a Newton-Raphson algorithm (Haberman, 1974, 1976, 1977); related programs based on Fisher's method of scoring (see Haberman, 1974, 1977; Dayton and Macready, 1976a, b; 1977a, b, c); Carroll's canonical decomposition algorithm (Carroll, 1975; Green, Carmone, and Wachspress, 1976); Formann's algorithm based on a logit-type transformation of model parameters and a certain gradient method (Formann, 1978); Goodman's (1974a, b) method based on iterative proportional scaling of parameters; and other approaches related to these and to the earlier estimation techniques. Estimation no longer poses a serious problem, since a wide variety of algorithms are available, and most of these algorithms produce efficient maximum likelihood solutions. The MLLSA program uses Goodman's (1974a, b) method, and we believe that users will find this algorithm preferable in certain respects to the others mentioned here. The algorithm used in MLLSA completely avoids the inversion of matrices (unlike Fisher scoring or Newton-Raphson algorithms), and is readily programmed to deal with a variety of unrestricted or restricted models. The program produces maximum likelihood solutions (unlike the Carroll method, or the older LASY methods), and always guarantees permissible parameter estimates (unlike LASY, or some of the older maximum likelihood methods). In applications on the IBM 370 I have found MLLSA to be reasonably cost-efficient, although comparisons with other programs have not been rigorously carried out. The program appears more flexible and more general than any of the other programs of which I am aware. We now briefly discuss the algorithm and indicate how it has been used in MLLSA.

Returning to the model parameters in (2), we can see that

$$(5) \quad \pi_t^X = \sum_{i,j,k} \pi_{ijkt}^{ABCX}$$

and

$$(6) \quad \pi_t^X \pi_{it}^{\bar{A}X} = \sum_{j,k} \pi_{ijkt}^{ABCX} .$$

Formulae similar to (6) can be written for the products $\pi_t^X \pi_{jt}^{\bar{B}X}$ and $\pi_t^X \pi_{kt}^{\bar{C}X}$. Now let $\pi_{ijkt}^{ABC\bar{X}}$ denote the conditional probability that an individual with responses pattern (i,j,k) is in the tth class of X. By applying the definition of conditional probability, we have

$$(7) \quad \pi_{ijkt}^{ABC\bar{X}} = \pi_{ijkt}^{ABCX} / \pi_{ijk} .$$

Using (7) we can rewrite (5) and (6) as

$$(8) \quad \pi_t^X = \sum_{i,j,k} \pi_{ijk} \pi_{ijkt}^{ABCX}$$

and

$$(9) \quad \pi_{it}^{AX} = \left(\sum_{j,k} \pi_{ijk} \pi_{ijkt}^{AB\bar{C}X} \right) / \pi_t^X$$

Formulae similar to (9) can be obtained for the other conditional probabilities.

We let circumflexes denote the maximum likelihood estimate of the model parameters, and we let P_{ijk} denote the observed sample proportion at level (i,j,k) with respect to the joint variable (A,B,C). Noting that the latent class model can be described in the shorthand notation of Goodman (1970) as $(A \otimes B \otimes C | X)$, we can see that estimates $\hat{\pi}_{ijkt}^{ABCX}$ will be such that the indirectly observed marginals (AX), (BX), and (CX) and their lower-order relatives are fit by the latent class model. These conditions can be shown to imply that the maximum likelihood estimates will satisfy the following system of equations:

$$(10) \quad \hat{\pi}_t^X = \sum_{i,j,k} P_{ijk} \hat{\pi}_{ijkt}^{ABC\bar{X}}$$

$$(11) \quad \hat{\pi}_{it}^{\bar{A}X} = \left(\sum_{j,k} P_{ijk} \hat{\pi}_{ijki}^{ABC\bar{X}} \right) / \hat{\pi}_t^X$$

$$(12) \quad \hat{\pi}_{jt}^{\bar{B}X} = \left(\sum_{i,k} P_{ijk} \, \hat{\pi}_{ijkt}^{ABC\bar{X}} \right) / \hat{\pi}_t^X$$

$$(13) \quad \hat{\pi}_{kt}^{\bar{C}X} = \left(\sum_{i,j} P_{ijk} \, \hat{\pi}_{ijkt}^{ABC\bar{X}} \right) / \hat{\pi}_t^X .$$

Now let π denote the vector of parameters $(\pi_t^X, \pi_{it}^{AX}, \pi_{jt}^{BX}, \pi_{kt}^{CX})$ and let $\hat{\pi}$ denote the corresponding maximum likelihood estimate of that vector. To calculate $\hat{\pi}$, start with an initial set of trial values, viz. $\hat{\pi}(0) = (\hat{\pi}_t^X(0), \hat{\pi}_{it}^{AX}(0), \hat{\pi}_{jt}^{BX}(0), \hat{\pi}_{kt}^{CX}(0))$, where the start values are chosen to ensure that (4) is satisfied. Then use a formula analogous to (2) to obtain a trial value $\hat{\pi}_{ijkt}^{ABCX}(0)$, replacing the parameters on the righthand side of (2) with the elements of $\hat{\pi}(0)$. (Note that the trial estimates $\hat{\pi}_{ijkt}^{ABCX}(0)$ will all be permissible probability estimates.) Then use (1) to obtain a trial value $\hat{\pi}_{ijkt}^{ABC\bar{X}}(0)$; viz.,

$$(14) \quad \hat{\pi}_{ijkt}^{ABCX}(0) = \hat{\pi}_{ijkt}^{ABC\bar{X}}(0) / \hat{\pi}_{ijk}(0).$$

Now obtain the proportionally rescaled estimates $\hat{\pi}(1)$ by substituting these trial values into (10)-(13). It is not difficult to show (Goodman, 1978) that, apart from round-off error, the estimates so obtained will all be permissible estimates of the model parameters, and they will satisfy identically the restrictions in equation (4).

Before beginning a second cycle of iteration, it is necessary to rescale the elements of $\hat{\pi}(1)$ to ensure that all the conditions of (4) are satisfied. By virtue of round-off error in the calculations, these restrictions need not be satisfied after completing a cycle, and this round-off error can cumulate from cycle to cycle complicating the procedure in unknown ways. For example, if $'\Sigma_{i=1}^I \pi_{it}^{\bar{A}X}(1) = C_t (\neq 1)$ then multiply $\pi_{it}^{AX}(1)$ by $(C_t)^{-1}$ for every i and use the result to begin the next cycle. If one or more of the elements $\pi_{1t}^{\bar{A}X}, \ldots, \pi_{It}^{\bar{A}X}$ are restricted in some way in addition to (4), then the algorithm can be modified to rescale only free parameters. (If all the parameters in the relevant set are restricted in some way, then similar, but more complicated, procedures for rescaling can be used. MLLSA will appropriately rescale model parameters under a wide variety of conditions, including some cases where all of the parameters in a given set are restricted in some way.) After rescaling $\hat{\pi}(1)$ to correct for round-off, the second cycle of iteration is begun. The procedure reported in this and the preceding paragraph is repeated until the desired level of convergence is obtained. The reader is referred to

Goodman (1974a) for a fuller discussion of the algorithm, the proper selection of start values, and related topics.

This algorithm may also be applied to estimate restricted latent structures. It is tedious to describe the manner in which various types of restrictions are dealt with in between cycles of the iterative procedure. Suffice it to say that each cycle begins with a set of trial values in which the restrictions of (4) as well as the other restrictions are satisfied. We emphasize that care must be taken to ensure that each cycle of the procedure begins with estimates that satisfy the necessary restrictions. Failure to correct for round-off can produce very misleading results indeed (cf. Formann, 1978; Goodman, 1978).

The MLLSA program using the algorithm described in this section has been used by approximately 30 researchers thus far, and the feedback from them has been very positive. All that is required for the user of MLLSA are the start values $\hat{\pi}(0)$ and some other information necessary to define the particular model under consideration.

IV. IDENTIFICATION OF MODEL PARAMETERS AND DEGREES OF FREEDOM

Not every conceivable latent structure model will have identifiable parameters, as is the case with various factor-analytic models analogous to latent structure models. Goodman presented a method for determining the identifiability of the parameters which is actually a generalization of an earlier result by McHugh (1956). This method is based on a standard result concerning Jacobians of transformations, and need not be fully discussed here. Briefly, the approach is as follows.

Equation (2) defines a transformation from the parameter vector π to the vector $\{\pi_{ijk}\}$. The transformation will be nonsingular if and only if the matrix H of first derivatives

$$(15) \quad H = \left\{ \frac{\partial \{\pi_{ijk}\}}{\partial \pi} \right\}$$

is of rank equal to the number of nonredundant components of π. The elements of H can be determined explicitly by using (1) and (2)

TABLE 1
An example of an unidentifable model

Model	Latent class t	$\hat{\pi}_t^X$	$\bar{A}X$ π_{1t}	$\bar{B}X$ π_{1t}	$\bar{C}X$ π_{1t}	$\bar{D}X$ π_{1t}
Goodman's	1	0.208	0.997	0.973	0.986	0.884
model H_2*	2	0.630	0.824	0.459	0.425	0.183
	3	0.162	0.404	0.052	0.256	0.067
Model using	1	0.195	0.909	0.998	0.979	0.998
different start	2	0.584	0.199	0.445	0.495	0.842
values**	3	0.221	0.075	0.268	0.092	0.475

* Based on the three-class unrestricted model applied to the Stouffer-Toby data on role conflict. See Goodman (1974a)

** Start values taken from H_2, with the modifications that $\hat{\pi}_2^X(0) = 0.555$, $\hat{\pi}_3^X(0) = 0.237$, and $\hat{\pi}_{13}^{AX}(0) = 0.504$

to calculate derivatives, and sample estimates of these derivatives can be obtained by substituting the corresponding estimates π into the results of the differentiation. For a given sample and a given latent structure model H can therefore be estimated (say, by $\hat{H}$), and the identifiability of the estimates parameter values can be determined by calculating the rank of $\hat{H}$. Care must be taken in calculating the rank of $\hat{H}$, because this matrix will not in general be square. Various procedures are available to calculate the rank of rectangular matrices, and one of these must be used.[1] The degrees of freedom associated with a particular model will be equal to $IJK - 1$ minus the rank of H (when the number of nonredundant elements of π is less than or equal to the number of nonredundant elements of $\{\pi_{ijk}\}$ — note that there are $IJK - 1$ such nonredundant elements, since $\sum_{i,j,k} \pi_{ijk} = 1$). In general, the degrees of freedom for a latent class model will be given by

(16) $df = IJK - 1 - $ (no. of nonredundant parameters in π).

We are now ready to examine the identification problem with an empirical example. Goodman (1974a) found that the three-class unrestricted model applied to the Stouffer-Toby data on role conflict was unidentifiable.[2] The (unidentified) parameters estimated with his model H_2 are presented in Table 1. Since $\sum \pi_t^X = 1$ there appear to be two nonredundant latent class proportions, and there appear to be 12 nonredundant conditional probabilities, for a total of 14 model parameters. However, when we calculate $\hat{H}$ we find that this matrix has rank 13, implying that the parameters are underidentified. A restriction of some kind must therefore be imposed.

An alternative way to examine the identifiability of Goodman's model H_2 is to refit the model using start values that are close to but slightly different from the estimates obtained from H_2. From Table 1 we find $\hat{\pi}_2^X = 0.630$, $\hat{\pi}_3^X = 0.162$, and $\hat{\pi}_{13}^{\bar{A}X} = 0.404$. For purposes of illustration we have modified the start values for a new attempt by taking $\hat{\pi}_2^X(0) = 0.555$, $\hat{\pi}_3^X(0) = 0.237$, and $\hat{\pi}_3^{\bar{A}x}(0) = 0.504$. The algorithm then converges to the solution shown in the second tier of Table 1. Both solutions produce a likelihood ratio χ^2 of 0.387, but we see that the parameter estimates from the second solution are *very* different from those of H_2. This procedure also shows that the solution to the system of equations $(10) - (13)$ is not unique. A procedure like this one can always be used if the identification of model parameters is in question.

Both of the methods discussed here can be used to check identification. MLLSA automatically calculates the rank of $\hat{H}$, but users without access to this program can use the other method based on an alteration of start values. Goodman's (1974a) paper demonstrates how unidentifiable models can be replaced by identifiable models.

V. PREDICTING LATENT CLASS MEMBERSHIP FROM OBSERVED RESPONSE PATTERNS

One of the objectives of latent structure analysis can be to 'reduce the dimensionality' of a set of items. This is done by estimating from the observed response patterns (i, j, k) the latent class variable. An estimate of this variable can be denoted by $\hat{X}$, although as in factor analysis there are important qualifications on the meaning of the *variable estimate* (rather than a *parameter* estimate) implied by this notation. The method of estimating X is described in Lazarsfeld and Henry (1968) and Goodman (1974b), and so we only briefly summarize the procedure here. In doing so, however, we will present a convenient index of the quality of the prediction (estimation) of X.

Returning to equation (7), we find an expression for π_{ijkt}^{ABCX} the conditional probability that an individual having observable response pattern (i, j, k) will be in latent class t. If t' is the class of X where π_{ijkt}^{ABCX} is a maximum, for given response pattern (i, j, k), then one prediction rule would be to assign all individuals with response pattern (i, j, k) to class t' of X. We can denote $\varepsilon_{ijk} = 1 - \pi_{ijkt'}^{ABCX}$ as the expected rate of misclassification, and the expected number of classification errors for response pattern (i, j, k) would be

$$(17) \quad E_{ijk} = n\, \varepsilon_{ijk}\, \pi_{ijk}.$$

The expected number of classification errors in the table would be

$$(18) \quad E_2 = \underset{ijx}{\Sigma} E_{ijk}\,.$$

The estimated expected numbers misclassified are obtained by substituting estimates $\hat{\varepsilon}_{ijk}$ and $\hat{\pi}_{ijk}$ into (17) and hence (18). Now suppose that the classes of X were to be predicted without knowledge of ABC (i.e., unconditionally). Assuming that π_1^X , ..., π_T^X were known, then the same prediction rule that defined the error rates of ε_{ijk} would assign all individuals into the t^*th class of X, where $\pi_{t^*}^X$, is the modal latent class proportion. The expected rate of error for this unconditional prediction would be $\varepsilon_1 = 1 - \pi_{t^*}^X{}^*$ and the expected number of errors for a sample of size n would be

$$(19) \quad E_1 = n\varepsilon_1.$$

In order to gauge the quality of the prediction of the classes of $\dot{X}$ (i.e., to judge the precision with which $\hat{X}$ estimates X), we recommend computing an asymmetric measure of association between X and the joint variable ABC. The measure that is consistent with the prediction rules used to estimate X and to define the errors E_1, E_2, is the lambda measure

$$(20) \quad \lambda_{X \cdot ABC} = (E_1 - E_2)/E_1.$$

This measure is discussed in Goodman and Kruskal (1954), and is essentially the same as Guttman's coefficient of scalability widely used in scalogram analysis (cf. Torgerson 1962).

TABLE 2
Assignment of respondents into latent classes
for a two-class unrestricted model*

Response pattern	Observed frequency	Expected frequency	Predicted class	Probability of error
(1,1,1,1)	42	41.84	1	0.04
(1,1,1,2)	23	23.28	1	0.48
(1,1,2,1)	6	6.30	1	0.50
(1,1,2,2)	25	21.49	2	0.04
(1,2,1,1)	6	6.05	2	0.42
(1,2,1,2)	24	23.66	2	0.03
(1,2,2,1)	7	6.58	2	0.03
(1,2,2,2)	38	41.80	2	0.00
(2,1,1,1)	1	0.96	2	0.28
(2,1,1,2)	4	4.60	2	0.02
(2,1,2,1)	1	1.28	2	0.02
(2,1,2,2)	6	8.25	2	0.00
(2,2,1,1)	2	1.42	2	0.01
(2,2,1,2)	9	9.19	2	0.00
(2,2,2,1)	2	2.56	2	0.00
(2,2,2,2)	20	16.74	2	0.00

* Percent correctly allocated in the latent classes $= 90.3$ percent. Lambda of the assignment $= 0.652$.

Table 2 presents quantities that allow a rigorous assessment of the quality of prediction of the classes of X for an unrestricted two-class model applied to thé same 2^4 table analyzed earlier in Table 1. We see that all individuals with response patterns (1,1,1,1), (1,1,1,2), or (1,1,2,1) would be predicted to be at level 1 of the X variable, and all other individuals would be predicted at level 2 of X. The estimated dichotomy $\hat{X}$ could, for example, be used in further substantive analysis where X is thought to be an explanatory variable 'causing' (in some sense) other variables. We see from Table 2 that the error rates $\hat{\varepsilon}_{ijk}$ are high for some cells, and this accounts for the lambda measure being estimated at 0.652 (less than one). Given the prediction rule used to estimate X, the errors are reduced by 65.2 percent when the response patterns of the observed variables are taken into account. Since λ is not dependent on n (as are, e.g., the χ^2 statistics), and since it takes account of the uncon-

FIGURE 1
Two path models with two latent variables Y and Z
for the Lazarsfeld panel data

Goodman's (1974b) model H_2

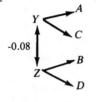

$$\chi^2 = 7.32 \text{ on } 4 \text{ d.f.*}$$

Multiple-Indicator, Multiple-Cause Model

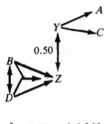

$$\chi^2 = 7.04 \text{ on } 2 \text{ d.f.**}$$

* In estimating this model for the Lazarsfeld panel data, we actually found one terminal estimate, so the d.f. should be increased to 5. See Goodman (1974b) for the justification for this convention, and compare our results with his Table 15.

** There are two additional paths in the multiple-indicator, multiple-cause model, viz. the path denoting association between the exogenous variables B and D, and the path denoting the effect of B on Z, which differs according to the level of D (or the path denoting the effect of D on Z, which differs according to the level of B); i.e., this model has two additional paths, and two fewer d.f. than Goodman's model H_2.

ditional distribution of X (i.e., π_5^x, ..., π_T^x), it is preferable to some other indexes that might be used. The utility of λ as an index of model adequacy when used in conjunction with other indexes of fit, appears to be substantial, especially in comparative work.

VI. MULTIPLE-INDICATOR, MULTIPLE-CAUSE MODELS

Werts, Linn, and Jöreskog (1971; 1973) and Jöreskog (1973), as well as others, have presented methods for the estimation and testing of structural equation models for quantitative data involving unobservables. Strictly speaking, these methods are appropriate whenever the variables in the models are distributed as multivariate normal random variables. Models that correspond to many of these were considered by Goodman (1974b), although the modified latent structure methods provide maximum likelihood solutions for discrete (multinomial) cross-classifications, regardless of the underlying distribution of the quantitative variables that might underly the discrete variables. In this section we reconsider one model presented by Goodman wholly analogous to the model in Werts, Linn, and Jöreskog (1971), and we also present a new model not actually considered by Goodman which is wholly analogous to the multiple-indicator, multiple-cause (MIMC) model. The MIMC model is a special case of the more general model presented in Jöreskog (1973). In considering this model we are suggesting (although certainly not proving in a rigorous sense) that many of the Jöreskog models possess counterparts in the modified latent structure approach. Since the latent structure methods do not make such stringent distributional assumptions as the Jöreskog methods, they can be used in cases where the variables in question are discrete (or discretized) in meaningful ways, but are not multivariate normal.

The data to be re-analyzed here are Lazarsfeld's panel data on voting intentions.[3] The reader is referred to Goodman (1974b) for the cross-classification to be analyzed; to save space, we do not present it here. That 16-fold table was obtained by cross-classifying 266 respondents by dichotomous measures of vote intention (1 = Republican, 2 = other) and opinion of the Republican candidate (1 = favorable, 2 = unfavorable) at two different points in time. We let A and C refer to vote intention for times 1 and 2, and we let B and D refer to opinion at times 1 and 2.

Goodman considered one model for these data which posited the existence of two latent dichotomous variables denoted here as Y (latent vote intention) and Z (latent opinion) which explained the $ABCD$ association according to the first path diagram in Figure 1. The variables A and C were considered as fallible indicators of Y which were not directly related to Z, and the variables B and D were considered as fallible indicators of Z which were not directly related to Y. This model had a likelihood ratio χ^2 of 7.32 of 4 d.f., and so explains the data very well. However, under this model the estimated effect between Y and Z turned out to be -0.08 (logarithmic scale), denoting a *negative* and negligible relationship between latent opinion and latent intention. On purely statistical grounds the model cannot be questioned, but the structural parameter just discussed turned out to have an estimate that would violate our understanding of the relationship between Y and Z.

One model that might be cosidered as an alternative would consider B and D as imperfect causes of latent opinion Z, Z a cause of latent vote intention Y, and Y a 'cause' of the indicators A and C. This would correspond to a multiple-indicator, multiple-cause model with two latent variables, and the path diagram would correspond to the second model in Figure 1. The reader may wish to compare this model with the somewhat different range of models considered in Goodman (1974b) — see his Figure 10 — or the corresponding models presented in Jöreskog (1973). We now consider how restrictions on the latent class model serve to define the given MIMC model.

First, consider a four-fold latent variable X with classes $(1,2,3,4)$ which correspond one-to-one with the joint (Y,Z) variable with classes $((1,1), (1,2), (2,1), (2,2))$. Next, consider the joint variable BD with classes $(1,2,3,4)$ corresponding one-to-one with the categories of (B,D), $((1,1), (1,2), (2,1), (2,2))$. Let π_{irs}^{AYZ} denote the conditional probability that an individual will be at level i of A, given that he is at level (r, s) on (Y, Z), and let π_{krs}^{CYZ} and $\pi_{j\lambda rs}^{B\bar{D}YZ}$ be similarly defined. The MIMC model says that the conditional probabilities $\pi^{\bar{A}YZ}$ and $\pi^{\bar{C}YZ}$ depend on the level r of Y (but not on the level s of Z), and that the conditional probabilities $\pi^{B\bar{D}YZ}$ the level s of variable Z (but not on the level r of Y). By taking account of the correspondence between X and (Y, Z) and the correspondence between BD and (B, D), this model must therefore satisfy the following set of equality restrictions:

$$(21) \quad \pi_{11}^{\bar{A}X} = \pi_{12}^{\bar{A}X}, \pi_{13}^{\bar{A}X} = \pi_{14}^{\bar{A}X}$$

$$(22) \quad \pi_{11}^{\bar{C}X} = \pi_{12}^{\bar{C}X}, \pi_{13}^{\bar{C}X} = \pi_{14}^{\bar{C}X}$$

$$(23) \quad \pi_{11}^{\bar{B}\bar{D}X} = \pi_{13}^{\bar{B}\bar{D}X}, \pi_{21}^{\bar{B}\bar{D}X} = \pi_{23}^{\bar{B}\bar{D}X}$$

$$(24) \quad \pi_{31}^{\bar{B}\bar{D}X} = \pi_{33}^{\bar{B}\bar{D}X}, \pi_{12}^{\bar{B}\bar{D}X} = \pi_{14}^{\bar{B}\bar{D}X}$$

$$(25) \quad \pi_{22}^{\bar{B}\bar{D}X} = \pi_{24}^{\bar{B}\bar{D}X}, \pi_{32}^{\bar{B}\bar{D}X} = \pi_{34}^{\bar{B}\bar{D}X}.$$

Equations (21)-(25) define the MIMC model applied to the $2 \times 2 \times 4$ $A \times C \times BD$ cross-table, and equations similar to them can be used to define other MIMC models. Upon estimating this model, we find a likelihood ratio χ^2 of 7.04 on 2 d.f., and we find the estimated effect of Z on Y to be $+0.50$. To save space, we do not discuss the other effects in the path models of Figure 1, but note here that the $Y - Z$ association (obtained directly from the estimates $\hat{\pi}_1^X, \hat{\pi}_2^X, \hat{\pi}_3^X, \hat{\pi}_4^X$) now corresponds more closely with our a priori expectations.

Other models considered by Jöreskog and others have counterparts as modified latent structure models, but we do not further discuss the matter here. Of course, these models (e.g. MIMC models) can be applied to cases with more than two causes and/or more than two indicators.

VII. LATENT STRUCTURE MODELS FOR ORDINAL INDICATORS

Ordinal indicators of underlying attributes are ubiquitous in social research, and have been analyzed by a variety of methods. Often researchers assign numeric scores to the rank-order categories of such variables, and then proceed in their statistical analysis as if the recoded variables were quantitative. We suggest a latent structure approach that exploits (a) the actual distributional properties of ordinal variables in a cross-classification, (b) the rank-order character of the variables, and (c) the status of the observed variables as indicators of unobservable or latent variables (cf. Clogg, 1979b). Table 3 is an example of the kind of data we have in mind. Three trichotomous indicators of life satisfaction are considered in that cross-classification, and the categories of the variables refer to high, medium, or low satisfaction with a particular facet of life.

TABLE 3
Observed cross-classification of three
trichotomous indicators of life satisfaction*

B	A	C = 1	C = 2	C = 3
1	1	466	27	16
1	2	191	38	14
1	3	64	18	5
2	1	126	31	5
2	2	117	58	12
2	3	45	23	3
3	1	54	12	7
3	2	49	26	11
3	3	23	16	15
$n = 1,472$				

* A = satisfaction with residence; B = satisfaction with hobbies; C = satisfaction with family

Source: 1975 General Social Survey. The original variables were coded 1-7, but we have recoded values so that code 1 refers to 'a very great deal' or 'a great deal'; code 2 refers to 'quite a bit' or 'a fair amount'; and code 3 refers to 'some', 'a little', or 'none.' The observed cross-classification pertains only to those who responded to all of the questions. Only 18 of the 1,490 original observations are missing from this table.

In Table 4 the fit of various latent structure models is presented. H_0 is the usual independence model, which can be thought of as a one-class latent structure. H_1 is the unrestricted two-class model, and with a χ^2 of 28.57 on 13 d.f. the fit is certainly acceptable. H_2 is the unrestricted three-class model, which turns out to be identifiable for these data, and with a χ^2 of 2.36 on 7 d.f. we have fit the data very well indeed. Unrestricted models (viz. H_1, H_2) do not take the order of the item categories into account, and so we now suggest a restricted latent structure model which overcomes this difficulty.

TABLE 4
Goodness-of-fit and likelihood ratio chi-square
statistics for some latent structure models
applied to the data of Table 3

Model	Degrees of freedom	Goodness-of-fit chi-square χ^2	Likelihood ratio chi-square L^2	$\dfrac{1 - L^2(H)}{L^2(H_0)}$
H_0	20	339.43	259.17	—
H_1	13	34.84	28.57	0.89
H_2	7*	2.32	2.36	0.99
H_3	14**	25.22	24.77	0.90
H_4	17	46.65	43.56	0.83

* Strictly speaking. there are 6 d.f. for the unrestricted three-class for the 3x3x3 table, but since $\hat{\pi}_{22}^{B} \cdot 0$, the large sample theory would not pertain to the unrestricted model for these data. We actually consider H_2 as the *restricted* model, where π_{22}^{BX} is set equal to zero. For the model restricted in this way there are 7 d.f., and this *restricted* model could be tested with the usual large sample theory. See related comments in the text.

** Degrees of freedom are actually 12 for this restricted model. See comments in note above and in the text.

We suppose that there exists a three-class latent structure where the following conditions are met:

1. In latent class 1 (corresponding to 'latent' high), an item response of 3 (low) is prohibited, but an item response of 2 (medium) is allowed, and is regarded as a 'response error' for members of this class.

2. In latent class 2 (corresponding to 'latent' medium), item responses of 1 or 3, as well as 2, are allowed.

3. In latent class 3 (corresponding to 'latent' low), an item response of 1 is prohibited, but item responses of 2 or 3 are allowed. Item responses of 2 to any item are regarded as 'response errors' for members of the class.

The latent variable X will possess a kind of rank order owing to the restrictions implied by these assumptions. The rule that defines that order can be described in the following more general manner: for a member of the tth latent class, only responses to the *same* or *immediately adjacent* item response categories ($t-1$, t, or $t+1$) are

TABLE 5
Latent structure parameters for three-class models H_2, H_3 of Table 4

	Proportion of respondents in latent class	
	H_2	H_3
Latent class 1	0.55	0.32
Latent class 2	0.41	0.66
Latent class 3	0.04	0.02

Proportion in latent class who respond 1, 2, or 3 on the indicators

	Latent class 1		Latent class 2		Latent class 3	
	H_2	H_3	H_2	H_3	H_2	H_3
$\hat{\pi}_{1t}^{\bar{A}X}$	0.72	0.84	0.26	0.35	0.16	0.00*
$\hat{\pi}_{2t}^{\bar{A}X}$	0.22	0.16	0.53	0.45	0.31	0.32
$\hat{\pi}_{3t}^{\bar{A}X}$	0.06	0.00*	0.21	0.20	0.53	0.68
$\hat{\pi}_{1t}^{\bar{B}X}$	0.79	0.92	0.32	0.42	0.15	0.00*
$\hat{\pi}_{2t}^{\bar{B}X}$	0.14	0.08	0.50	0.39	0.00**	0.00**
$\hat{\pi}_{3t}^{\bar{B}X}$	0.07	0.00*	0.18	0.19	0.85	1.00
$\hat{\pi}_{1t}^{\bar{C}X}$	0.95	1.00	0.58	0.68	0.24	0.00*
$\hat{\pi}_{2t}^{\bar{C}X}$	0.02	0.00**	0.36	0.25	0.28	0.39
$\hat{\pi}_{3t}^{\bar{C}X}$	0.03	0.00*	0.06	0.07	0.48	0.61

* Restricted by hypothesis

** Estimated at 0.00

permissible. It is not difficult to generalize this model to cases where there are more than three items and/or more than three ordered response categories per item.

We denote the hypothesis just described as H_3, which imposes the following restrictions on a three-class latent structure.

(26) $\pi_{31}^{\bar{A}X} = \pi_{31}^{\bar{B}X} = \pi_{31}^{\bar{C}X} = 0,$

(27) $\pi_{13}^{\bar{A}X} = \pi_{13}^{\bar{B}X} = \pi_{13}^{\bar{C}X} = 0.$

From Table 4 we find a likelihood ratio χ^2 for H_2 of 24.77 on 14 d.f., certainly an acceptable fit for these data. (See the notes to Table 4 for a discussion of the calculation of degrees of freedom.) Table 5 presents the parameter estimates for this three-class restricted model, and compares them with those obtained from H_2 discussed earlier. Note that the ordering of item categories has been taken into account in defining the permissible 'adjacent responses' for members of the ordered latent classes, but no assumption of spacing has been made. I am not aware of other applications of latent structure models to non-dichotomous data (except for the ones in Clogg, 1979a), although it is my understanding that Dean Harper has also considered similar models.

Another model for the data in Table 3 is hypothesis H_4. This model is actually motivated by Goodman's (1975) new model for scaling response patterns, but is also related to the underlying rationale used to develop Cohen's kappa measure of agreement (cf. Fleiss, 1973). It bears similarity as well to a model considered by Henry (1975) for the analysis of a scale of relative deprivation. A natural manner in which to view the cross-classification of Table 3 is to examine the extent to which items *agree* in their recording of high, medium, or low responses. We now consider one model emphasizing this point of view.

We now assume that there exist four latent types in the population, which are characterized by the following conditions:

1.   a latent 'high' class exists, and members of this class will respond 'high' to each of the items A, B, and C with certainty;
2.   a latent 'medium' class exists, and members of this class will respond 'medium' to each of the items A, B and C with certainty;
3.   a latent 'low' class exists, and members of this class will respond 'low' to each of the items A, B, and C with certainty;

4. a latent 'unscalable' or latent 'disagreement' class exists, and for members of this class responses to each of the items A, B, and C are mutually independent.

Restrictions on the four-class latent structure which define the model are the following:

(28) $\quad \pi_{11}^{\bar{A}X} = \pi_{11}^{\bar{B}X} = \pi_{11}^{\bar{C}X} = 1$

(29) $\quad \pi_{22}^{\bar{A}X} = \pi_{22}^{\bar{B}X} = \pi_{22}^{\bar{C}X} = 1$

(30) $\quad \pi_{33}^{\bar{A}X} = \pi_{33}^{\bar{B}X} = \pi_{33}^{\bar{C}X} = 1.$

The parameters π_1^X, π_2^X, π_3^X denote the proportions in latent agreement on the items (viz. agreement on high, medium, or low satisfaction with life), and π_4^X denotes the proportion in latent disagreement. Because of the restrictions in (28)-(30) there are 17 degrees of freedom, three less than for the independence model H_0. Model H_4 is thus very parsimonious. We find a χ^2 for H_4 of 43.56, which is a dramatic improvement over the independence model, even though still unacceptable on purely statistical grounds. The latent class proportions π_1^X, π_2^X, π_3^X, π_4^X were estimated at

0.22, 0.01, 0.01, 0.76

respectively; i.e., under H_4 76 percent of the population are estimated to be in latent disagreement, while 22 percent are in latent agreement that all facets of life are very satisfying.

Model H_4 can also be generalized, much as the Goodman scale model (Goodman, 1975) is generalized. A method of measuring agreement also stems from this model which is similar to but different from Cohen's kappa. Cohen's kappa makes an implicit comparison of observed agreement with agreement that would be expected under a relationship of mutual independence (model H_0 above), but the indexes of agreement discussed above and based on the latent class proportions make an implicit comparison with a model of latent agreement which in this context comes very close to fitting the data. For related comments, the reader is referred to Hildebrand, Laing, and Rosenthal (1974) and Goodman and Kruskal (1974).

The models presented in this section are only indications of the potential utility of latent structure methods in the analysis of ordinal data. These models exploit the distributional properties corresponding to the sampled cross-classification; they avoid the assumption of intervalness of item categories while exploiting the ordinality of those categories (see H_3); and they are suited to the treatment of ordinal items as indicators of unobservables. In addition, they can be easily considered with the MLLSA computer program.

VIII. SOME LATENT STRUCTURE MODELS OF MOBILITY

In this final section we consider latent structure models of social mobility. The objective is to demonstrate how a subject that has received sustained attention in mathematical sociology can be approached from a latent structure point of view. This development actually has roots in the models of 'perfect mobility,' and 'quasi-perfect mobility' (Goodman, 1969; 1972; 1978; Duncan, 1979; Hauser, 1978). Indeed, many of the models that have been proposed in the mobility context can be interpreted as latent structures, restricted latent structures, or quasi-latent structures.

The mobility tables analyzed here are the classic British and Danish tables which have been frequently analyzed in the mobility literature. To save space, those tables will not be reproduced here; the reader is referred to Goodman (1972) for the data. The 5×5 tables of that paper will be re-analyzed here. One zero cell frequency in the British table has been replaced by a one in order to simplify the calculation of degrees of freedom for some of the models (e.g., model M_1 to be considered shortly, estimates an *expected* count of zero for this cell in the British table, implying that degrees of freedom should be adjusted). This ad hoc adjustment does little to alter the conclusions that follow. In principle, the models to be proposed could be applied to any cross-classification of origin status by destination status, for instance 'turnover' tables which arise from panel studies.

We let F refer to the 'father's status' variable, with categories $i = 1, \ldots, 5$, and we let S refer to 'son's status,' with categories $j = 1, \ldots, 5$. The categories of F and S are *observable status* categories, and need not correspond to *latent class* categories which may underlie the mobility table. A latent structure approach to the mobility table assumes that latent classes in some way govern the mobility process among observed status categories. Given this assumption, the latent structure model should allow a characterization of the class variable underlying the status variables in the observed table.

Table 6 presents the fit of some latent structure models of the British and Danish mobility tables, and we now discuss them in turn. Model M_0 is the independence model, termed a model of 'perfect mobility' by Goldhammer, Rogoff, and others. Since the independence model can be thought of as a one-class latent structure, another interpretation of this model is to describe it as a model of no (latent) class structure. M_0 assumes that there is only one 'underlying' class in the mobility table, and that within this one class mobility chances are completely random, depending only on the distribution of observable origin statuses and observable destination statuses. We see, of course, that M_0 does not fit the data. The failure of this model to fit these cross-classifications and others like them lead to the development of the model of 'quasi-perfect mobility' (cf. Goodman, 1969; 1972; and references cited there). The quasi-perfect mobility model assumes that there are some persons in each of the five observed statuses who will 'stay' in those statuses with certainty; i.e., immobility is deterministic in character for the latent 'stayers.' In addition, one latent class is posited to exist in which mobility chances are random, depending only upon the distribution of origin statuses and the distribution of destination statuses in the conditional table which applies to all latent 'movers.' The quasi-perfect mobility hypothesis thus says that there is perfect 'inheritance' of the observed statuses for some persons, and it says that there exists only one additional class defined as a homogeneous class because it has random mobility chances.

Another way to generalize M_0 is to proceed directly to the latent structure approach. Models M_1 and M_2 are two- and three-class unrestricted models, respectively, and would be interpreted in the following way. For the two-class model, two latent classes are posited to exist, and within each latent class the perfect mobility hypothesis holds. The term 'class' is used here very deliberately, because there is a high degree of isomorphism between a 'class' in, say, the Weberian sense of the term, and a latent class of persons in the observed mobility table.[4] Statistical independence between origin statuses and destination statuses is here taken as a defining characteristic of class. Model M_3, of course, has a similar inter-

TABLE 6
Latent structure and quasi-latent structure models of mobility

| Model | British 5×5 table | | | Danish 5×5 table | | | |
	d.f.*	Likelihood ratio chi-square	Goodness-of-fit chi-square	Index of dissimilarity	d.f.*	Likelihood ratio chi-square	Goodness-of-fit chi-square	Index of dissimilarity
M_0 (Independence)	16	821.89	1225.59	—** %	16	654.20	754.10	—** %
M_1 (Two-class latent structure)	9	177.97	202.14	7.9	8	116.23	133.64	8.8
M_2 (Three-class latent structure)	2	50.85	50.55	4.6	2	32.67	33.28	5.0
M_4 (Two-class quasi-latent structure)	6	9.76	9.35	1.5	6	8.23	8.06	1.7
M_5 (Restricted two-class quasi-latent structure)	13	41.18	41.44	3.7	14	32.87	32.47	3.6

* Degrees of freedom adjusted for some terminal estimates (e.g. zero estimates of conditional probabilities)
** Index of dissimilarity was not obtained for the independence model

pretation. In Table 6 we see that M_1 does not fit the data well, and that while M_2 has a considerably better fit it is not parsimonious. We now consider modifications of M_1 and M_2 that do fit the data, and are also generalizations of the perfect mobility model (M_0) and the model of quasi-perfect mobility.

Consider a model in which there is status inheritance in observed statuses 1, 3, and 5 (but not statuses 2 or 4), and in which there are *two* latent classes (unlike the *single* class considered under M_0 or under the quasi-perfect mobility model), in each of which the relationship between origin and destination is one of independence. Restrictions that define this model (a kind of 'quasi-latent structure' — see Goodman, 1974b) are as follows. Consider a five-class latent structure, where

(31) $\quad \pi_{11}^{\bar{F}X} = \pi_{11}^{\bar{S}X} = 1$

(32) $\quad \pi_{32}^{\bar{F}X} = \pi_{32}^{\bar{S}X} = 1$

(33) $\quad \pi_{53}^{\bar{F}X} = \pi_{53}^{\bar{S}X} = 1$

and where latent classes four and five are completely unrestricted. We denote this model as M_4, and we find (cf. Table 6) that it fits both the British and the Danish tables very well indeed. With model M_4 we would misclassify only 1.5 percent of the British and 1.7 percent of the Danish observed frequencies. (See the indices of dissimilarity reported in Table 6.) Apart from persistence in three of the observed status categories, a two-class latent structure will explain the pattern of mobility.

Now let us turn to M_5, a special type of restricted quasi-latent structure. M_5 imposes on M_4 the following additional restrictions:

(34) $\quad \pi_{it}^{\bar{F}X} = \pi_{it}^{\bar{S}X}$, for $i = 1, \ldots, 5; t = 4,5$.

These restrictions say that in the two conditional tables formed by considering the mobility table for each of classes four and five, the origin and destination marginals are identical; i.e., in each latent class the actual distribution of status categories remained constant over time. We see that M_5 is not an acceptable fit on purely statistical grounds (cf. Table 6), but it nevertheless fits the data very well.

For the purposes of comparing the mobility structure in Britain and Denmark, the parameters of M_5 are provided in Table 7. We see that latent class four is a class with typically high observed status, and latent class five is a class with typically low observed status. The parameters in Table 7 can be employed in various ways to provide indices of class structure (or mobility structure), but we do not pursue these matters in the present report. Models M_1-M_5 are, to our knowledge, new models of mobility; and their interpretation coincides very closely with specific stratification-mobility concepts. There indeed appears to be much potential for a rigorous latent structure approach to the analysis of social mobility.

TABLE 7
**Parameter estimates from model M_5 applied
to British and Danish mobility tables**

Latent class proportions*	$\hat{\pi}_1^X$	$\hat{\pi}_2^X$	$\hat{\pi}_3^X$	$\hat{\pi}_4^X$	$\hat{\pi}_5^X$
Britain	0.012	0.013	0.061	0.212	0.701
Denmark	0.006	0.058	0.059	0.335	0.541

Conditional probability that an individual in latent class 4 (high) will have status j $(j = 1, \ldots, 5)$**

Status	1	2	3	4	5
Britain	0.095	0.479	0.173	0.226	0.026
Denmark	0.067	0.363	0.340	0.179	0.051

Conditional probability that an individual in latent class 5 (low) will have status j $(j = 1, \ldots, 5)$**

Status	1	2	3	4	5
Britain	0.000	0.056	0.128	0.532	0.285
Denmark	0.000	0.000	0.209	0.510	0.281

* Latent class 1 refers to persons who are latent stayers in the observed status 1; latent class 2 refers to persons who are latent stayers in the observed status 3; latent class 3 refers to persons who are latent stayers in the observed status 5.

** Model M_5 says that an individual in latent class 4 has the same probability of having origin i and destination i. A similar comment applies to latent class 5, a 'latent lower class'.

IX. CONCLUSION

All of the models proposed in this paper, and many others, can be estimated and tested with the MLLSA computer program. There are several other programs now available for latent structure work, and these other programs could also be used. Latent structure methods are now feasible for the empirical social researcher (cf. Sections 2-5 above), and the further elaboration of existing latent structure models promises the development of a rich language for the expression of social theory (cf. Sections 6-8 above). We hope that this survey and review has provided ample testimony to the truth of these claims.

NOTES

1. MLLSA uses a modified Gram-Schmidt procedure to calculate the rank of $\hat{H}$. Because $\hat{H}$ will contain estimates that are subject to round-off error, care must be taken to ensure that the algorithm appropriately takes this into account. Experimentation with trial data sets demonstrated which level of numerical precision should be used to calculate the rank of $\hat{H}$. Of course, if excessive precision were used, then virtually all estimates of $\hat{H}$ (calculated with less precision) would produce an impression that the model in question were locally identifiable.

2. Lazarsfeld and Henry (1968) show that three-class models for the 2^4 table are not identifiable in general, using techniques different from the one used here.

3. The Lazarsfeld panel data are selected here merely as an illustrative example. Actually, it would be very difficult to posit a MIMC model for these panel data on substantive grounds. However, the results of this section are only intended to demonstrate the possibility of using the MIMC model with the latent structure approach; we use the Lazarsfeld panel data only so that comparisons of this new model with those presented in Goodman (1974b) can be made.

4. Some readers will undoubtedly object to this seemingly casual indentification of latent classes with traditional sociological concepts of 'class.' In the context of a mobility table a latent class is one that shares the same (random) mobility chances, and it is in this specific sense that the term 'class' is used. We find this conception of class congruent with at least some uses of the term.

REFERENCES

Carroll, J. D. (1975) 'Application of CANDECOMP to Solving for Parameters of Lazarsfeld's Latent Class Model,' paper presented at the Society for Multivariate Experimental Psychology Meeting, Gleneden Beach, Oregon, November 1975.

Chen, T., and S. E. Fienberg (1976) 'The Analysis of Contingency Tables with Incompletely Classified Data,' *Biometrics*, vol. 32:133-44.

Clogg, C. C. (1977) 'Unrestricted and Restricted Maximum Likelihood Latent Structure Analysis: A Manual for Users,' University Park, Pennsylvania: Population Issues Research Office, Working Papers, 1977-09.

Clogg, C. C. (1979a) *Measuring Underemployment: Demographic Indicators for the United States*. New York: Academic Press.

Clogg, C. C. (1979b) 'Some Latent Structure Models for the Analysis of Likert-type Data,' *Social Science Research*, vol. 8:287-301.

Coleman, J. S. (1964) *Introduction to Mathematical Sociology*. New York: Free Press.

Dayton, C. M. and G. B. Macready (1976a) 'Computer Programs for Probabilistic Models,' Department of Measurement and Statistics, University of Maryland.

Dayton, C. M. and G. B. Macready (1976b) 'A Probabilistic Model for Validation of Behavioral Hierarchies,' *Psychometrika*, vol. 41:189-204.

Dayton, C. M. and G. B. Macready (1977a) 'Statistical Comparisons Among Hierarchies Based on latent Structure Models,' paper presented to the Annual Meeting of the American Educational Research Association.

Dayton, C. M. and G. B. Macready (1977b) 'The Use of Probabilistic Models in the Assessment of Mastery,' *Journal of Educational Statistics*, vol. 2:99-120.

Dayton, C. M. and G. B. Macready (1977c) 'The Validation of Models Based on Latent Structures,' paper presented to American Statistical Association Annual Meeting.

Duncan, O. D. (1979) 'How Destination Depends on Origin in the Occuptional Mobility Table,' *American Journal of Sociology*, vol. 84:793-803.

Fielding, A. (1977) 'Latent Structure Models,' pp. 125-57 in C. A. O'Muircheartaigh and C. Payne (eds), *The Analysis of Survey Data*, Volume I: *Exploring Data Structures*. New York: John Wiley.

Fleiss, J. L. (1973) *Statistical Methods for Rates and Proportions*. New York: John Wiley.

Formann, A. K. (1978) 'A Note on Parameter Estimation for Lazarsfeld's Latent Class Analysis,' *Psychometrika*, vol. 43:123-6.

Goodman, L. A. (1969) 'How to Ransack Social Mobility Tables and Other Kinds of Cross-classification Tables,' *American Journal of Sociology*, vol. 75:1-40.

Goodman, L. A. (1970) 'The Multivariate Analysis of Qualitative Data: Interactions Among Multiple Classification,' *Journal of the American Statistical Association*, vol. 65:225-56.

Goodman, L. A. (1972) 'Some Multiplicative Models for the Analysis of Cross-classified Data, pp. 649-95 in J. L. Cam (ed.), *Proceedings of the Sixth Berkeley Symposium on Mathematical Statistics and Probability*. Berkeley: University of California Press.

Goodman, L. A. (1974a) 'Exploratory Latent Structure Analysis Using Both Identifiable and Unidentifiable Models,' *Biometrika*, vol. 61:215-31.

Goodman, L. A. (1974b) 'The Analysis of Systems of Qualitative Variables When Some of the Variables are Unobservable. Part I: A Modified Latent Structure Approach,' *American Journal of Sociology*, vol. 79:1179-259.

Goodman, L. A. (1974c) 'The Analysis of Systems of Qualitative Variables When Some of the Variables are Unobservable. Part II: The Use of Modified Latent Distance Models,' unpublished manuscript.

Goodman, L. A. (1975) 'A New Model for Scaling Response Patterns: An Application of the Quasi-independence Concept,' *Journal of the American Statistical Association*, vol. 70:755-68.

Goodman, L. A. (1978) 'A Note on the Estimation of Parameters in Latent Structure Analysis,' Technical Report No. 59, Department of Statistics, University of Chicago (forthcoming in *Psychometrika*).

Goodman, L. A. (1979a) 'Multiplicative Models for the Analysis of Occupational Mobility Tables and Other Kinds of Cross-classification Tables,' *American Journal of Sociology*, vol. 84:804-19.

Goodman, L. A. (1979b) 'The Analysis of Qualitative Variables Using More Parsimonious Quasi-Independent Models, Scaling Models, and Latent Structures that Fit the Observed Data,' in R. M. Merton, J. S. Coleman and P. H. Rossi (eds), *Qualitative and Quantitative Social Research: Papers in Honor of Paul F. Lazarsfeld*. New York: Free Press.

Goodman, L. A. and W. H. Kruskal (1954) 'Measures of Association for Cross-classifications,' *Journal of the American Statistical Association*, vol. 49:732-64.

Goodman, L. A. and W. H. Kruskal, 'Empirical Evaluation of Formal Theory', *Journal of Mathematical Sociology*, vol. 3:187-96.

Green, P. E., F. J. Carmone and D. P. Wachspress (1976) 'Consumer Segmentation via Latent Class Analysis,' *Journal of Consumer Research*, vol. 3:170-4.

Haberman, S. J. (1974) 'Log-linear Models for Frequency Tables Derived by Indirect Observation: Maximum Likelihood Equations,' *Annals of Statistics*, vol. 2:911-24.

Haberman, S. J. (1976) 'Iterative Scaling Procedures for Log-linear Models for Frequency Tables Derived by Indirect Observation,' 1975 Statistical Computing Section, *Proceedings of the American Statistical Association*, pp. 45-50.

Haberman, S. J. (1977) 'Product Models for Frequency Tables Involving Indirect Observation,' *Annals of Statistics*, vol. 5:1124-47.

Haberman, S. J. (1979) *The Analysis of Qualitative Data: vol. 2. New Development*. New York: Academic Press.

Harper, D. (1972) 'Local Dependence Latent Structure Models,' *Psychometrika*, vol. 37:53-9.

Hauser, R. M. (1978) 'A Structural Model of the Mobility Table,' *Social Forces*, vol. 56:919-53.

Hays, D. G., and E. F. Borgatta (1954) 'An Empirical Comparison of Restricted and General Latent Distance Analysis,' *Psychometrika*, vol. 19:271-9.

Henry, N. W. (1975) 'Latent Structure Analysis of a Scale of Relative Deprivation,' unpublished manuscript.

Hildebrand, D. K., J. D. Laing and H. L. Rosenthal (1974) 'Prediction Logic: A Method for Empirical Evaluation of Formal Theory,' *Journal of Mathematical Sociology*, vol. 3:163-85.

Jöreskog, K. G. (1973) 'A General Method for Estimating a Linear Structural Equation System,' pp. 85-112 in A. S. Goldberger and O. D. Duncan (eds), *Structural Equation Models in the Social Sciences*. New York: Seminar Press.

Lazarsfeld, P. F. (1950) 'The Logical and Mathematical Foundation of Latent Structure Analysis,' in S. A. Stouffer et al. (eds), *Measurement and Prediction*. Princeton: Princeton University Press.

Lazarsfled, P. F. and N. W. Henry (1968) *Latent Structure Analyis*. Boston: Houghton Mifflin.

Madansky, A. (1960) 'Determinantal Methods in Latent Class Analysis,' *Psychometrika*, vol. 25:183-98.

McHugh, R. B. (1956) 'Efficient Estimation and Local Identification in Latent Class Analysis,' *Psychometrika*, vol. 21:331-47.

McHugh, R. B. (1958) 'Note on "Efficient Estimation and Local Identification in Latent Class Analysis",' *Psychometrika*, vol. 23:273-4.

Press, S. J. (1972) *Applied Multivariate Analysis*. New York: Holt, Rinehart, and Winston.

Proctor, C. A. (1970) 'A Probabilistic Formulation and Statistical Analysis of Guttman Scaling,' *Psychometrika*, vol. 35:73-8.

Proctor, C. A. (1971) 'Reliability of a Guttman Scale Score,' *Proceedings of the Social Statistics Section of the American Statistical Association*, pp. 348-9.

Pullum, T. W. (1975) *Measuring Occupational Inheritance*. New York: Elsevier.

Rosenberg, M. (1968) *The Logic of Survey Analysis*. New York: Basic Books.

Torgerson, W. S. (1962) *Theory and Methods of Scaling*. New York: John Wiley.

Werts, C. E., R. L. Linn and K. G. Jöreskog (1971) 'Estimating the Parameters of Path Models Involving Unmeasured Variables,' pp. 400-09 in H. M. Blalock (ed.), *Causal Models in the Social Sciences*. Chicago: Aldine.

Werts, C. E., R. L. Linn, and K. G. Jöreskog (1973) 'Identification and Estimation in Path Analysis with Unmeasured Variables,' *American Journal of Sociology*, vol. 78:1469-84.

Wiggins, L. M. (1973) *Panel Analysis: Latent Probability Models for Attitude and Behavior Processes*. San Francisco: Jossey-Bass.

III

MEASUREMENT MODELS
AND RESEARCH APPLICATIONS

9

APPLICATIONS OF SIMULTANEOUS
FACTOR ANALYSIS TO ISSUES
OF FACTORIAL INVARIANCE

Duane F. Alwin
University of Michigan

David J. Jackson
*National Institute of Mental Health,
Adelphi, Maryland*

INTRODUCTION

Following Thurstone's (1935, 1947) discussions of factorial invariance, students of factor analysis have been concerned with the problem of the correspondence of factors identified in separate studies or in subgroups of the same study. This concern with the comparison of factors over samples or sub-samples has generated an array of methods for comparing factors (see reviews by Leyden, 1953; Barlow and Burt, 1954; Wrigley, 1958; Pinneau and Newhouse, 1964; Harman, 1967; Rummel, 1970; Mulaik, 1972). The most common ad hoc approach to the problem involves the computation of an index of factor similarity for corresponding factors given estimates of a factor model using the same variables in two or more samples. The major indices that have been proposed

---

Authors' Note. This research was supported in part by a grant from the Spencer Foundation through the School of Education, Indiana University. The authors wish to thank Ted Davies for valuable computer assistance.

include the 'coefficient of similarity' (Burt, 1939) (also referred to as the 'unadjusted correlation' (Barlow and Burt, 1954), the 'coefficient of congruence' (Tucker, 1951), and the 'degree of factor similarity' (Wrigley and Newhouse, 1955);[1] the 'coefficient of pattern similarity' (Cattell, 1949); and the 'index of root mean square' (Mosier, 1939; see also Harman, 1967). A second approach to the problem of factorial invariance defines it essentially as a problem of rotation (see Meredith, 1964a, b).

These methods were developed primarily for results obtained from exploratory factor analysis, and it can be argued that the issues of factorial invariance are not adequately addressed using exploratory factor analysis. More recently, the problem of factorial invariance has been phrased within a confirmatory factor analysis, hypothesis-testing framework (Jöreskog, 1971b; Lawley and Maxwell, 1971), and Jöreskog (1971b) has proposed a method of simultaneous factor analysis for dealing with factorial invariance using confirmato maximum likelihood methods (see Sörbom and Jöreskog, 1976). Several applications of Jöreskog's methods have appeared in the psychometric literature (e.g. McGaw and Jöreskog, 1971; Bloxom, 1972; Bechtoldt, 1974; Sörbom, 1974), but few applications of these methods exist using sociological or social psychological data.

The objectives of this paper are twofold. First, we present a general framework for examining issues of factorial invariance. For this we rely heavily on Jöreskog's (1971b) and Sörbom's (1974) presentation of similar material. Second, we present several applications of the Jöreskog-Sörbom methods to questions of factorial invariance using illustrations from the sociological literature.

THE GENERAL COMMON FACTOR MODEL

The common factor model for an observed vector of variables y_g (of order p) in population (or subpopulation) g ($g = 1, 2, \ldots m$) may be written as:

(1) $\quad y_g = v_g + \Lambda_g \xi_g + \varepsilon_g$

where v_g is a vector (of order p) of constants representing the origins of measurement for the p variables, ξ_g is a vector (of order k) of hypothetical common factors, ε_g is a vector (of order p) of disturbances unique to each of the p variables, and Λ_g is a $(p \times k)$ matrix of regression coefficients relating the p variables to the k latent factors.

The vector of constants representing the origins of measurement for the p variables are arbitrary and may under certain circumstances be equal to the vector of means for the p variables (viz. when $E(\xi_g) = 0$); but, in the general case they are not.[2] The metrics for the latent factors in ξ_g are also arbitrary, but it is often convenient to assign the metric of one of the variables measuring a given factor to that factor. Although most statements of the common factor model center the latent factors (i.e. $E(\xi_g) = 0$), in the general case this is unnecessary and in some cases undesirable. The present discussion assumes that the factors of the model are represented in an interpretable metric. The vector of disturbances, ε_g, contains both random errors of measurement and reliable variation specific to each observed variable, but in certain special cases of the general model the vector of disturbances contains only random measurement error. This is the case for the true score models (see Jöreskog, 1971a; Alwin and Jackson, 1979).

The properties of the model, assumed to hold in population g, are as follows:

(1) $E(\xi_g) = \theta_g$
(2) $E(\varepsilon_g) = 0$
(3) $E(\varepsilon_g \varepsilon_g') = \text{diagonal}$
(4) $E(\xi_g \varepsilon_g') = 0$.

The disturbances are, then, centered, and are randomly distributed with respect to other disturbances and the latent common factors. The expected value of the common factors, θ_g, represents the means of the factors in the metrics that they have been assigned.

Given the above properties (2)-(4), the covariance structure for y_g may be written as:

(2) $\quad \Sigma_g = \Lambda_g \, \Phi_g \, \Lambda_g' + \Psi_g^2$

where Φ_g is the covariance matrix for the latent common factors, i.e. $E(\xi_g \xi_g')$, and Ψ_g^2 is the covariance matrix for the disturbances, i.e. $E(\varepsilon_g \varepsilon_g')$. As indicated above, the model used here assumes that Ψ_g^2 is diagonal, which is a property of the common factor model in its conventional statement (see Lawley and Maxwell, 1971), but under certain circumstances Ψ_g^2 may be nondiagonal. Note also that Φ_g may be nondiagonal; i.e., the latent common factors may have nonzero covariances. Finally, it is important to note that the covariance structure for y_g is independent of the origins of measurement, ν_g, and the factor means, θ_g.

The means of the observed variables in y_g are expressed in terms of the model as:

(3) $E(y_g) = \mu_g = \nu_g + \Lambda_g \theta_g.$

In other words, the mean vector is a linear function of the factor means. There are two special cases of this general model with respect to equation (3) which have some convenient properties (see Sörbom and Jöreskog, 1976). First is the case where $\theta_g = 0$. Here $\nu_g = \mu_g$; i.e., the origins of measurement are equal to the variable means. This statement of the model is useful when the factor means are of no inherent interest (see Alwin and Jackson, 1979). Second is the case where $\nu_g = 0$. Here $\mu_g = \Lambda_g \theta_g$. The observed variable means in this case are still a linear function of the factor means, but there is no additive constant in the relationship. This statement of the model is useful when the factor means are of substantive interest, but the location of the origins of measurement is of no particular interest.[3] Given the present interest in issues of factorial invariance, the following discussion will assume that $E(\nu_g) = 0$ in all populations, and henceforth we will ignore these parameters.

The parameters of the common factor model may be estimated if the model is identified. A necessary condition for the identification of the model is a minimum of k^2 independent constraints on Λ_g, Φ_g, and θ_g (Jöreskog, 1971a; Sörbom, 1974; Sörbom and Jöreskog, 1976). A number of possibilities for doing this are available, and some of these are illustrated below.

ISSUES OF FACTORIAL INVARIANCE

As indicated in the above discussion, there are four aspects of the common factor model that are potentially of interest in the investigation of issues of factorial invariance, Λ_g, θ_g, Ψ_g^2 and Φ_g. These parameter matrices may exhibit degrees of invariance over populations or sub-populations, and if an investigator is concerned with issues of factorial invariance, then the questions involved may be phrased with respect to the invariance of the parameters of these matrices. There are actually two subsets of issues here. First, there are two issues involving measurement structure invariance, the invariance of Λ_g and Ψ_g^2. Recall that Λ_g represents the regression of the measured variables, y_g, on the latent factors, ξ_g; and Ψ_g^2 represents the covariance structure of the disturbances, ε_g, in the measured variables. Second, there are two issues involving the invariance of the model in the factor space, the invariance of θ_g and Φ_g. These matrices represent the vector of factor means and the covariance structure for the factors, respectively.

Beginning with Thurstone's discussion of factorial invariance, the most frequent concern with issues of factorial invariance is with the invariance of the factor pattern, Λ_g, over populations (e.g. Harman, 1967; Rummel, 1970). Indeed, the proposed measures of factor similarity involve computations based solely on the factor pattern. Measures of factor similarity as they are used in practice, however, actually confound some of the issues of factorial invariance inasmuch as the deal with 'standardized' factor pattern matrices. If we define $S = (\text{diag. } \Phi)^{-1/2}$ and $D = (\text{diag. } \Sigma)^{-1/2}$, then we may rescale Λ to Λ^* as follows:

(4) $\quad \Lambda^* = D\Lambda S^{-1}$.

This represents a 'standardized' factor pattern, the coefficients of which range, under most conditions, between ± 1.0. This is the type of factor pattern matrix obtained in most applications of exploratory factor analysis. It is clear, then, that Λ^* is affected by both Λ and Φ, and the investigation of the invariance of this matrix confounds two separate and distinct issues of factorial invariance.[4] Consequently, the use of measures of factor similarity using the factor loadings in Λ^* mask some distinct issues of factorial invariance. The position taken in the present paper is that the use of exploratory factor analysis in its conventional form to examine issues of factorial invariance is of limited utility.

By contrast, Jöreskog's (1971b) discussion of simultaneous factor analysis makes clear the distinction between the invariance of Λ_g, Φ_g and Ψ_g^2, and Sörbom's (1974) discussion extends Jöreskog's treatment to include the issue of the invariance of θ_g. These papers place the issues of factorial invariance in a hypothesis-testing framework, and the following discussion reveiws the specification of hypotheses of invariance within this framework.

THE EVALUATION OF ISSUES
OF FACTORIAL INVARIANCE

Hypothesis 1.1

A preliminary, conclusive test for the invariance of three of the parameter matrices of the model, Λ_g, Φ_g and Ψ_g^2 involves the hypothesis of the equality of the covariance structure of the observed variables, Σ_g, over populations, i.e. H_0: $\Sigma_1 = \Sigma_2 \ldots = \Sigma_m$. If the covariance structures in all populations are found to be equal, within sampling error, the components of the models generating the covariance structures may be assumed to be equal (Jöreskog, 1971b:419); i.e. $\Lambda_1 = \Lambda_2 \ldots = \Lambda_m$; $\Phi_1 = \Phi_2 \ldots = \Phi_m$; and $\Psi_1^2 = \Psi_2^2 \ldots \Psi_m^2$. A test statistic for this hypothesis is given by Jöreskog (1971b:419), which is distributed approximately as χ^2 with $0.5 (m-1)p(p+1)$ degrees of freedom. This hypothesis may be investigated using COFAMM (Sörbom and Jöreskog, 1976) by specifying that the latent factors are centered, $k_g = p$, $\Lambda_g = I$, $\Psi_g^2 = 0$, and $\Phi_1 = \Phi_2 \ldots = \Phi_m$.[5] An analysis of the sample covariance matrices from m populations using this set of specifications provides the necessary test statistic, referred to as χ_1^2. If this χ^2 value is judged to be statistically significantly greater than zero, the null hypothesis of equality of covariance matrices may be rejected. If this hypothesis cannot be rejected, it may be concluded, with some level of error, that $\Lambda_1 = \Lambda_2 \ldots = \Lambda_m$; $\Phi_1 = \Phi_m \ldots \Phi_m$; and $\Psi_2^1 = \Psi_2^2 \ldots = \Psi_m^2$.

Hypothesis 1.2

If, in the examination of hypothesis 1.1, one accepts the hypothesis of equality of covariance structures over populations, and thereby concludes that the factor pattern matrices are equal over populations, one may then examine the equivalence of the factor means in the m populations; i.e., H_0: $\theta_1 = \theta_2 \ldots \theta_m$. A preliminary test for this, given the equality of Σ_g over populations, involves the hypothesis of the equality of the vector of observed means, μ_g, in all populations. This hypothesis may be investigated using COFAMM (Sörbom and Jöreskog, 1976) by specifying that the factor means are non-centered and equal over populations, $k_g = p$, $\Lambda_g = I$, $\Psi_g^2 = 0$, and $\Phi_1 = \Phi_2 = \ldots = \Phi_m$.[6] An analysis of the sample covariance matrices and the observed mean vectors produces a χ^2 statistic, referred to as $\chi^2_{\Sigma\theta}$, with $0.5\ (m-1)p(p+1)+p(m-1)$ degrees of freedom. This χ^2 value is then compared with the χ^2_{Σ} value obtained from the examination of hypothesis 1.1, as follows:

(5) $\quad \chi^2_{\theta}|_{\Sigma} = \chi^2_{\Sigma\theta} - \chi^2_{\Sigma}.$

The $\chi^2_{\theta}|_{\Sigma}$ statistic has $p(m-1)$ degrees of freedom. If $\chi^2_{\theta}|_{\Sigma}$ is statistically significant, then the factor means are assumed to be different, and if the statistic is non-significant, it may be concluded that $\theta_1 = \theta_2 \ldots \theta_m$, since $\mu_g = \Lambda_g \theta_g$.

Hypothesis 2.1

If, in the examination of hypothesis 1.1, one rejects the null hypothesis that $\Sigma_1 = \Sigma_2 \ldots = \Sigma_m$, then it becomes necessary to examine the issues of factorial invariance separately. Jöreskog (1971b) suggests that the issues of measurement structure invariance, i.e. Λ_g and Ψ^2_g, be examined first. The first of these to be examined involves the hypothesis of an invariant factor pattern, $\Lambda_1 = \Lambda_2 \ldots = \Lambda_m$. The examination of this hypothesis assumes that the number of factors in each population is known a priori and that a subset of these factors is held in common over all populations. Here we examine the case in which k_g factors exist in all populations (see Jöreskog, 1971b:420). In order to examine the hypothesis that the factor pattern, Λ_g, is the same in all populations, it is necessary to estimate a model that constrains a common factor pattern over the m populations. Then this model is compared with a model that places no between-population constraints on the factor pattern in the m populations. To do this one must impose the same set of k^2 constraints (at a minimum) in the Λ_g, consisting of $k-1$ zero elements and one nonzero element (usually a unity) in each column. This model may be estimated using COFAMM (Sörbom and Jöreskog, 1976), in which the parameter matrices, Λ, θ_1, θ_2, $\ldots \theta_m$, Φ_1, Φ_2, $\ldots \Phi_m$, Ψ^2_1, Ψ^2_2, $\ldots \Psi^2_m$ are estimated. This analysis produces a χ^2 value, referred to as χ^2_{Λ}, with degrees of freedom equal to $d_{\Lambda} = 0.5mp(p+1) - pk + q - 0.5mk(k+1) - mk$, where q is the number of fixed elements in Λ (a minimum of k^2).

In order to examine the hypothesis that the constrained model described here fits the data as well as the unconstrained model, Jöreskog (1971b:420) gives the following test statistic:

(6) $\quad \chi^2_{\Lambda|k} = \chi^2_{\Lambda} - \chi^2_k$

where χ^2_k is the sum of the within population χ^2 values for the k factor model which imposes the same set of k^2 constraints. The $\chi^2_{\Lambda|k}$ statistic has degrees of freedom equal to $d_{\Lambda|k} = d_{\Lambda} - d_k$, where d_k is the sum of degrees of freedom in the m within-population models. In general d_k is equal to $m[0.5p(p+1) + p - pk + q - 0.5k(k-1) - p - k]$, where q is the number of fixed elements in Λ_g. If the χ^2 value for the constrained model is significantly greater than the χ^2 value for the unconstrained model, i.e., $\chi^2_{\Lambda|k} > 0$, given the degrees of freedom involved, the hypothesis of invariance in the factor pattern may be rejected. If, on the other hand, $\chi^2_{\Lambda|k}$ is not significantly greater than zero, the invariance of the factor pattern is suggested.

If one is not interested in the factor means, a simpler version of this model may be estimated in which $\theta_g = 0$ (see Jöreskog, 1971b:420; Alwin and Jackson, 1979). In this model the vectors of observed means, μ_g, are ignored. Here the degrees of freedom associated with χ^2_{Λ} are $d_{\Lambda} = 0.5mp(p+1) - pk + q - 0.5mk(k+1) - mp$, and the degrees of freedom associated with χ^2_k are $d_k = m[0.5p(p+1) - pk + q - 0.5k(k+1) - p]$.

Hypothesis 2.2

If the hypothesis of invariance in the factor pattern is not rejected, it is then possible to examine the invariance of the factor means, i.e. $\theta_1 = \theta_2 \ldots \theta_m$. To examine this hypothesis a model is estimated which constrains both Λ_g and θ_g over populations. Using COFAMM (Sörbom and Jöreskog, 1976) a model is estimated which obtains estimates of Λ, θ, Φ_1, Φ_2, $\ldots\Phi_m$, Ψ^2_1, Ψ^2_2, $\ldots\Psi^2_m$. The constraints placed on Λ in this analysis should be the same as those imposed in the examination of hypothesis 2.1. This analysis produces a χ^2 value, referred to as $\chi^2_{\Lambda\theta}$, with degrees of freedom equal to $d_{\Lambda\theta} = 0.5mp(p+1) - pk - k + q - 0.5mk(k+1)$, where q is the number of fixed elements in Λ. Then the hypothesis of invariance in the factor means may be examined using the following test statistic:

(7) $\quad \chi^2_\theta | \Lambda = \chi^2_{\Lambda\theta} - \chi^2_\Lambda$

with degrees of freedom $d_\theta |_\Lambda = d_{\Lambda\theta} - d_\Lambda$.

Hypothesis 2.3

A second hypothesis which may be examined if the hypothesis of an invariant factor pattern is accepted involves the second aspect of measurement structure invariance, namely the invariance of the covariance structure of the disturbances, i.e. $\Psi^2_1 = \Psi^2_2 \ldots = \Psi^2_m$. Following Jöreskog (1971b), this hypothesis (like hypothesis 2.2) is tested conditional on the finding of an invariant factor pattern, and it is unlikely that it will be meaningful when the invariance of the factor pattern has been rejected. In this case it is necessary to obtain a model in which the parameters in Λ, Ψ^2, θ_1, θ_2, $\ldots \theta_m$, Φ_1, Φ_2, $\ldots \Phi_m$ are estimated. This analysis yields a χ^2 value, referred to as $\chi^2_{\Lambda\psi2}$, with degrees of freedom equal to $d_{\Lambda\psi2} = 0.5mp(p+1) + mp - pk + q - 0.5mk(k+1) - p - mk$, where again q is the number of fixed elements in Λ. The hypothesis of invariance in Ψ^2_g may then be examined using the following test statistic:

(8) $\quad \chi^2_{\psi2} | \Lambda = \chi^2_{\Lambda\psi2} - \chi^2_\Lambda$

with degrees of freedom $d_{\psi2} |_\Lambda = d_{\Lambda\psi2} - d_\Lambda$. If this value of χ^2 is significantly greater than zero, the hypothesis of an invariant disturbance covariance structure may be rejected, but if the difference in equation (8) is not significant, invariance in Ψ^2_g is suggested.[7]

Again, if the factor means are of no interest, a simpler version of the above model may be used by setting $\theta_g = 0$. Here the degrees of freedom for $\chi^2_{\Lambda\psi2}$ equal $d_{\Lambda\psi2} = 0.5mp(p+1) - pk + q - 0.5 mk(k+1) - p$ (see Jöreskog, 1971b:420; Alwin and Jackson, 1979).

Hypothesis 2.4

A third hypothesis that may be evaluated if the hypothesis of an invariant factor pattern is accepted involves the covariance structure of the latent factors, i.e. $\Phi_1 = \Phi_2 \ldots \Phi_m$. Jöreskog (1971b:420) suggests that this hypothesis be made conditional on the acceptance of invariance in both Λ_g and Ψ_g^2. We take the view here, however, that it is meaningful to examine the invariance of Φ_g independent of any constraints on Ψ_g^2. We do agree with Jöreskog (1971b) that the examination of the invariance of Φ_g should depend on the prior finding of the same factor pattern over populations, i.e. $\Lambda_1 = \Lambda_2 \ldots \Lambda_m$. In the present case it is necessary to obtain a model in which the parameters in Λ, Φ, θ_1, θ_2, $\ldots \theta_m$, Ψ_1^2, Ψ_2^2, $\ldots \Psi_m^2$ are estimated. This analysis yields a χ^2 value, referred to as $\chi^2_{\Lambda_\Phi}$, with degrees of freedom equal to $d_{\Lambda_\Phi} = 0.5mp(p+1) - pk + q - 0.5k(k+1) - mk$, where again q is the number of fixed elements in Λ. The hypothesis of invariance in Φ_g may then be examined using the following test statistic:

(9) $\quad \chi^2_{\Phi|\Lambda} = \chi^2_{\Lambda_\Phi} - \chi^2_\Lambda$

with degrees of freedom $d_{\Phi|\Lambda} = d_{\Lambda_\Phi} - d_\Lambda$. If this value of χ^2 is significantly greater than zero, the hypothesis of an invariant factor covariance structure may be rejected, but if the difference in equation (9) is not significant, invariance in the factor covariance structure, Φ_g, is suggested.

As with hypotheses 2.2 and 2.3, if the factor means are of no interest, it is possible to use a simpler version of the present model in which $\theta_g = 0$. In this case the degrees of freedom for $\chi^2_{\Lambda_\Phi}$ are $d_{\Lambda_\Phi} = 0.5mp(p+1) - pk + q - 0.5k(k+1) - mp$.

Hypothesis 3.1

Following Jöreskog's (1971b) exposition, it may be desirable to examine the invariance of Φ_g, conditional on the finding of the invariance of Λ_g and Ψ_g^2. As noted above (hypothesis 2.4), it is possible to consider the invariance of Φ_g independent of any constraints on Ψ_g^2 as well. Here we consider a model in which the parameters in Λ, Ψ^2, Φ, θ_1, θ_2, $\ldots \theta_m$ are estimated. The estimates of these parameters may be obtained using COFAMM (Sörbom and Jöreskog, 1976). Such an analysis produces a χ^2 value, referred to as $\chi^2_{\Lambda_\Psi^2\Phi}$, with degrees of freedom equal to $d_{\Lambda_\Psi^2\Phi} = 0.5mp(p+1) + mp - pk + q - 0.5k(k+1) - p - mk$. The hypothesis that this set of constraints on the model produces a fit to the data that is as good as the fit provided by the model examined in hypothesis 2.3 (involving the invariance of Λ_g and Ψ_g^2) may be examined using the following test statisic:

$$(10) \quad \chi^2_{\Phi}|_{\Lambda\Psi2} = \chi^2_{\Lambda\Psi2\Phi} - \chi^2_{\Lambda\Psi2}$$

with degrees of freedom $d_{\Lambda\Psi^2\Phi} - d_{\Lambda\Psi^2}$. Again, if the factor means are of no interest, a simpler form of the hypothesis may be examined in which $\theta_g = 0$. Here the parameters in only Λ, Ψ^2 and Φ are estimated. Here $\chi^2_{\Lambda\Psi^2\Phi}$ has degrees of freedom equal to $d_{\Lambda\Psi^2\Phi} = 0.5mp(p+1) - pk + q - 0.5k(k+1) - p$. This form of the hypothesis is included in hypothesis 1.1, but as Jöreskog (1971b:420) notes, this is a stronger hypothesis because it specifies a particular form of invariance.

SUMMARY OF INVARIANCE HYPOTHESES

In the foregoing presentation we have indicated that the issues of factorial invariance can be separated into two subsets of issues. First, there are issues related to the invariance of the measurement structure, Λ_g and Ψ_g^2, and second, there are issues related to the properties of the latent factors themselves, the invariance of θ_g and Φ_g. In the above discussion, we have first suggested some preliminary tests for invariance involving Σ_g and μ_g (hypotheses 1.1 and 1.2). In most situations, however, the examination of issues of factorial invariance must be pursued beyond the examination of Σ_g and μ_g, and consequently the invariance of the parameters of the model must be undertaken separately. The most critical of these issues, upon which the others depend, is the invariance of Λ_g, the set of regression parameters relating the variables to the latent factors. The invariance of Λ_g, along with the invariance of Ψ_g^2, constitute the subset of issues involved in the examination of measurement structure invariance. It is suggested that the invariance of Ψ_g^2 must be examined conditional on the acceptance of an invariant factor pattern, Λ_g (see hypothesis 2.3).

As noted above, the second set of invariance issues of interest involves the parameters describing the latent factors — their covariance structure, Φ_g, and their means, θ_g. The examination of the invariance of these parameter matrices is also contingent on the acceptance of an invariant Λ_g. So, given the finding of an invariant Λ_g (hypothesis 2.1), the hypotheses that the factor means in θ_g are invariant over populations (hypothesis 2.2) and that the factor covariance structure, Φ_g, is invariant over populations (hypothesis 2.4) may be examined. In the above presentation neither of these invariance issues is made conditional on the invariance of the disturbance covariance structure, Ψ_g^2. However, Jöreskog's (1971b) discussion of similar material suggests that the investigation of the invariance of Φ_g may be made conditional on the invariance of both Λ_g and Ψ_g^2. This hypothesis is given as hypothesis 3.1 above.

The hypotheses presented above are summarized as follows:

Preliminary hypotheses

1.1 H_0: $\Sigma_1 = \Sigma_2 \ldots = \Sigma_m$
1.2 H_0: $\Sigma_1 = \Sigma_2 \ldots = \Sigma_m$ and $\mu_1 = \mu_2 \ldots \mu_m$

Specific invariance hypotheses

2.1 H_0: $\Lambda_1 = \Lambda_2' \ldots = \Lambda_m$
2.2 H_0: $\Lambda_1 = \Lambda_2 \ldots = \Lambda_m$ and $\theta_1 = \theta_2 \ldots \theta_m$
2.3 H_0: $\Lambda_1 = \Lambda_2 \ldots = \Lambda_m$ and $\Psi_1^2 = \Psi_2^2 \ldots \Psi_m^2$
2.4 H_0: $\Lambda_1 = \Lambda_2 \ldots = \Lambda_m$ and $\Phi_1 = \Phi_2 \ldots = \Phi_m$
3.1 H_0: $\Lambda_1 = \Lambda_2 \ldots = \Lambda_m$, $\Psi_1^2 = \Psi_2^2 \ldots \Psi_m^2$, and $\Phi_1 = \Phi_2 \ldots \Phi_m$

The investigation of hypotheses 2.2, 2.3 and 2.4 assumes that hypothesis 2.1 is not rejected. Also, the examination of hypothesis 3.1 assumes that hypothesis 2.3 is not rejected. Finally, we should note that, although these issues of factorial invariance have been set forth in terms of the examination of a sequence of hypotheses, the suggested statistical tests are not independent (Jöreskog, 1971b). The acceptance of any of these models cannot be based on statistical grounds alone. It should also be noted that the use of data from samples of large size will almost always guarantee the rejection of models that otherwise provide a reasonable representation of the data. While statistical criteria provide one basis for making an interpretation of the fit of a model to the data, substantive considerations and the objectives of the research should also help in the choice of a model.

APPLICATIONS OF SIMULTANEOUS
FACTOR ANALYSIS

In this section we demonstrate the application of the Jöreskog-Sörbom methods of simultaneous factor analysis to the examination of issues of factorial invariance. The first example uses data analyzed by Haller et al. (1974; see also Otto et al., 1973; 1974) on eight measures of occupational aspirations in a national survey of US high school youth. The measures were obtained as follows:

> The subject is asked to respond to stimulus questions in terms of ten ordered response alternatives consisting of occupations at equally spaced levels of occupational prestige. The stimulus questions are: (1) realistic short-range — the occupation 'you are really sure you can get when your schooling is over'; (2) ideal short-range — the occupation 'you would choose if you were free to choose any of them you wished when your schooling is over'; (3) realistic long-range — the occupation 'you are really sure you can have by the time you are 30 years old'; (4) ideal long-range — the occupation 'you would choose to have when you are 30 years old if you were free to have any of them.' [Haller et al., 1974:118]

Two measures of each of the four facets of occupational aspirations were obtained yielding the following array of measures:

y_1 — realistic short-range 1
y_2 — ideal short-range 1
y_3 — realistic short-range 2
y_4 — ideal short-range 2
y_5 — realistic long-range 1
y_6 — ideal long-range 1
y_7 — realistic long-range 2
y_8 — ideal long-range 2

Haller et al. (1974) investigate the issue of factor pattern invariance for these eight measures in sixteen sub-populations (defined by sex, grade level, and parental socioeconomic status) using methods of exploratory factor analysis. The present analysis focuses on the male subpopulation ($N=17,205$) only. The correlations and standard deviations of the eight measures of occupational aspirations in the eight sub-samples of males analyzed here are given by Otto et al. (1973) and are not reproduced here.[8]

We estimate the parameters of three models within each sub-sample and over the sub-sample of males, as follows: (1) $k = 1$ unrestricted-factor model, (2) $k = 2$ unrestricted-factor model, and (3) $k = 2$ congeneric-measures model. Recall that in order to identify the parameters of the general common factor model, it is necessary to place a minimum of k^2 restrictions on the parameters of θ_g, Λ_g and θ_g. This may be satisfied by placing a unit in each column of Λ_g and $k - 1$ zeros in each column of Λ_g. In the $k = 1$ factor model it is necessary only to fix a unit for one of the variables in the column of Λ_g. The Λ_g matrix we use for the two-factor unrestricted model is of the form (asterisks indicate fixed parameters):

$$
\begin{array}{c}
 \\
y_1 \\
y_2 \\
y_3 \\
y_4 \\
y_5 \\
y_6 \\
y_7 \\
y_8
\end{array}
\begin{bmatrix}
\xi_1 & \xi_2 \\
1.0^* & 0.0^* \\
0.0^* & 1.0^* \\
\lambda_{31} & \lambda_{32} \\
\lambda_{41} & \lambda_{42} \\
\lambda_{51} & \lambda_{52} \\
\lambda_{61} & \lambda_{62} \\
\lambda_{71} & \lambda_{72} \\
\lambda_{81} & \lambda_{82}
\end{bmatrix}
$$

The pattern coefficient matrix for the $k = 2$ congeneric measures model is of the form:

$$
\begin{array}{c}
 \\
y_1 \\
y_2 \\
y_3 \\
y_4 \\
y_5 \\
y_6 \\
y_7 \\
y_8
\end{array}
\begin{bmatrix}
\xi_1 & \xi_2 \\
1.0^* & 0.0^* \\
0.0^* & 1.0^* \\
\lambda_{31} & 0.0^* \\
0.0^* & \lambda_{42} \\
\lambda_{51} & 0.0^* \\
0.0^* & \lambda_{62} \\
\lambda_{71} & 0.0^* \\
0.0^* & \lambda_{82}
\end{bmatrix}
$$

This congeneric measures model postulates a latent variable for the realistic aspirations measures and a latent variable for the ideal aspirations measures. Given the restrictions on the above models, the remaining parameters in θ_g, Λ_g, Φ_g and Ψ_g^2 are estimated using COFAMM (Sörbom and Jöreskog, 1976).

TABLE 1
Goodness of fit information for within-group factor models for eight sub-samples of males in the Haller et al. (1974) data on level of occupational aspirations

Sub-sample**	$k = 1$ (27 d.f.) χ^2	χ^2/d.f.	$k = 2u$ (19 d.f.)* χ^2	χ^2/d.f.	$k = 2r$ (25 d.f.)* χ^2	χ^2/d.f.
1. Seniors, high SES	870.43	32.24	178.67	9.40	412.67	16.51
2. Seniors, low SES	861.25	31.90	153.60	8.08	358.91	14.36
3. Juniors, high SES	991.49	36.72	136.93	7.21	373.86	14.95
4. Juniors, low SES	792.09	29.34	145.30	7.65	361.80	14.47
5. Sophomores, high SES	924.49	34.24	145.43	7.65	364.75	14.59
6. Sophomores, low SES	838.38	31.05	129.22	6.80	264.49	10.58
7. Freshmen, high SES	649.46	24.05	105.92	5.57	298.50	11.94
8. Freshmen, low SES	790.12	29.26	163.80	8.62	536.49	21.46
Total	6,717.71	31.10	1,158.86	7.62	2,971.46	14.86

* The $k = 2u$ is the two-factor unrestricted model and the $k = 2r$ is the two-factor congeneric measures model.

** The sample sizes for the eight groups are as follows: (1) 2,206, (2) 2,157, (3) 2,324, (4) 2,419, (5) 2,513, (6) 2,521, (7) 1,713, (8) 1,352.

Table 1 presents the descriptive information regarding the fit of these three models to each sub-sample covariance structure. It is clear from these results that the two-factor models fit the data better in all sub-samples than does the single-factor model. In fact, either two-factor model provides a statistically significant improvement in the fit to the data over and above the single-factor model in all cases. Exploratory analyses of these data indicate that in some cases a three-factor model enhances the fit to the data using statistical criteria as a basis for evaluating goodness of fit, but the theoretical meaning of the additional factor was not always apparent. The two-factor congeneric measures model is the more parsimonious of the two-factor models, involving six more degrees of freedom than the unrestricted two-factor model. However, given the large sample sizes involved in this example, the unrestricted two-factor model provides the best overall fit to the data using statistical criteria alone for evaluating the goodness of a model. For example, in the high socioeconomic, senior sub-sample of males, the difference between the χ^2 values associated with the $k=2$ unrestricted and $k=2$ congeneric models is $412.666-178.669 = 233.997$. This value, itself distributed as χ^2, is statistically significant at low levels of type I error, and therefore from a statistical point of view the hypothesis that the added restrictions of the congeneric model preserve the fit to the data must be rejected. So, even though the congeneric model has a certain appeal based on substantive considerations, it must be rejected on statistical grounds, primarily because of large sample sizes involved.

The analysis of factorial invariance involving the two-factor models described above is presented in Table 2. The preliminary hypothesis of the invariance of the covariance structure must be rejected since the χ^2 value of 908.994 with 252 degrees of freedom is statistically significant at very low levels of type I error. Of course, the size of the samples involved contribute to the rejection of the null hypothesis, but it is virtually impossible to isolate the effect of sample size on this statistical test. In Table 3 we present the results of estimating the models involving an invariant factor pattern, i.e. $\Lambda_1 = \Lambda_2 \ldots \Lambda_m$ for both the $k=2$ unrestricted and $k=2$ congeneric models. The values for the Λ and Φ_g parameter matrices are presented in standardized form, although the models were estimated in their metric form.[9]

There is considerable similarity in the factor patterns for these models over the sub-samples examined here, as evidenced by the χ^2

TABLE 2
Goodness of fit information for between-group factor models for eight sub-samples of males in the Haller et al. (1974) data on level of occupational aspirations

Model		χ^2	d.f.
1. $\Sigma_1 = \Sigma_2 \ldots = \Sigma_m$		908.994	252
2. $\Lambda_1 = \Lambda_2 \ldots = \Lambda_m$	$(k=2u)$	1343.103	236
	$(k=2r)$	3059.609	242
3. $\Lambda_1 = \Lambda_2 \ldots = \Lambda_m$ and $\Theta_1 = \Theta_2 \ldots = \Theta_m$	$(k=2u)$	2534.856	250
	$(k=2r)$	4223.820	256
4. $\Lambda_1 = \Lambda_2 \ldots = \Lambda_m$ and $\Phi_1 = \Phi_2 \ldots = \Phi_m$	$(k=2u)$	1492.639	257
	$(k=2r)$	3162.096	263
5. $\Lambda_1 = \Lambda_2 \ldots = \Lambda_m$ and $\Psi_1^2 = \Psi_2^2 \ldots = \Psi_m^2$	$(k=2u)$	1767.161	292
	$(k=2r)$	3481.281	298

values obtained for the constrained models. However, it is not possible to accept the hypothesis of factor pattern invariance on statistical grounds. The examination of hypothesis 2.1 yields statistically significant χ^2 values for both two-factor models. In the unrestricted model, $\chi^2_{\lambda|k} = 1343.103 - 1158.856 = 184.247$ with $236 - 152 = 84$ degrees of freedom (d.f.), and in the congeneric model $\chi^2_{\lambda|k} = 3059.609 - 2971.464 = 88.145$ with $242 - 200 = 42$ d.f. Both of these χ^2 values are significant at very low levels of type I error, and therefore the hypothesis of factor pattern invariance must be rejected. Again, however, it is difficult to determine the exact contribution of sample sizes to this result, although it is apparent that the large samples may cause us to reject a theoretically reasonable model using statistical criteria of goodness of fit. Owing to the possibility that we have falsely rejected the hypothesis of invariance in the factor pattern in these subsamples, we present the information regarding the fit of models that constrain θ_g, Φ_g and Ψ_g^2 over subsamples in addition to Λ_g (hypotheses 2.2, 2.3, and 2.4) for the $k = 2$ models. Despite the apparent similarities of values in the θ_g, Φ_g and Ψ_g^2 matrices over groups (see Table 3), the application of the relevant test statistic to χ^2 values in Table 2 causes us to reject the hypothesis of invariance in θ_g, Φ_g and Ψ_g^2 (given a common Λ) in these groups.

TABLE 3
Simultaneous factor analysis of eight sub-samples of males in the Haller et al. (1974) data on level of occupational aspirations

Two-factor unrestricted model

$$
\begin{aligned}
\Theta_1 &= [3.953 \quad 6.656] \\
\Theta_2 &= [3.274 \quad 6.176] \\
\Theta_3 &= [3.949 \quad 6.708] \\
\Theta_4 &= [3.185 \quad 6.016] \\
\Theta_5 &= [4.131 \quad 6.727] \\
\Theta_6 &= [3.247 \quad 6.009] \\
\Theta_7 &= [4.180 \quad 6.717] \\
\Theta_8 &= [3.415 \quad 6.132]
\end{aligned}
\qquad
\Lambda =
\begin{bmatrix}
0.640 & 0.000 \\
0.000 & 0.462 \\
0.785 & -0.059 \\
0.124 & 0.432 \\
0.358 & 0.207 \\
-0.188 & 0.703 \\
0.378 & 0.235 \\
0.057 & 0.526
\end{bmatrix}
$$

$\Phi_1 = [0.603]$	$\Psi_1^2 =$	[3.27	4.15	2.31	2.96	4.35	2.26	3.64	2.78]
$\Phi_2 = [0.673]$	$\Psi_2^2 =$	[2.62	5.27	2.07	3.14	4.69	2.54	3.40	2.95]
$\Phi_3 = [0.634]$	$\Psi_3^2 =$	[3.31	4.48	2.28	3.00	4.30	2.21	3.62	2.91]
$\Phi_4 = [0.710]$	$\Psi_4^2 \cdot$	[2.76	5.72	2.40	3.24	5.21	2.74	3.48	3.41]
$\Phi_5 = [0.720]$	$\Psi_5^2 =$	[3.53	4.11	2.40	3.08	4.29	2.43	3.42	2.81]
$\Phi_6 = [0.773]$	$\Psi_6^2 =$	[3.06	5.67	2.73	3.31	5.07	2.74	3.45	3.60]
$\Phi_7 = [0.629]$	$\Psi_7^2 =$	[3.47	4.22	2.76	3.34	4.24	2.62	3.54	3.42]
$\Phi_8 = [0.862]$	$\Psi_8^2 =$	[3.24	5.09	2.41	3.50	5.61	2.83	3.40	3.76]

Two-factor congeneric measures model

$$
\begin{aligned}
\Theta_1 &= [3.974 \quad 6.643] \\
\Theta_2 &= [3.415 \quad 6.162] \\
\Theta_3 &= [3.964 \quad 6.707] \\
\Theta_4 &= [3.304 \quad 6.017] \\
\Theta_5 &= [4.078 \quad 6.730] \\
\Theta_6 &= [3.326 \quad 6.026] \\
\Theta_7 &= [4.085 \quad 6.734] \\
\Theta_8 &= [3.455 \quad 6.154]
\end{aligned}
\qquad
\Lambda =
\begin{bmatrix}
0.510 & 0.000 \\
0.000 & 0.464 \\
0.526 & 0.000 \\
0.000 & 0.492 \\
0.636 & 0.000 \\
0.000 & 0.619 \\
0.701 & 0.000 \\
0.000 & 0.555
\end{bmatrix}
$$

$\Phi_1 = [0.653]$	$\Psi_1^2 =$	[3.84	4.11	3.44	3.01	3.82	2.42	3.10	2.75]
$\Phi_2 = [0.744]$	$\Psi_2^2 =$	[3.10	5.21	3.06	3.10	4.23	2.70	2.93	2.89]
$\Phi_3 = [0.655]$	$\Psi_3^2 =$	[3.84	4.45	3.38	3.05	3.79	2.32	3.07	2.88]
$\Phi_4 = [0.799]$	$\Psi_4^2 =$	[3.18	5.67	3.36	3.22	4.77	2.91	3.08	3.35]
$\Phi_5 = [0.751]$	$\Psi_5^2 =$	[4.02	4.09	3.39	3.08	3.87	2.55	2.96	2.81]
$\Phi_6 = [0.847]$	$\Psi_6^2 =$	[3.45	5.60	3.64	3.26	4.53	2.90	2.91	3.53]
$\Phi_7 = [0.649]$	$\Psi_7^2 =$	[4.18	4.18	4.05	3.36	3.79	2.76	3.09	3.40]
$\Phi_8 = [0.925]$	$\Psi_8^2 =$	[3.70	5.01	3.53	3.46	5.21	2.96	2.92	3.71]

Note: The diagonal elements of the Φ_g matrices are not presented. Only the diagonal elements of the Ψ_g^2 matrices are presented. The subscripts correspond to the sub-samples enumerated in Table 1.

The second example presented here uses data on adolescent self-esteem obtained from Rosenberg and Simmons's (1971) study of youth in Baltimore public schools.[10] A stratified cluster sample of students in grades 7-12 responded to several questions dealing with global self-esteem, as follows:

y_1 — A kid told me: 'I am able to do things as well as most other kids. Do you feel like this about yourself?

y_2 — Another kid said: 'I am no good at all. Do you ever feel like this?'

y_3 — A kid said: 'I am satisfied with myself. Do you feel like this?'

y_4 — A kid told me: 'I do not like myself. Do you ever feel like this?'

y_5 — A kid said: 'I am as good as most other kids I know. Do you feel like this?'

y_6 — Another kid said: 'I think I am no good at all. Do you ever feel like this?'

y_7 — Everybody has some things about him which are good and some things about him which are bad. Are more things about you good, bad or both the same?

y_8 — Another kid said: 'I'm not much good at anything. Do you ever feel like this?'

y_9 — How happy are you with the kind of person you are?

y_{10} — Another kid said: 'I like the kind of person I am. Do you feel like this?'

y_{11} — A kid told me: 'There's a lot wrong with me. Do you ever feel like this?'

Three response categories were provided for all questions, with the exception of y_9, where four response categories were available. The correlations among these variables are given in Table 4 along with their means and standard deviations. Note that items 1, 3, 5, 9, and 10 emphasize positive features of self-conception, items 2, 4, 6, 8, and 11 involve negative content, and item 7 essentially balances positive and negative features of self-concept. The model we analyze here takes these differences in question wording into account.[11] We hypothesize that positively worded questions share variance in common apart from their measurement of global self-esteem, and, similarly, that negatively worded questions covary as a function of question wording apart from their measurement of global self-esteem.

TABLE 4
Correlations, means and standard deviations for Rosenberg and Simmons (1971) measures of adolescent self-esteem for blacks ($N = 840$; above diagonal) and whites ($N = 531$; below diagonal)

Variable	y_1	y_2	y_3	y_4	y_5	y_6	y_7	y_8	y_9	y_{10}	y_{11}	$\bar{y}$	s_y
y_1	1.0	-0.020	0.057	-0.028	0.506	-0.044	0.122	0.004	0.075	0.178	-0.013	2.05	0.836
y_2	0.076	1.0	0.088	0.293	0.024	0.455	0.110	0.320	0.097	0.104	0.314	2.63	0.588
y_3	0.116	0.238	1.0	0.050	0.055	0.097	0.023	0.054	0.282	0.325	0.163	2.31	0.797
y_4	0.023	0.452	0.108	1.0	-0.027	0.343	0.094	0.278	0.176	0.120	0.217	2.70	0.554
y_5	0.509	0.144	0.150	0.113	1.0	-0.016	0.139	-0.003	0.027	0.175	-0.014	1.93	0.858
y_6	0.096	0.592	0.192	0.524	0.088	1.0	0.100	0.431	0.178	0.083	0.346	2.70	0.538
y_7	0.191	0.212	0.208	0.167	0.241	0.168	1.0	0.111	0.099	0.120	0.138	2.24	0.489
y_8	0.115	0.440	0.100	0.353	0.135	0.459	0.217	1.0	0.126	0.052	0.310	2.67	0.578
y_9	0.044	0.247	0.344	0.218	0.120	0.215	0.189	0.237	1.0	0.412	0.188	3.25	0.812
y_{10}	0.204	0.221	0.371	0.181	0.313	0.152	0.218	0.225	0.485	1.0	0.194	2.53	0.721
y_{11}	-0.021	0.369	0.217	0.424	-0.055	0.424	0.233	0.470	0.298	0.165	1.0	2.60	0.650
$\bar{y}$	2.23	2.40	2.14	2.46	2.14	2.50	2.24	2.51	3.12	2.43	2.46		
s_y	0.786	0.639	0.805	0.614	0.822	0.608	0.461	0.634	0.710	0.711	0.661		

The analysis presented here proposes the following structure for the factor pattern (asterisks indicate fixed parameters):

$$
\begin{array}{c}
 & \begin{array}{ccc} \xi_1 & \xi_2 & \xi_3 \end{array} \\
\begin{array}{c} y_1 \\ y_2 \\ y_3 \\ y_4 \\ y_5 \\ y_6 \\ y_7 \\ y_8 \\ y_9 \\ y_{10} \\ y_{11} \end{array}
\left[
\begin{array}{ccc}
0.0^* & 0.0^* & 1.0^* \\
1.0^* & \lambda_{22} & 0.0^* \\
\lambda_{31} & 0.0^* & \lambda_{33} \\
\lambda_{41} & 1.0^* & 0.0^* \\
0.0^* & 0.0^* & \lambda_{53} \\
\lambda_{61} & \lambda_{62} & 0.0^* \\
\lambda_{71} & 0.0^* & \lambda_{73} \\
\lambda_{81} & \lambda_{82} & 0.0^* \\
\lambda_{91} & 0.0^* & \lambda_{93} \\
\lambda_{101} & 0.0^* & \lambda_{103} \\
\lambda_{111} & \lambda_{112} & 0.0^*
\end{array}
\right]
\end{array}
$$

This model sets forth a general common factor (ξ_1) underlying all of the self-esteem measures (with the exception of items 1 and 5), a common factor (ξ_2) underlying the negatively worded items, and a common factor (ξ_3) underlying the positively worded items. The model is identified by placing a unit in each column of λ_g and at least $k-1$ zeros in each column of Λ_g.

Table 5 presents the estimates of the parameters of this three-factor model for white and black youth in the Baltimore sample, in which the factor pattern proposed above is constrained equal over groups, and Table 6 presents goodness-of-fit information for the within and between group factor analyses.[12] The χ^2 value for the model which constrains the factor pattern to be equal over groups is not significantly greater than the χ^2 value for the unconstrained model, i.e. $405.521 - 372.504 = 33.017$ with $97 - 80 = 17$ d.f. ($p > 0.01$). This provides statistical support for the acceptance of the hypothesis of factor pattern invariance and provides a basis for the examination of other issues of factorial invariance. The necessary information for examining these issues is given in Table 6. In all three cases (hypotheses 2.2, 2.3, and 2.4) the relevant χ^2 values are statistically significant ($\chi^2_{\theta\Lambda} - \chi^2_\Lambda = 92.498$ (3 d.f.), $\chi^2_{\theta\Lambda} - \chi^2_\Lambda = 29.112$ (6 d.f.), and $\chi^2_{\psi2\Lambda} - \chi^2_\Lambda = 37.971$ (11 d.f.), suggesting that these additional forms of invariance are implausible.

The third and final example presented here is based on Kluegel et al.'s (1977) study of subjective class identification. Using data from a modified probability sample of 800 adults (432 whites and 368

TABLE 5
Simultaneous factor analysis of white and black sub-samples of the Baltimore data on measures of self-esteem

$$\Theta_W = [2.923 \quad 0.927 \quad 2.743]$$
$$\Theta_B = [3.109 \quad 1.050 \quad 2.501]$$

$$\Phi_W = \begin{bmatrix} -0.272 & \\ -0.039 & 0.217 \end{bmatrix}$$

$$\Phi_B = \begin{bmatrix} -0.390 & \\ -0.161 & 0.095 \end{bmatrix}$$

$$\Lambda = \begin{bmatrix} 0.000 & 0.000 & 0.731 \\ 0.473 & 0.628 & 0.000 \\ 0.378 & 0.000 & 0.107 \\ 0.545 & 0.549 & 0.000 \\ 0.000 & 0.000 & 0.674 \\ 0.513 & 0.736 & 0.000 \\ 0.506 & 0.000 & 0.395 \\ 0.509 & 0.582 & 0.000 \\ 0.577 & 0.000 & 0.121 \\ 0.410 & 0.000 & 0.240 \\ 0.497 & 0.385 & 0.000 \end{bmatrix}$$

$$\Psi_W^2 = [0.289 \; 0.199 \; 0.510 \; 0.223 \; 0.343 \; 0.139 \; 0.169 \; 0.245 \; 0.277 \; 0.333 \; 0.273]$$
$$\Psi_B^2 = [0.331 \; 0.219 \; 0.534 \; 0.229 \; 0.390 \; 0.137 \; 0.214 \; 0.225 \; 0.447 \; 0.377 \; 0.312]$$

Note: The diagonal elements of the Φ_g matrices are not presented, and only the diagonal elements of the Ψ_g^2 matrices are presented

TABLE 6
Goodness of fit information for within- and between-group factor models in the Rosenberg and Simmons (1971) data on adolescent self-esteem

		Within-group models		
Model		χ^2	d.f.	χ^2/d.f.
Whites		191.50	40	4.788
Blacks		181.00	40	4.525
Sum		372.50	80	
		Between-group models		
Model		χ^2	d.f.	
1. $\Sigma_W = \Sigma_B$		159.10	66	
2. $\Lambda_W = \Lambda_B$		405.52	97	
3. $\Lambda_W = \Lambda_B$ $\Theta_W = \Theta_B$		498.02	100	
4. $\Lambda_W = \Lambda_B$ $\Phi_W = \Phi_B$		434.63	103	
5. $\Lambda_W = \Lambda_B$ $\Psi_W^2 = \Psi_B^2$		443.49	108	

blacks) in Gary, Indiana, in 1969,[13] Kluegel et al. analyze several measures of objective social class, subjective social class and political alienation. The variables analyzed by Kluegel et al. are as follows:

y_1 — educational level — five categories ranging from less than ninth grade to college graduate

y_2 — occupational status — Duncan SEI score.

y_3 — family income — coded in units of \$2,000.

y_4 — subjective class, occupation indicator — respondents were asked to place themselves in one of four class categories: lower, working, middle, or upper, in terms of their occupation.

y_5 — subjective class, income indicator — respondents were asked to place themselves in one of four class categories (see y_4) in terms of their income

y_6 — subjective class, life-style indicator — respondents were asked to place themselves in one of four class categories (see y_4) in terms of their life-style

y_7 — subjective class, influence indicator — respondents were asked to place themselves in one of four class categories (see y_4) in terms of their influence.

y_8 — subjective class, general indicator — respondents were asked to place themselves in one of four class categories (see y_4) in general terms

y_9 — political alienation indicator 1 — response (four-point Likert scale) to the statement, 'People like me don't have any say about what the government does.'

y_{10} — political alienation indicator 2 — response (four-point Likert scale) to the statement, 'I don't think public officials care much what people like me think.'

y_{11} — political alienation indicator 3 — response (four-point Likert scale) to the statement, 'The leaders of the federal government don't care what happens to people like me.'

y_{12} — political alienation indicator 4 — response (four-point Likert scale) to the statement, 'This nation is run by the few people in power, and there is not much the little guy can do about it.'

The correlations, means and standard deviations for these measures are given for blacks and whites by Kluegel et al. (1977:603) and are not reproduced here. Kluegel et al. (1977)

analyze several models for blacks and whites with the goal of obtaining the best fitting factor model for each group, but they make no comparisons between blacks and whites in a simultaneous analysis. Their analysis assumes that y_1, y_2, and y_3 are perfect measures of education, occupational status and family income, and we carry these assumptions into our analysis. They begin with a model in which there are five latent variables, one each for education, occupational status and income and two sets of congeneric measures for subjective social class and political alienation (see Kluegel et al.:604, Figure 1). They reject this model for both blacks and whites on the basis of statistical goodness of fit. We refer to this model as model I here. The factor pattern that Kluegel et al. select for whites is as follows:

$$
\begin{array}{c@{\quad}ccccc}
 & \xi_1 & \xi_2 & \xi_3 & \xi_4 & \xi_5 \\
y_1 & 1.0^* & 0.0^* & 0.0^* & 0.0^* & 0.0^* \\
y_2 & 0.0^* & 1.0^* & 0.0^* & 0.0^* & 0.0^* \\
y_3 & 0.0^* & 0.0^* & 1.0^* & 0.0^* & 0.0^* \\
y_4 & 0.0^* & \lambda_{42} & 0.0^* & 1.0^* & 0.0^* \\
y_5 & 0.0^* & 0.0^* & \lambda_{53} & \lambda_{54} & 0.0^* \\
y_6 & 0.0^* & 0.0^* & 0.0^* & \lambda_{64} & 0.0^* \\
y_7 & 0.0^* & 0.0^* & 0.0^* & \lambda_{74} & 0.0^* \\
y_8 & 0.0^* & 0.0^* & 0.0^* & \lambda_{84} & 0.0^* \\
y_9 & 0.0^* & 0.0^* & 0.0^* & 0.0^* & 1.0^* \\
y_{10} & 0.0^* & 0.0^* & 0.0^* & 0.0^* & \lambda_{105} \\
y_{11} & 0.0^* & 0.0^* & 0.0^* & 0.0^* & \lambda_{115} \\
y_{12} & 0.0^* & 0.0^* & 0.0^* & 0.0^* & \lambda_{125}
\end{array}
$$

As above, the asterisks denote fixed parameters, and we should note that we have stated the model in metric form so that we may compare this model in the two sub-populations of blacks and whites. Also, the models we estimate here do not center the factors as Kluegel et al.'s analysis does, and this allows us to obtain estimates of the factor means in θ_g for both subgroups. The above factor pattern departs from a congeneric measurement model in that y_4 and y_5 are allowed to depend upon the occupational status and income measures respectively. As Kluegel et al. point out, this specification embodies a form of nonrandom measurement error for these indicators of subjective social class. Under this specification, however, Kluegel et al. assume that Ψ^2 for whites is diagonal; i.e., the remaining errors of measurement operate randomly.

The factor pattern corresponding to the model selected for blacks by Kluegel et al. is as follows:

	ξ_1	ξ_2	ξ_3	ξ_4	ξ_5
y_2	1.0*	0.0*	0.0*	0.0*	0.0*
y_2	0.0*	1.0*	0.0*	0.0*	0.0*
y_3	0.0*	0.0*	1.0*	0.0*	0.0*
y_4	0.0*	λ_{42}	0.0*	1.0*	0.0*
y_5	0.0*	0.0*	λ_{53}	λ_{54}	0.0*
y_6	0.0*	0.0*	0.0*	λ_{64}	0.0*
y_7	0.0*	0.0*	0.0*	λ_{74}	λ_{75}
y_8	0.0*	0.0*	0.0*	λ_{84}	0.0*
y_9	0.0*	0.0*	0.0*	0.0*	1.0*
y_{10}	0.0*	0.0*	0.0*	0.0*	λ_{105}
y_{11}	0.0*	0.0*	0.0*	0.0*	λ_{115}
y_{12}	0.0*	0.0*	0.0*	0.0*	λ_{125}

The factor pattern Kluegel et al. select for blacks, when, is similar to that proposed for whites, except that y_7 (the subjective class, influence indicator) is allowed to depend on the political alienation latent construct. In addition, for blacks the measurement error terms for y_4 and y_9 are allowed to covary, so Ψ_s^2 for blacks is non-diagonal. Here we refer to the model Kluegel et al. select for whites as model II and the model they select for blacks as model III.

The present analysis extends the work of Kluegel et al. by examining several models for blacks and whites using simultaneous factor analysis. We first reproduce the three Kluegel et al. models within each group with the additional specification that the factor means are to be estimated. Table 7 presents the goodness of fit information for models I, II, and III in both the black and white subsamples. Consistent with the analysis carried out by Kluegel et al., model II represents a significant improvement in the fit to the data over model I for whites, and model III represents a significant improvement over model I for blacks. However, the differences between models II and III for either blacks or whites are trivial, although for blacks the reduction in the χ^2 value resulting from the addition of the parameters in model III ($x^2 = 7.2$ with 2 d.f.) is significant at the 0.05 level. These within-group analyses essentially replicate the Kluegel et al. findings and support their choice of models describing the two groups.

TABLE 7
Goodness of fit information for within- and between-group
factor models in the Kluegel et al. (1977) data on objective
and subjective social class and political alienation

Model		Within-group models χ^2	d.f.	χ^2/d.f.
I	Whites	109.28	54	2.024
	Blacks	136.70	54	2.532
	Sum	245.98	108	
II	Whites	75.40	52	1.450
	Blacks	107.26	52	2.063
	Sum	182.67	104	
III	Whites*	75.40	51	1.470
	Blacks**	100.06	50	2.001
	Sum	175.46	101	

Model		Between-group models χ^2	d.f.
	$\Sigma_W = \Sigma_B$	203.21	78
I	$\Lambda_W = \Lambda_B$	264.88	115
II	$\Lambda_W = \Lambda_B$	524.44	113
III	$\Lambda_W = \Lambda_B$	520.38	112

* Ψ^2 is diagonal
** Ψ^2 is nondiagonal

Table 7 also presents the simultaneous factor analysis of the white and black sub-samples in the Kleugel et al. data. These analyses show that, regardless of the model used to compare blacks and whites, there is no basis of support for hypotheses of similarity in the factor patterns of the two groups, again replicating Kluegel et al.'s conclusions.

SUMMARY AND CONCLUSIONS

This paper has emphasized the utility of phrasing questions of factorial invariance within a confirmatory factor analysis framework, and we have argued that methods of exploratory factor analysis are inadequate for these purposes. The general common factor model involves two subsets of issues regarding the degree of invariance in parameters of the model over populations (or sub-populations) which can be addressed using the methods of confirmatory factor analysis. The first subset of issues involves the parameters representing the measurement structure. Here two separate parameter matrices are involved: (1) the set of regression parameters relating the measured variables to the latent factors, i.e. the factor pattern matrix, λ_g, and (2) the covariance matrix of the residuals in the measured variables, Ψ_g^2. In the above presentation we have assumed that Ψ_g^2 is diagonal, although in the general case it is not. The second subset of invariance issues involves the parameters describing the properties of the factors of the model. Again, two parameter matrices are involved: (1) the means of the factors, θ_g, and (2) the covariance matrix of the factors, Φ_g.

The four parameter matrices described above are all potentially of interest in the investigation of factorial invariance, but the most central issue is the invariance of the factor pattern, Λ_g. If the fundamental relationships between the variables and the factors of the model are not held in common over populations (or sub-populations), it is difficult to argue that the same factors exist across populations. Therefore the examination of the other issues of factorial invariance hinges on the acceptance of the hypothesis that the same factor pattern may be used to describe all populations. The difficulty with assessing factor pattern invariance using conventional methods of exploratory factor analysis is that the issue of factor pattern invariance is confounded with the issue of invariance in the covariance structure for the factors of the model.

Within this framework we have outlined a sequence of hypotheses, derived in part from the presentation of similar material by Jöreskog (1971b) and Sörbom (1974), which may be examined to address the issues of factorial invariance. The examination of these hypotheses using COFAMM (Sörbom and Jöreskog, 1976) provides a statistical basis for the investigation of these issues, although we have pointed out that the acceptance of any particular model cannot in general be based on statistical grounds alone. One of the main difficulties with using statistical criteria alone for the evaluation of the fit of any of these models to the data at hand is that maximum likelihood χ^2 test statistics are influenced by the sizes of the samples used. There is, therefore, no unequivocal measure of the fit of any particular invariance hypothesis to the data, although the examination of the χ^2 values can be used to arrive at a reasonable interpretation of the data.

Finally, we have presented the application of the Jöreskog-Sörbom methods of simultaneous factor analysis to the investigation of issues of factorial invariance in three separate bodies of data. Our illustrations, however, are confined to the comparison of factor models among sub-populations within a particular body of data. Although the use of these methods is not limited to sub-population comparisons, our analyses demonstrate the general strategy that may be used to investigate invariance issues where their examination speaks to relevant theoretical and methodological questions. The investigation of invariance issues among sub-populations within a particular body of data can be used as a basis for determining whether it is feasible to assume that the variables involved indeed measure the same construct(s), and this has implications for the use of the variables involved to represent theoretical constructs in other forms of data anlysis. If it can be assumed that the same constructs are represented by a given set of variables across sub-populations, then it is relevant to assess the degree to which other parameters of the model are similar for the sub-populations involved. Our empirical analyses demonstrate how these issues may be addressed.

NOTES

1. A coefficient similar to this which is sometimes used is the ordinary product-moment correlation of the factor loadings over variables, sometimes referred to as the adjusted correlation (see Fiske, 1949; Cattell, 1952), but this coefficient has not been strongly proposed as a measure of factor similarity (see Barlow and Burt, 1954; Pinneau and Newhouse, 1964).

2. Sörbom and Jöreskog (1976) refer to this vector of constants as 'location parameters.'

3. The present discussion considers the model in the gth population or sub-population. When multiple populations are considered simultaneously, other special cases may be of interest (see Sörbom and Jöreskog, 1976); for example, the case where v_g are equal over groups or where θ_g are equal over groups, but not necessarily set equal to zero.

4. It should be obvious that Λ^* is also affected by D, which is a function of the population variances of the variables. This point has been recognized by the literature on factorial invariance since Thurstone.

5. Note that the variable means are ignored in the examination of this hypothesis.

6. We present this hypothesis as theoretically feasible, although we have been unsuccessful in our attempts to estimate this model using COFAMM.

7. As we noted above, while the model used here assumes Ψ_g^2 is diagonal, under some circumstances it may be nondiagonal. In such cases the form of the invariance hypothesis involving Ψ_g^2 is the same, but the degrees of freedom involved will depend upon the number of free parameters in Ψ_g^2.

8. The authors wish to thank Luther Otto for kindly making these correlations available.

9. The standardized values for the maximum likelihood solution are obtained as follows. Let Φ_p be the pooled factor covariance matrix over groups, defined as:

$$\Phi_p = (1/N) \sum_{g=1}^{m} N_g \Phi_g$$

where N_g is the sample size for the gth group and N is the sum of sample sizes over groups. Define $S_p = (\text{diag. } \Phi_p)^{-\frac{1}{2}}$. Let Σ_p be the pooled variable covariance matrix over groups, defined as:

$$\Sigma_p = (1/N) \sum_{g=1}^{m} N_g \Sigma_g$$

Define $D_p = (\text{diag. } \Sigma_p)^{-\frac{1}{2}}$. The standardized factor pattern in this case is defined as $\Lambda\% = D\Lambda S^{-1}$, and the standardized factor covariance matrix for the gth group is $\Phi_g^* S$. (Note that our notation here varies from that used by Sörbom and Jöreskog, 1976:p.18.)

10. The authors wish to thank Professor Morris Rosenberg for access to the data upon which the present analysis is based.

11. The authors wish to thank Dr Neal Krause for his help in specifying the form of the factor model used here.

12. Again, in Table 5 the standardized values are presented for Λ and Φ_g.

13. These data were collected in the 1969 Gary Area Project of the Institute of Social Research at Indiana University under the direction of Professor Sheldon Stryker.

REFERENCES

Alwin, D. F. and D. J. Jackson (1979) 'Measurement Models for Response Errors in Surveys: Issues and Applications,' pp. 68-119 in K. F. Schuessler (ed.), *Sociological Methodology 1980*, San Francisco: Jossey-Bass.

Barlow, J. B. and C. Burt (1954) 'The Identification of Factors from Different Experiments,' *British Journal of Statistical Psychology*, vol. 7:52-6.

Bechtoldt, H. P. (1974) 'A Confirmatory Analysis of the Factor Stability Hypothesis,' *Psychometrika*, vol. 39:319-26.

Bloxom, B. (1972) 'Alternative Approaches to Factorial Invariance,' *Psychometrika*, vol. 37:425-40.

Burt, C. (1939) 'The Relations of Educational Abilities,' *British Journal of Educational Psychology*, vol. 9:45-71.

Cattell, R. B. (1949) 'r_p and Other Coefficients of Pattern Similarity,' *Psychometrika*, vol. 14:279-98.

Cattell, R. B. (1952) *Factor Analysis*. New York: Harper.

Fiske, D. (1949) 'Consistency of the Factorial Structures of Personality Ratings from Different Sources,' *Journal of Abnormal and Social Psychology*, vol. 44:329-44.

Haller, A. O., L. B. Otto, R. F. Meier and G. W. Ohlendorf (1974) 'Level of Occupational Aspiration: An Empirical Analysis,' *American Sociological Review*, vol. 39:113-21.

Harman, H. H. (1967) *Modern Factor Analysis*. Chicago: University of Chicago Press.

Jöreskog, K. G. (1971a) 'Statistical Analysis of Sets of Congeneric Tests,' *Psychometrika*, vol. 36:109-33.

Jöreskog, K. G. (1971b) 'Simultaneous Factor Analysis in Several Populations,' *Psychometrika*, vol. 36:409-26.

Kluegel, J. R., R. Singleton and C. E. Starnes (1977) 'Subjective Class Identification: A Multiple Indicator Approach', *American Sociological Review*, vol. 42:599-611.

Lawley, D. N. and A. E. Maxwell (1971) *Factor Analysis as a Statistical Method*. New York: American Elsevier.

Leyden, T. (1953) 'The Identification and Invariance of Factors,' *British Journal of Statistical Psychology*, vol. 6:119.

McGaw, B. and K. G. Jöreskog (1971) 'Factorial Invariance of Ability Measures in Groups Differing in Intelligence and Socioeconomic Status,' *British Journal of Mathematical and Statistical Psychology*, vol. 24:154-68.

Meredith, W. (1964a) 'Notes on Factorial Invariance,' *Psychometrika*, vol. 29:177-85.

Meredith, W. (1964b) 'Rotation to Achieve Factorial Invariance,' *Psychometrika*, Vol. 29:187-206.

Mosier, C. I. (1939) 'Determining a Simple Structure When Loadings for Certain Tests are Known,' *Psychometrika*, vol. 4:149-62.

Mulaik, S. A. (1972) *The Foundations of Factor Analysis*. New York: McGraw-Hill.

Otto, L. B., A. O. Haller, R. F. Meier and G. W. Ohlendorf (1973) 'An Empirical Evaluation of an Occupational Aspiration Scale,' paper presented at the Annual Meeting of the American College Personnel Association. Cleveland, Ohio. April 1973.

Otto, L. B., A. O. Haller, R. F. Meier and G. W. Ohlendorf (1974) 'An Empirical Evaluation of a Scale to Measure Occupational Aspiration Level,' *Journal of Vocational Behavior*, vol. 5:1-11.

Pinneau, S. and A. Newhouse (1964) 'Measures of Invariance and Comparability in Factor Analysis for Fixed Variables,' *Psychometrika*, vol. 29:271-81.

Rosenberg, M. and R. G. Simmons (1971) *Black and White Self-Esteem: The Urban School Child*, Rose Monograph Series. Washington, DC: American Sociological Association.

Rummel, R. J. (1970) *Applied Factor Analysis*. Evanston, Ill.: Northwestern University Press.

Sörbom, D. (1974) 'A General Method for Studying Differences in Factor Means and Factor Structure Between Groups,' *British Journal of Mathematical and Statistical Psychology*, vol. 27:229-39.

Sörbom, D. and K. G. Jöreskog (1976) *COFAMM — Confirmatory Factor Analysis with Model Modification*. Chicago: National Educational Resources, Inc.

Thurstone, L. L. (1935) *The Vectors of the Mind*. Chicago: University of Chicago Press.

Thurstone, L. L. (1947) *Multiple Factor Analysis*. Chicago: University of Chicago Press.

Tucker, L. (1951) 'A Method for Synthesis of Factor Analysis Studies,' Personnel Research Section Report No. 984. Washington, DC: Department of the Army.

Wrigley, C. (1958) 'Objectivity in Factor Analysis,' *Educational and Psychological Measurement*, vol. 18:463-76.

Wrigley, C. and A. Newhouse (1955) 'The Matching of Two Sets of Factors,' *American Psychologist*, vol. 10:418-19.

JOB CONDITIONS AND INTELLECTUAL FLEXIBILITY: A LONGITUDINAL ASSESSMENT OF THEIR RECIPROCAL EFFECTS

Melvin L. Kohn
Carmi Schooler
National Institute of Mental Health, Adelphi, Maryland

This paper illustrates the application of a new and powerful methodology to an old and important substantive problem — assessing the reciprocal relationships between job conditions and individual psychological functioning. The combination of confirmatory factor analysis and linear structural equations causal analysis, as developed by Karl Jöreskog and his associates and applied to longitudinal data, provides an effective way of analyzing these complex reciprocal relationships.

Cross-sectional data cannot provide definitive evidence of the directions and magnitudes of effects in reciprocal relationships (Kohn and Schooler, 1973; Kohn, 1976). In particular, even though it is possible to obtain retrospective information about past jobs, it

Authors' Note. This is a greatly revised version of a paper presented at the Ninth World Congress of Sociology, Uppsala, Sweden, 14-19 August 1978. We are indebted to Ronald Schoenberg for a critical appraisal of the causal models in an earlier version of this paper. We are also indebted to Bruce Roberts, Carrie Schoenbach, and Margaret Renfors for their assistance in carrying out the analyses and to Virginia Marbley for typing innumerable revisions of the manuscript.

is not possible in a cross-sectional study to obtain trustworthy information about men's levels of psychological functioning when they held those jobs. Thus, cross-sectional data provide no way of taking into account earlier levels of, say, intellectual flexibility in assessing the effects of job conditions (or anything else) on current intellectual flexibility. But even with longitudinal data, two major methodological problems remain: how to deal with measurement error and how to model complex causal processes.

Measurement error is always problematic in causal analyses, because the magnitudes of regression coefficients are underestimated in direct proportion to the unreliability of the independent variables. Such error is particularly problematic in analyses of reciprocal effects, where each variable in a pair is an independent variable vis-à-vis the other. The problem is further exacerbated in longitudinal analyses because of the high probability that errors in the measurement of any indicator in the original data will be correlatec ·vith errors in the measurement of that same indicator at a later time. For example, any errors in the information obtained in a baseline survey about the complexity of men's work with things or in coding that information might well be correlated with errors in the same type of information in a follow-up survey. Such correlated errors in any pair of constituent items might make the overtime stability of the underlying concept — the substantive complexity of work — seem greater or less than it really is. Thus, before assessing changes in substantive complexity and the reasons for such changes, we must remove the effects of correlated errors in measurement of the indicators of this concept.

Confirmatory factor analysis provides an excellent method for accomplishing this difficult task. The essence of the method lies in the use of multiple indicators for each principal concept, inferring from the covariation of the indicators the degree to which each reflects the underlying concept that they all are hypothesized to reflect and the degree to which each reflects anything else, which for measurement purposes is considered to be error. This method enables one explicitly to model correlations in the errors. The test of one's success in differentiating underlying concepts from errors in the indicators is how well the hypothesized model reproduces the original variance-covariance matrix of the indicators.

In addition to measurement error, the major problem in longitudinal analysis is that it is difficult to estimate complex causal models, particularly when there is a priori reason to believe, not only that occupational conditions can both affect and be affected by the personalities of the people who hold the jobs, but also that these effects can occur both contemporaneously and over time. We shall discuss the ramifications of this problem at length. For now, it is sufficient to say that the method for solving linear structural equations employed in the LISREL computer program is an effective way of estimating such models. LISREL is not easy to learn or simple to employ; and it is expensive in computer time. But it has the crucial advantage of allowing the analyst to make deliberate choices about all the parameters of the model, thus making explicit and subject to theoretical determination decisions that are otherwise arbitrary, often made without the investigator being fully aware of the issues.

We have employed LISREL in a prototypic analysis of our longitudinal data, an analysis of the relationship between the substantive complexity of work and intellectual flexibility (Kohn and Schooler, 1978).[1] Now we expand that analysis greatly, to deal not only with the substantive complexity of work, but also with a wide variety of other job conditions. We continue, however, to focus on intellectual flexibility, mainly because it offers us the greatest challenge — intellectual flexibility obviously affects recruitment into complex jobs, and there is every reason to expect it to be one of the most resistant to change of all the facets of psychological functioning we have studied. Yet, intellectual flexibility is so important a part of psychological functioning that we must not unthinkingly assume it to be entirely the product of genetics and early life experience. Rather, we should empirically test the possibility that intellectual flexibility may be responsive to adult occupational experience.

DATA

The baseline data come from interviews conducted in 1964 with a sample of 3,101 men, representative of all men employed in civilian occupations in the United States. (For more specific information on sample and research design, see Kohn, 1969:235-64.) In 1974 the National Opinion Research Center (NORC) carried out a follow-up survey for us, interviewing a representative sub-sample of approximately one-fourth of those men who were then less than 65 years old. The age limitation was imposed to increase the probability that the men in the follow-up study would still be in the labor force.

In this as in all longitudinal studies, the question of the representativeness of the original and follow-up samples is crucial for assessing the generalizability of any analyses we do. For an assessment of the representativeness of the original sample, see Kohn, 1969: Appendix C. As for the follow-up sample, of the 883 men whom we randomly selected for re-interview, NORC succeeded in locating 820 (i.e., 93 percent) ten years after the original survey. Of the 820 men located, 35 had died. Of the remaining 785 men, NORC actually re-interviewed 687, i.e., 78 percent of those originally selected and 88 percent of those located and found to be alive. A systematic comparison of the social and psychological characteristics of the men who were re-interviewed with those of a truly representative sample of employed men in the 16-64 age group, namely the men who were randomly excluded from the follow-up study, shows that the men who were re-interviewed were, as of the time of the original interviews, a little more intellectually flexible than were those in the comparison group. But the two groups do not differ significantly in other characteristics important to our analyses, e.g. education and major occupational characteristics.

A MEASUREMENT MODEL FOR
INTELLECTUAL FLEXIBILITY

Our index of intellectual flexibility is meant to reflect men's actual intellectual performance in the interview situation. In the 1964 interview, we used a variety of indicators — including the men's answers to seemingly simple but highly revealing cognitive problems, their handling of perceptual and projective tests, their propensity to agree when asked 'agree-disagree' questions, and the impression they made on the interviewer during a long session that required a great deal of thought and reflection. None of these indicators is believed to be completely valid; but we do believe that all the indicators reflect, to some substantial degree, men's flexibility in coping with an intellectually demanding situation.

We claim neither that this index measures innate intellectual ability, nor that intellectual flexibility evidenced in the interview situation is necessarily identical to intellectual flexibility as it might be manifested in other situations; we do not have enough informa-

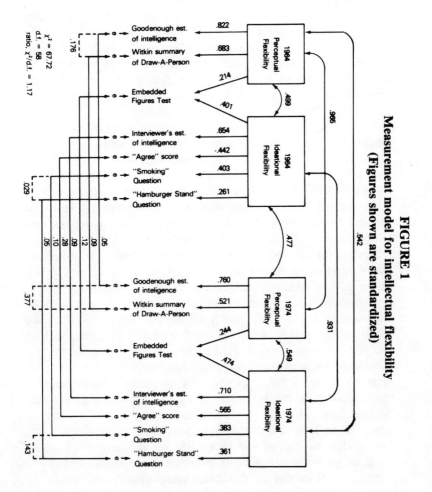

FIGURE 1

Measurement model for intellectual flexibility

(Figures shown are standardized)

tion about the situational variability of intellectual functioning to be certain. What we do claim is that our index reflects men's actual intellectual functioning in a non-work situation that seemed to elicit considerable intellectual effort from nearly all the respondents. That our index is not artifactual, and that it measures an enduring characteristic, is attested to by the evidence — to be presented shortly — of its remarkably high stability over time. Spaeth's (1976) analysis adds to the credibility of the index by showing that the correlations between an earlier variant of our index and various social phenomena are similar to those for more conventional indices of intellectual functioning.

More concretely, our index uses seven indicators of each man's intellectual performance (see Figure 1).[2] These are: (1) the Goodenough estimate of his intelligence (see Witkin et al., 1962), based on a detailed evaluation of the draw-a-person test; (2) Witkin's (Witkin et al., 1962) appraisal of the sophistication of body-concept in the draw-a-person test; (3) a summary score for his performance on a portion of the Embedded Figures test (see Witkin et al., 1962); (4) the interviewer's appraisal of the man's intelligence; (5) the frequency with which he agreed when asked the many agree-disagree questions included in the interview; (6) a rating of the adequacy of his answer to the apparently simple cognitive problem, 'What are all the arguments you can think of for and against allowing cigarette commercials on TV?' (7) a rating of the adequacy of his answer to another relatively simple cognitive problem, 'Suppose you wanted to open a hamburger stand and there were two locations available. What questions would you consider in deciding which of the two locations offers a better business opportunity?' In the follow-up study, we secured entirely comparable data, after elaborate pre-testing to be certain that the cognitive problems had the same meaning in 1974 as in 1964.

In earlier analysis of the 1964 data, we had performed an orthogonal principal components factor analysis, which yielded two dimensions of intellectual flexibility, one primarily perceptual, the other ideational. The measurement model we now employ for intellectual flexibility follows the logic of the two-factor model derived from that exploratory factor analysis, but uses confirmatory factor analysis (Jöreskog, 1969; 1970; 1973a; 1978; Jöreskog and Sörbom, 1976). We conceive of the seven indicators of intellectual flexibility as reflecting the underlying concepts, which they measure only imperfectly, together with some degree of 'error' in measurement. We allow for the possibility that errors of measurement are correlated over time — that whatever errors there were in the measurement of the Embedded Figures Test in 1964, for example, may be correlated with errors in the measurement of the same test in 1974. We also allow the possibility of intra-time error correlations. Specifically, to take into account that the Goodenough estimate of intelligence and the Witkin appraisal of body-concept are based on the same task, the Draw-a-Person test, we allow their errors to be correlated; we also allow for the possibility of correlated error between the two cognitive problems.[3]

The model depicted in Figure 1 shows that some of the paths from concepts to indicators are not especially strong; this is the very reason we thought it necessary to construct a measurement model that would differentiate unreliability of measurement from actual intellectual functioning. Judging by the goodness-of-fit test, the model is successful in achieving this objective: The overall chi-square is 67.72, with 58 degrees of freedom, for a ratio of 1.17, which means that the model provides a very good approximation to the actual variances and covariances of the indicators.

Our concern in the causal analyses is entirely with the ideational component of intellectual flexibility, which is of greater theoretical interest than is the perceptual component.[4] From the measurement model, we learn that the correlation between men's levels of ideational flexibility in 1964 and their levels of ideational flexibility in 1974, shorn of measurement error, is a very substantial 0.93. Clearly, there has been great stability in men's levels of ideational flexibility over the 10-year period. The question for causal analysis is whether, despite this overall stability, job conditions have had some effect.

Parenthetically, the correlation between an index of ideational flexibility derived from factor loadings in exploratory factor analysis of the 1964 data and a similar index derived from the same factor loadings for 1974 is a much lower 0.59. If we were to do a causal analysis using factor scores based on exploratory factor analysis, most of the 'change' in ideational flexibility that we would be analyzing would in actuality be not change, but measurement error.[5]

JOB CONDITIONS

Our surveys include information about more than 50 separable facets of work. Not all of them need be considered here, for earlier analyses (Kohn and Schooler, 1973) indicate that many occupational conditions do not have any substantial impact on men's psychological functioning, independent of other pertinent occupational conditions and of education. The present analysis focuses on fourteen job conditions, which together identify a man's place in the organizational structure, his opportunities for occupational self-direction, the principal job pressures to which he is subject, and the principal extrinsic risks and rewards built into his job. Specifically, we measure three aspects of an individual's place in the organizational structure — ownership, bureaucratization, and hierarchical position; the conditions determinative of occupational self-direction are the substantive complexity of work, routinization, and closeness of supervision; the job pressures considered here are time-pressure, heaviness, dirtiness, and the number of hours worked in the average week; and the extrinsic risks and rewards are the risk of losing one's job or business, the probability of being held responsible for things outside one's control, job protections, and job income. We call this set of job conditions 'the structural imperatives of the job.'[6] These job conditions are 'structural' in two senses: they are built into the structure of the job, and they are largely determined by the job's location in the structures of the economy and the society.

Previous analyses have indicated that the three conditions determinative of occupational self-direction — substantive complexity, closeness of supervision, and routinization — are of critical importance for psychological functioning (Kohn and Schooler, 1969; 1973; Kohn, 1969; 1976; 1977). We therefore initially focus on these three. We then go on to enlarge the analysis to include all the structural imperatives of the job.

A MEASUREMENT MODEL FOR OCCUPATIONAL SELF-DIRECTION

By occupational self-direction, we mean the use of initiative, thought, and independent judgment in work. Since the three principal determinants of occupational self-direction are theoretically

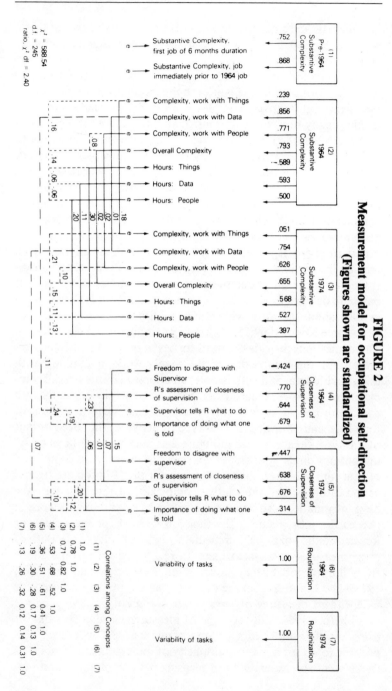

FIGURE 2
Measurement model for occupational self-direction
(Figures shown are standardized)

interrelated, and since we have multiple indicators of two of them, we have developed a single measurement model that encompasses all three (see Figure 2).

We define the substantive complexity of work as the degree to which performance of the work requires thought and independent judgment. Substantively complex work by its very nature requires making many decisions that must take into account ill-defined or apparently conflicting contingencies. Although, in general, work with data or with people is likely to be more complex than work with things, this is not always the case, and an index of the overall complexity of work should reflect the degree of complexity of each of these three types of activity. Work with things can vary in complexity from ditch-digging to sculpting; similarly, work with people can vary in complexity from receiving simple directions or orders to giving legal advice; and work with data can vary from reading instructions to synthesizing abstract conceptual systems.

Our information about the substantive complexity of work is based on detailed questioning of each respondent in 1964 and again in 1974 about his work with things, with data or ideas, and with people (see Kohn, 1969:153-5, 271-6; or Kohn and Schooler, 1978). These questions provide the basis for seven ratings of each job: appraisals of the complexity of the man's work in that job with things, with data, and with people; an appraisal of the overall complexity of his work, regardless of whether he works primarily with data, with people, or with things; and estimates of the amount of time he spends working at each type of activity. The seven ratings of the 1964 job are treated in Figure 2 as indicators of the underlying but not directly measured concept, the substantive complexity of that job; similarly, the seven ratings of the 1974 job are treated as indicators of the substantive complexity of the 1974 job. We have information also about the complexity of each man's work in two earlier jobs, namely, the first job he held for six months or longer and the job he held immediately before his 1964 job. Both of these measures are approximate scores, based on extrapolations from limited job history information (see Kohn and Schooler, 1973:111-12, note 21). In the present analysis, we have no need for independent measures of substantive complexity at two separate times before 1964. But the logic of measurement models calls for using multiple indicators of important concepts whenever it is possible to do so; it is the multiplicity of indicators that enables us to differentiate unreliability of measurement from an accurate index of the underlying concept. We therefore treat these two measures as indicators of a single concept, 'earlier' (pre-1964) substantive complexity.

Closeness of supervision is a limiting condition on occupational self-direction: workers cannot exercise occupational self-direction if they are closely supervised, although not being closely supervised does not necessarily mean that workers are required or even free to use initiative, thought, and independent judgment. Closeness of supervision is measured by a worker's assessment of: his freedom to disagree with his supervisor, how closely he is supervised, the extent to which his supervisor tells him what to do rather than discussing it with him, and the importance in his job of doing what one is told to do.[7]

Routinization is the final determinant of occupational self-direction; highly routinized (repetitive and predictable) jobs restrict possibilities for exercising initiative, thought, and judgment, while jobs with a variety of unpredictable tasks may facilitate or even require the use of self-direction. Our present treatment of routinization is a sharp departure from our treatment of routinization in earlier analyses. In those analyses, we indexed routinization by two questions, one about the repetitiveness of the work tasks, the other about the complexity of the 'units' of which the work is comprised. Now we find, in confirmatory factor analysis, that the question about the nature of the units of work reflects not only the routinization of work but also its substantive complexity and even how closely it is supervised. Faced with the choice of a single indicator of routinization or a needlessly complex measurement model, we elect to use the single indicator. We have, however, improved the index of repetitiveness by including further information from the interviews about the predictability of non-repetitive work. Respondents' work was coded from most variable (the work involves doing different things in different ways and one cannot predict what may come up) to least variable (the work is unvaryingly repetitive).

The measurement model for occupational self-direction, including the error correlations depicted in Figure 2, provides an excellent fit to the variance-covariance matrix of the indicators. The chi-square is 588.54, with 245 degrees of freedom, a ratio of 2.40.

THE RECIPROCAL EFFECTS OF OCCUPATIONAL
SELF-DIRECTION AND IDEATIONAL FLEXIBILITY

To do causal analyses, we have computed the covariances among job complexity at the various stages of career, closeness of supervision, routinization, and ideational flexibility in 1964 and in 1974, and all the other variables (specified below) that enter into the analyses.[8] These covariances are the data on which the causal model of the reciprocal relationships between occupational self-direction and ideational flexibility is based.[9]

A reciprocal relationship can occur contemporaneously (albeit not necessarily instantaneously) or over time. We therefore want to assess a causal model that allows the possibility of both contemporaneous and lagged reciprocal effects. (By contemporaneous reciprocal effects, we mean the effects of present job conditions and present ideational flexibility on each other; by lagged reciprocal effects we mean the effects of earlier conditions of work and earlier ideational flexibility both on current conditions of work and on current ideational flexibility.)[10]

Our model (see Figure 3) includes as potentially pertinent exogenous variables all social characteristics that the research literature and our own earlier analyses give us any reason to believe might affect either job placement or ideational flexibility. We thus include in the model the respondent's age and his level of education, his race, national background, and religious background, the educational levels of both parents, his father's occupational status, his maternal and paternal grandfathers' occupational statuses, the urbanness and region of the country of the principal place where he was raised, and even the number of brothers and sisters he had.[11] We also include as exogenous variables the respondent's 1964 levels of ideational flexibility, substantive complexity, routinization, and closeness of supervision, as well as the level of substantive complexity of his 'earlier' (pre-1964) jobs.

To assess the reciprocal effects of occupational self-direction and ideational flexibility, we have to make some assumptions that limit the number of parameters to be estimated. Otherwise, the number of parameters to be estimated would surpass the amount of information available and it would be impossible to obtain unique estimates of the parameters. The assumptions we use to identify the equations are that some effects cannot be direct, but only indirect. (A variable that identifies an equation by not being allowed to have

FIGURE 3

Occupational self-direction and ideational flexibility: A priori model emphasizing contemporaneous effects of routinization and closeness of supervision

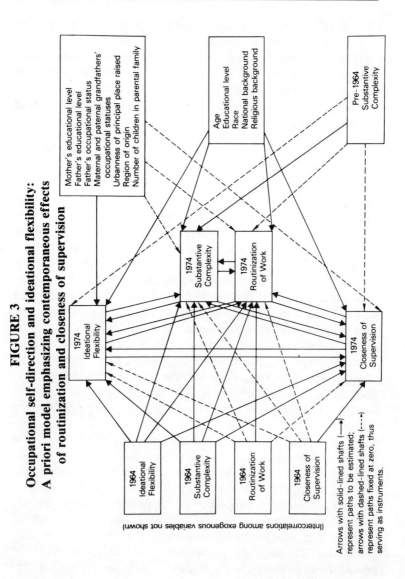

a direct effect on the dependent variable of that equation is called an instrument. For an instrument to identify an equation meaningfully, there must be theoretical justification that its effect should be only indirect and the instrument must be correlated with the variable it is not allowed to affect directly. The stronger the correlation between the instrument and the dependent variable, the more efficacious the instrument for identifying the equation.)[12]

To allow ideational flexibility to have both contemporaneous and lagged effects on occupational conditions, we posit that background characteristics that would not be interpreted as job credentials by employers (even by discriminatory employers) do not directly affect 1974 job conditions. These non-credentialing background characteristics are thus used as instruments to identify the contemporaneous effects of ideational flexibility on job conditions. The paths from non-credentialing background characteristics to 1974 job conditions are therefore fixed at zero. (Paths fixed at zero to provide instrumentation are depicted in Figure 3 by arrows with broken lines for shafts.) The rationale is that maternal and paternal education, paternal occupational status, maternal and paternal grandathers' occupational statuses, urbanness and region of origin, and number of children in the parental family may have affected job placements earlier in the men's careers. But by 1974, when all men in the sample were at least ten years into their careers, these variables should no longer have had any direct effects on the substantive complexity, closeness of supervision, or routinization of their jobs.

To allow the possibility that substantive complexity may have both contemporaneous and lagged effects on ideational flexibility, we posit that the substantive complexity of pre-1964 jobs should have no direct effect on the men's ideational flexibility in 1974, when the substantive complexity of their 1964 and 1974 jobs are taken into account. Thus, 'earlier' (pre-1964) substantive complexity serves as an instrument for the path from 1974 substantive complexity to 1974 intellectual flexibility. Similarly, to allow the possibility that substantive complexity may have both contemporaneous and lagged effects on routinization and closeness of supervision, we again take advantage of pre-1964 substantive complexity as an instrument. But since we have no pre-1964 measures of routinization or closeness of supervision to serve as instruments, we have no way of simultaneously assessing the contemporaneous and lagged effects of these occupational conditions on each other, on ideational flexibility, or on substantive complexity. We are therefore forced to follow a two-phase strategy. In this strategy, we give priority to contemporaneous effects, by using the 1964 measures of routinization and closeness of supervision as instruments to identify the effects of 1974 routinization and closeness of supervision on each other, on substantive complexity, and on ideational flexibility. We give priority to contemporaneous effects for two reasons.

The first reason applies particularly to the effects of routinization and closeness of supervision on each other and on substantive complexity. In assessing inter-occupational effects, we must recognize the structural integrity of the job. It would deny the reality of job structure to assume, for example, that the substantive complexity of the present job is more affected by how closely some past job was supervised than by how closely the present job is supervised.

The second reason for giving priority to contemporaneous effects is particularly important in assessing the effects of these job conditions on ideational flexibility. We are attempting to disaggregate a correlation between, for example, the routinization of men's jobs in 1974 and their ideational flexibility at that same time. This can be done most effectively by simultaneously assessing the effect of 1974 routinization on 1974 ideational flexibility and of 1974 ideational flexibility on 1974 routinization. Assessing the lagged effects — of 1964 routinization on 1974 ideational flexibility and of 1964 ideational flexibility on 1974 routinization — while clearly pertinent, does not disaggregate the critical correlation so directly. Similarly for the correlation between closeness of supervision and ideational flexibility: an unequivocal test of reciprocity can be done only by allowing simultaneously reciprocal contemporaneous effects.

Although we give priority to contemporaneous effects, our principal concern is not whether some effect is contemporaneous or lagged, but whether it occurs at all. It is therefore necessary to allow the possibility of a lagged effect when there is no demonstrated contemporaneous effect. A model that left out such lagged effects would be seriously incomplete. Concretely, if any contemporaneous effect of routinization or closeness of supervision is statistically nonsignificant, we fix it at zero and then (no longer needing an instrument to identify that contemporaneous effect) are

FIGURE 4
Occupational self-direction and ideational flexibility
(Statistically significant paths only)

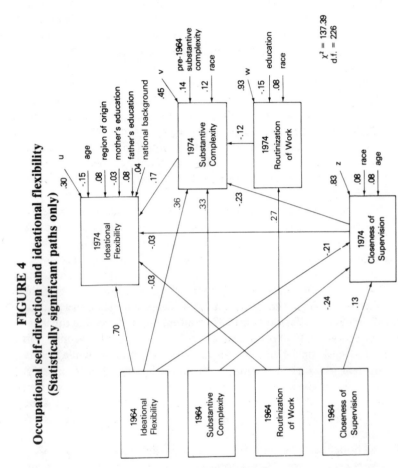

(Intercorrelations among exogenous variables not shown)

free to test the corresponding lagged effect of that occupational condition.

Estimating the model by this two-phase procedure, we arrive at a model (see Figure 4) similar to, but richer than, the one we earlier depicted (in Kohn and Schooler, 1978) for the reciprocal effects of substantive complexity and ideational flexibility. (Nonsignificant paths have been deleted from the model.) The contemporaneous effect of substantive complexity on ideational flexibility is as great in this model as in the earlier analysis; at 0.17, it is approximately one-fourth as large as the direct effect of men's earlier levels of ideational flexibility. To this impressive effect of substantive complexity on ideational flexibility are now added the small but statistically significant direct effects of routinization and closeness of supervision, the former lagged, the latter contemporaneous. Routinization and closeness of supervision also have indirect contemporaneous effects on ideational flexibility, in that both affect substantive complexity. Thus, substantive complexity is the keystone of an intricately interlocking system. It is important not only in its own right, but also as a mechanism by which the other aspects of occupational self-direction affect ideational flexibility.

The effect of ideational flexibility on substantive complexity, in this model as in our earlier analysis, is entirely lagged. In this model, with routinization and closeness of supervision allowed to affect substantive complexity, the effect of ideational flexibility on substantive complexity is somewhat reduced (0.36 instead of 0.41), but it is still very substantial indeed. Ideational flexibility is also shown to have a moderately strong lagged effect on closeness of supervision. Thus, we confirm that the effects of ideational flexibility on job conditions, while entirely lagged, are appreciable.

THE STRUCTURAL IMPERATIVES OF THE JOB AND IDEATIONAL FLEXIBILITY

Now we enlarge the model even further, adding to the three job conditions determinative of occupational self-direction all the other structural imperatives of the job.[13] Since we do not have multiple indicators of any of these job conditions, it is not possible to develop measurement models for any of them. Nor can we combine them into measurement models of organizational structure, job pressures, and extrinsic risks and rewards without losing our ability to assess the separate effects of particular job conditions. For example, if we used time pressure, heaviness, dirtiness, and number of hours worked as indicators in a measurement model of job pressure, we would no longer be able to examine the separate effects of each of the four types of job pressures. We chose therefore to use the single-indicator measures of each of these occupational conditions, recognizing that each is subject to some unknown degree of measurement error.[14]

We should also recognize that, since we have a sample of men rather than of jobs, our estimates of the effects of these fourteen occupational conditions on one another will be weighted in proportion to the numbers of men who experience the various job conditions. This is entirely reasonable for a social-psychological inquiry whose purpose is to assess the reciprocal effects of job conditions and psychological functioning. It might not be as reasonable for a social-structural analysis of occupations, for which a sample, of say, all the occupations enumerated in the Dictionary of Occupational Titles might be more appropriate.

Our model of job conditions and ideational flexibility, schematically outlined in Figure 5, is identified through much the same procedures as those employed in the model of occupational self-direction and ideational flexibility. We again use noncredentialing background variables and pre-1964 substantive complexity as instruments, and again give priorty to the contemporaneous effects of job conditions, allowing lagged effects only when the contemporaneous effects are not statistically significant.

One new consideration is that position in the organizational structure — as defined by ownership, bureaucratization, and hierarchical position — cannot be contemporaneously affected by ideational flexibility or by any occupational condition. This is definitially true, for a change from ownership to nonownership, or the reverse; or from a more bureaucratic to a less bureaucratic firm or organization, or the reverse; or from a higher to a lower position in the supervisory hierarchy, or the reverse, would signify a change in job. It is not even possible for these three aspects of organizational structure to affect each other without the person changing jobs.[15] But there is no reason why ideational flexibility or any occupational condition could not have a lagged effect on ownership, bureaucratization, or hierarchical position, for people

FIGURE 5

A priori model: occupational structure and ideational flexibility — contemporaneous effects

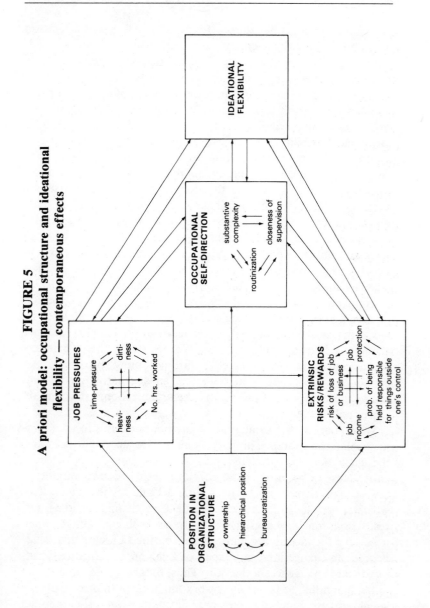

can change jobs in the course of ten years. All lagged effects on these three occupational conditions are identified and can be tested.

The logic of our assessment of the directions of effects in the relationships between occupational conditions and ideational flexibility requires the simultaneous testing of pairs of reciprocal paths — from some occupational condition to ideational flexibility and from ideational flexibility to that occuaptional condition. But, if ideational flexibility cannot have direct contemporaneous effects on ownership, bureaucratization, and hierarchical position, then these occuaptional conditions should not be allowed to have direct contemporaneous effects on ideational flexibility; otherwise, we would be prejudging the very issue we are trying to evaluate. Fortunately, there is nothing to preclude us from allowing ownership, bureaucratization, and hierarchical position to have either lagged effects or indirect contemporaneous effects on ideational flexibility. In fact, an earlier analysis (Kohn, 1971) found that bureaucratization's effects on ideational flexibility are primarily indirect, mediated through substantive complexity, income, and job protections. Extending the logic of this argument, we initially test a model that posits that not only bureaucratization, but also the other aspects of organizational structure, exert their primary psychological impact indirectly, through more proximate occupational conditions. Later, we test an alternative model that allows direct effects of position in the organizational structure on ideational flexibility.

We recognize that some other contemporaneous effects are improbable; for example, it is difficult to see how time-pressure, though it may be correlated with heaviness and dirtiness, could either cause or be caused by them. But it seems wiser to impose the fewest a priori restrictions on the model and let the data tell us which effects do, in fact, occur. We deliberately impose no a priori restrictions on lagged effects (except, as explained above, when necessary for identifying an equation) on the rationale that, since people can change jobs, any aspect of a job might influence the individual to change to another job. Thus, to take a trite example, an individual doing heavy or dirty work might be prompted to open a small business. Similarly, ideational flexibility at an earlier time can affect any aspect of occupation at a later time, even the individual's place in the organizational structure.

The actual model of job conditions and ideational flexibility is presented in Table 1. (The model, unfortunately, is too large and complex to capture in a figure.) Four things stand out in this model.

First, the effects of ideational flexibility on occupational conditions are impressive, albeit entirely lagged. Greater ideational flexibility in 1964 is conducive to working at jobs of greater substantive complexity in 1974, with less supervision, fewer hours of work, and fewer job protections. Ideational flexibility also increases the probability of becoming an owner or working in a bureaucratic firm or organization. These effects occur only over time. But over the course of ten years their importance is considerable.

Second, many conditions of work have statistically significant effects on 1974 ideational flexibility, even with 1964 ideational flexibility, pertinent social characteristics, and other job conditions statistically controlled. Substantive complexity, closeness of supervision, heaviness, being held responsible for things outside one's control, the risk of losing one's job or business, and income all have statistically significant contemporaneous effects on ideational flexibility, while routinization, time-pressure, and job protections have significant lagged effects. The magnitudes of these effects are small to moderate (they range from 0.03 to 0.13), but it is nevertheless noteworthy that so many of the structural imperatives of the job significantly affect ideational flexibility, even under such stringent statistical controls. Moreover, these direct effects, contemporaneous and lagged, are only part of the story. There is an intricate network of interrelationships among job conditions, with all of the structural imperatives of the job linked to one another and thus, ultimately, to ideational flexibility.

Third, the substantive complexity of work plays a pivotal role in this network. In terms of its direct effect on ideational flexibility, substantive complexity is clearly the most important job condition; its contemporaneous effect (of 0.13) being greater than the contemporaneous or lagged effect of any other occupational condition. In terms of its indirect effect on ideational flexibility, substantive complexity stands out as the keystone of the job structure. On the one hand, substantive complexity has contemporaneous effects on time-pressure, dirtiness, hours of work, the probability of being held responsible for things outside one's control, and income, as well as lagged effects on closeness of supervision and hierarchical position; several of these jobs conditions, in turn, directly affect ideational flexibility. On the other hand, the indirect effects of other occupational conditions on intellectual flexibility are to a

TABLE 1
The reciprocal effects of job conditions and ideational flexibility

	Ideational flexibility	Substantive complexity	Routinization	Closeness of supervision	Ownership	Bureau-cratization	Position in hierarchy	Time-pressure
				Statistically significant effects of:				
On 1974:								
Ideational flexibility	0.70(L)	0.13(C)	-0.04(L)	-0.03(C)	0.0	0.0	0.0	0.10(L)
Substantive complexity	0.31(L)	0.26(L)	-0.11(C)	-0.21(C)	0.07(C)	0.11(C)	0.19(C)	0.06(C)
Routinization	0.0	0.0	0.26(L)	0.0	0.0	0.0	-0.09(C)	0.0
Closeness of supervision	-0.17(L)	-0.20(L)	0.0	0.09(L)	0.0	0.0	-0.15(C)	0.0
Ownership	0.07(L)	0.0	0.0	0.0	0.54(L)	0.0	0.0	0.0
Bureaucratization	0.07(L)	0.0	0.0	0.0	-0.14(L)	0.46(L)	0.0	0.0
Position in hierarchy	0.0	0.21(L)	0.0	0.0	0.0	0.0	0.29(L)	0.11(L)
Time-pressure	0.0	0.11(C)	0.0	0.0	0.0	0.0	0.0	0.30(L)
Heaviness	0.0	0.0	-0.12(C)	0.0	0.0	-0.15(C)	-0.10(C)	0.0
Dirtiness	0.0	-0.40(C)	-0.11(C)	0.0	0.0	0.0	0.0	0.0
Hours of work	-0.23(L)	0.32(C)	0.0	0.0	0.0	-0.22(C)	0.0	0.0
'Held responsible'	0.0	0.16(C)	-0.08(L)	0.0	0.0	0.0	0.0	0.17(C)
Risk of loss of job	0.0	0.0	0.0	0.0	0.32(C)	0.0	0.0	0.0
Job protections	-0.13(L)	0.0	0.10(L)	0.0	0.0	0.37(C)	0.0	0.0
Job income	0.0	0.15(C)	0.0	0.0	0.36(C)	0.28(C)	0.14(C)	0.0

TABLE 1 (continued)

	Heaviness	Dirtiness	Hours of work	'Held responsible'	Risk of loss of job	Job protections	Job income
Ideational flexibility	-0.07(C)	0.0	0.0	-0.06(C)	0.03(C)	-0.09(L)	0.06(C)
Substantive complexity	0.0	0.0	0.0	0.0	0.0	0.05(L)	0.0
Routinization	0.0	0.0	0.0	0.0	0.0	0.0	-0.10(L)
Closeness of supervision	-0.11(C)	0.09(L)	0.0	0.11(C)	0.18(C)	0.06(C)	-0.10(L)
Ownership	0.0	0.0	0.0	0.0	0.0	-0.11(L)	0.0
Bureaucratization	0.0	0.0	0.0	-0.08(L)	0.0	0.0	0.0
Position in hierarchy	0.0	0.0	0.0	0.0	0.0	0.0	0.0
Time-pressure	0.21(L)	0.0	0.08(L)	-0.07(C)	0.0	0.0	0.12(C)
Heaviness	0.0	0.26(C)	0.15(C)	0.0	0.0	0.0	0.0
Dirtiness	0.0	0.39(L)	0.18(L)	0.0	0.0	0.0	0.0
Hours of work	0.0	0.10(L)	0.08(C)	0.24(L)	0.0	0.0	0.19(C)
'Held responsible'	0.0	0.0	0.0	0.0	0.0	0.0	0.0
Risk of loss of job	0.0	0.0	0.0	0.0	0.21(L)	0.0	0.0
Job protections	0.12(C)	0.0	0.0	0.0	0.0	0.34(L)	0.0
Job income	0.0	-0.12(C)	0.0	0.0	0.0	0.0	0.33(L)

TABLE 1 (continued)

	Pre-1964 substantive complexity	Education	Race	Age	National background	Religious background	Number of siblings	Region of origin
Ideational flexibility	0.17	0.0	0.0	-0.14	0.04	0.0	0.0	0.08
Substantive complexity		0.0	0.11	0.0	0.0	0.0		
Routinization		-0.11	0.0	0.0	0.0	0.0		
Closeness of supervision		0.0	0.08	0.09	0.0	0.0		
Ownership		0.0	0.0	0.10	0.0	0.0		
Bureaucratization		0.0	0.0	-0.09	0.0	0.0		
Position in hierarchy		0.0	0.0	-0.09	0.0	0.0		
Time-pressure		0.0	0.0	0.0	0.0	0.0		
Heaviness		-0.17	0.0	0.0	0.0	0.0		
Dirtiness		0.0	0.0	0.0	0.0	0.0		
Hours of work		0.0	0.0	0.0	0.0	0.0		
'Held responsible'		0.0	0.0	0.0	0.0	0.0		
Risk of loss of job		-0.08	0.0	0.0	0.0	0.0		
Job protections		0.0	0.0	0.0	0.0	0.0		
Job income		0.0	0.0	-0.14	0.0	0.0		

TABLE 1 (continued)

	Urbanness of place raised	Mother's education	Father's education	Father's occupational status	Maternal grandfather's occupational status	Paternal grandfather's occupational status
Ideational flexibility	-0.03	-0.03	0.07	0.0	-0.03	0.0
Substantive complexity						
Routinization						
Closeness of supervision						
Ownership						
Bureaucratization						
Position in hierarchy						
Time-pressure						
Heaviness						
Dirtiness						
Hours of work						
'Held responsible'						
Risk of loss of job						
Job protections						
Job income						

Note: (L) means a lagged effect (e.g., of 1964 ideational flexibility on 1974 flexibility); (C) means a contemporaneous effect (e.g., of 1974 substantive complexity on 1974 ideational flexibility).

large degree mediated through substantive complexity. Since substantive complexity has the greatest direct effect on ideational flexibility, other occupational conditions all indirectly affect ideational flexibility in rough proportion to their effects on substantive complexity.

Finally, although ownership, bureaucratization, and hierarchical position are not permitted to have direct contemporaneous effects on ideational flexibility in this model, and although they do not have significant lagged effects on ideational flexibility, they do have impressive indirect effects. Hierarchical position, for example, affects substantive complexity, routinization, closeness of supervision, heaviness of the work, and income, several of which directly affect ideational flexibility and all of which are linked to still other occupational conditions and thus ultimately to ideational flexibility. Ownership and bureaucratization have similar indirect effects.

Even though these indirect effects are impressive, we may nonetheless be underestimating the importance of position in the organizational structure by not allowing ownership, bureaucratization, and hierarchical position to have direct, contemporaneous effects on ideational flexibility. The difficulty, of course, is that allowing such effects when we cannot allow ideational flexibility to affect position in the organizational structure would assume the very unidirectionality of effects that our entire analysis is designed to transcend. Still, a model permitting organizational structure to have direct, contemporaneous effects on ideational flexibility would set upper limits for our estimates of the direct effects of ownership, bureaucratization, and hierarchical position on ideational flexibility, and lower limits for our estimates of the direct effects of all other job conditions on ideational flexibility. Testing such a model, we find that neither ownership nor bureaucratization would have a statistically significant direct effect on ideational flexibility.[16] Hierarchical position would have a significant direct effect, a contemporaneous path of 0.09. The direct effects of other occupational conditions would be somewhat reduced; in particular, the direct effect of substantive complexity on ideational flexibility would be reduced from 0.13 to 0.10. Thus, we can conclude that hierarchical position has a direct effect on ideational flexibility of no more than 0.09, while substantive complexity has a direct effect on ideational flexibility of no less than 0.10 and no more than 0.13. The unresolved issue is the degree to which the effect of hierarchical position is mediated through substantive complexity. In any case, both substantive complexity and hierarchical position clearly have decided importance for ideational flexibility.

CONCLUSION

These findings confirm and extend the conclusions we reached in our more limited analysis of the reciprocal effects of the substantive complexity of work and intellectual flexibility (Kohn and Schooler, 1978). The substantive complexity of work affects ideational flexibility not only when prior levels of ideational flexibility and pertinent aspects of social background are taken into account, but also when all other structural imperatives of the job are taken into account as well. We further find that substantive complexity is not the only job condition that directly affects ideational flexibility; several other job conditions that stimulate and challenge the individual are conducive to ideational flexibility. But, clearly, substantive complexity plays a key role, not only because of the magnitude of its effect on ideational flexibility, but because it plays a pivotal role in the structure of the job. It provides the principal mechanism through which other job conditions affect intellectual functioning.

We confirm that ideational flexibility has a very decided lagged effect on the substantive complexity of work; and we learn that ideational flexibility has lagged effects on several job conditions other than substantive complexity. The picture of how job affects and is affected by ideational flexibility has become more sharply delineated.

Yet, these very findings underline how much more there is to learn. Many of the reservations were expressed in our earlier paper apply as well to this analysis.[17] In particular, we must acknowledge that we have not been able to take account of unreliability in measurement of several of the major variables; we have done no systematic analysis of career patterns; we do not know whether the effects we have found are essentially the same for all age-cohorts and for all segments of the work force; and we have not taken into account other important events that may have occurred in the lives of these men during the 10-year interval between the baseline and the follow-up interviews. And, of course, our analyses have thus far been limited to one aspect of psychological functioning — ideational flexibility. In our ongoing research, we shall expand the analysis to include such other aspects of psychological functioning as authoritarian conservatism, self-esteem, standards of morality, and anxiety.

The most important issue, which our research will next address, is: which occupational conditions affect (and are affected by) which aspects of psychological functioning? Does substantive complexity play the pivotal role vis-à-vis all aspects of psychological functioning? Or might time-pressure or job protections or dirtiness be more important for such aspects of psychological functioning as anxiety or self-esteem? Doing the analyses reported in this paper has convinced us that Jöreskog's methods for confirmatory factor analysis and linear structural equations causal analysis are a most effective way to answer such questions.

NOTES

1. We have also employed these methods in a much broader cross-sectional analysis of the relationships between women's occupational conditions and psychological functioning (Miller et al., 1979).

2. In Figure 1, in all subsequent figures, and in the text, all paths and correlations are expressed in standardized form. Standardized values are more easily comprehended than are metric values, and the use of standardized values makes it possible to compare paths from concepts to indicators in the measurement models and to compare causal paths in the structural equation models. But all computations have been based on unstandardized variance-covariance matrices.

3. Allowing error correlations between the two cognitive problems was suggested by an examination of the first-order partial derivatives of the minimization function, which indicates whether the freeing of a parameter might improve the fit of model to data; see Sörbom (1975).

4. Moreover, the over-time stability of perceptual flexibility is so high ($r = 0.96$) that we encounter insuperable problems of multicollinearity when trying to estimate its contemporaneous and lagged effects on job conditions. Our analyses do indicate, though, that at least one job condition — the substantive complexity of work — affects perceptual flexibility as strongly as it does ideational flexibility.

5. Instructive discussions of the issues involved in separating unreliability from change are Alwin (1973; 1976), Blalock (1969), Burt (1973), Hauser and Goldberger (1971), Heise (1969; 1970; 1975), Heise and Bohrnstedt (1970), Lord and Novick (1968), and Wheaton et al. (1977). Informative applications of confirmatory factor analysis are provided in Bielby, Hauser, and Featherman (1977), Kohn and Schooler (1978), Mason et al. (1976), Miller et al. (1979), and Otto and Featherman (1975).

6. In an earlier paper (Kohn and Schooler, 1973), we used the term 'structural imperatives of the job' to describe a similar but not identical set of job conditions. Three occupational conditions have been added to those we then called the structural imperatives of the job and one has been deleted. We add job protections and job income because earlier analysis (Kohn, 1971) suggested that these, along with the substantive complexity of work, might be important mediating conditions through which the individual's position in the organizational structure affects his psychological functioning. And, of course, they might well be important in their own right. Hours worked per week was added because our analysis of women's occupational conditions and psychological functioning (Miller et al., 1979) indicated that, for women, where the hours of work are highly variable, this is an important job condition; for comparability, we now include it in the analysis of men. Deleted from the model is the respondent's estimate of the probability, in his field, of a 'sudden and dramatic change in income, reputation, or position.' There are three reasons for doubting that this is really a job condition. First, the question refers to the field in which the respondent works, not to his specific job; the referent is really a career contingency. Second, we have only limited information about whether the individual believes that the 'sudden and dramatic change' might result from externally imposed conditions or from his own achievements or failures. Finally, the question does not differentiate between changes for the better and changes for the worse.

7. Except for our dropping one question (about the supervisor's control over the pace of work), which had a highly skewed distribution, this treatment of closeness of supervision is conceptually no different from the Guttman Scale we earlier employed (e.g., in Kohn and Schooler, 1969). But using confirmatory factor analysis enables us to make a much more precise specification of the relationships of indicators to concept.

8. Our procedure has been to develop models that combine the principal features of two or more measurement models, compute the covariances of the concepts, and use these covariances as the data for causal analysis. In developing these combined models, the crucial requirement is to fix, at the values derived from the measurement models, those parameters that define the relationships between concepts and their indicators (i.e., the paths from concepts to indicators, the residuals for the indicators, and the correlations among those residuals) while not inadvertently fixing parameters that constrain the interrelationships of the concepts.

9. In developing the linear structural equation models, we employed the LISREL computer program (Jöreskog and van Thillo, 1972), as subsequently modified by Ronald Schoenberg. Pertinent writings on the strategy of this type of analysis are Burt (1976), Duncan (1975), Heise (1970; 1975), Jöreskog (1973b; 1977; 1978), Jöreskog and Sörbom (1976), Werts, Jöreskog, and Linn (1973), and Werts, Linn, and Jöreskog (1971).

10. A qualifying note is in order here. With a 10-year interval between measurements, all we can mean by a contemporaneous effect is an effect of the job

currently held (however long it has been held, short of 10 years) or of current ideational flexibility, not an effect of some previous job or of ideational flexibility at the time of that previous job. A more exact appraisal of the timing of effects would be exceedingly difficult to accomplish without measuring both job conditions and ideational flexibility at more frequent intervals than we have done.

11. The indices of national background, region of origin, and religious background are linear approximations to these concepts. In our present use, these indices represent slight underestimates of what would be shown in a more complicated dummy variable analysis. The rationale for these linearizations is given in Schooler (1972; 1976). Essentially, all three indices are ordered in terms of environmental complexity: national background, on the basis of how long it has been since the social organization of the nation's agriculture passed beyond feudalism; region of the United States, on the basis of industrialization and expenditures for education; and religion, on the basis of fundamentalism.

12. For lucid discussions of the topic of identification, see Duncan (1975:81-90), and Heise (1975:160-81).

13. The three aspects of the man's position in the organizational structure that we measure are the bureaucratization of the firm or organization in which he is employed, ownership/no ownership, and the number of people over whom he says he has direct or indirect supervisory authority. Of the four job pressures, three are measured by the respondent's appraisals of frequency of time pressure, how dirty he gets in his work, and the number of hours he works in the average week. The fourth, heaviness of work, is our appraisal, based on his description of his work with things. Extrinsic risks and rewards are measured by the individual's perceptions of the likelihood of being held responsible for things outside his control and of the risk of losing his job or business, his reported income, and a simple additive index of whether or not his job provides such benefits as job security and sick leave. These measures are described more fully in Kohn (1971) and Kohn and Schooler (1973).

14. Unfortunately, this means that we may underestimate the effects of these occupational conditions. The same problem exists, of course, for routinization and for the social background variables. We see no satisfactory way of compensating for the unreliability of these indices, since we do not have adequate data about their actual reliabilities.

15. Since we do not allow any variable to affect ownership, bureaucratization, or hierarchical position contemporaneously, we allow their residuals to correlate with those of all other endogenous variables, whenever such correlations are statistically significant.

16. More precisely: ownership would not have a significant contemporaneous effect on ideational flexibility. Bureaucratization would have a small, negative, contemporaneous effect, which is inconsistent both with its mainly positive indirect effects (mediated in large part through substantive complexity and job income) and with a positive lagged effect, which becomes statistically significant only when the contemporaneous effect is in the model.

17. One reservation no longer applies. At that time we had no information about whether job conditions affect women's psychological functioning similarly to men's. This question has now been answered affirmatively; see Miller et al. (1979).

REFERENCES

Alwin, Duane F. (1973) 'Making Inferences from Attitude-Behavior Correlations,' *Sociometry*, vol. 36:253-78.

Alwin, Duane F. (1976) 'Attitude Scales as Congeneric Tests: A Re-examination of an Attitude-Behavior Model,' *Sociometry*, vol. 39:377-83.

Bielby, William T., Robert M. Hauser and David L. Featherman (1977) 'Response Errors of Nonblack Males in Models of the Intergenerational Transmission of Socioeconomic Status,' *American Journal of Sociology*, vol. 82:1242-88.

Blalock, Hubert M., Jr (1969) 'Multiple Indicators and the Causal Approach to Measurement Error,' *American Journal of Sociology*, vol. 75:264-72.

Burt, Ronald S. (1973) 'Confirmatory Factor-Analytic Structures and the Theory Construction Process,' *Sociological Methods and Research*, vol. 2:131-90.

Burt, Ronald S. (1976) 'Interpretational Confounding of Unobserved Variables in Structural Equation Models,' *Sociological Methods and Research*, vol. 5: 3-52.

Duncan, Otis Dudley (1975) *Introduction to Structural Equation Models*. New York: Academic Press.

Hauser, Robert M. and Arthur S. Goldberger (1971) 'The Treatment of Unobservable Variables in Path Analysis,' pp. 81-117 in Herbert L. Costner (ed.) *Sociological Methodology*. San Francisco: Jossey-Bass.

Heise, David R. (1969) 'Separating Reliability and Stability in Test-Retest Correlation,' *American Sociological Review*, vol. 34:93-101.

Heise, David R. (1970) 'Causal Inference from Panel Data,' pp. 3-27 in Edgar F. Borgatta (ed.) *Sociological Methodology*. San Francisco: Jossey-Bass.

Heise, David R. (1975) *Causal Analysis*. New York: John Wiley.

Heise, David R. and George W. Bohrnstedt (1970) 'Validity, Invalidity, and Reliability,' pp. 104-29 in Edgar F. Borgatta (ed.) *Sociological Methodology*. San Francisco: Jossey-Bass.

Jöreskog, Karl G. (1969) 'A General Approach to Confirmatory Maximum Likelihood Factor Analysis,' *Psychometrika*, vol. 34:183-202.

Jöreskog, Karl G. (1970) 'A General Method for Analysis of Covariance Structures,' *Biometrika*, vol. 57:239-51.

Jöreskog, Karl G. (1973a) 'Analysis of Covariance Structures,' pp. 263-85 in P. R. Krishnaiah (ed.), *Multivariate Analysis*, vol. III. New York: Academic Press.

Jöreskog, Karl G. (1973b) 'A General Method for Estimating a Linear Structural Equation System,' pp. 85-112 in Arthur S. Goldberger and Otis Dudley Duncan (eds), *Structural Equation Models in the Social Sciences*. New York: Seminar Press.

Jöreskog, Karl G. (1977) 'Structural Equation Models in the Social Sciences: Specification, Estimation, and Testing,' pp. 265-286 in P. R. Krishnaiah (ed.), *Applications of Statistics*. Amsterdam: North Holland.

Jöreskog, Karl G. (1978) 'Structural Analysis of Covariance and Correlation Matrices,' *Psychometrika*, vol. 43:443-77.

Jöreskog, Karl G. and Sörbom D. (1976) 'Statistical Models and Methods for Analysis of Longitudinal Data,' pp. 235-85 in D. J. Aigner and A. S. Goldberger (eds), *Latent Variables in Socioeconomic Models*. Amsterdam: North Holland.

Jöreskog, Karl G. and Marielle van Thillo (1972) 'LISREL: A General Computer Program for Estimating a Linear Structural Equation System Involving Multiple Indicators of Unmeasured Variables,' *Research Bulletin 72-56*. Princeton, NJ: Educational Testing Service.

Kohn, Melvin L. (1969) *Class and Conformity: A Study in Values*. Homewood, Illinois: Dorsey Press 2nd edn., 1977, published by the University of Chicago Press.

Kohn, Melvin L. (1971) 'Bureaucratic Man: A Portrait and an Interpretation,' *American Sociological Review*, vol. 36:461-74.

Kohn, Melvin L. (1976) 'Occupational Structure and Alienation,' *American Journal of Sociology*, vol. 82:111-30.

Kohn, Melvin L. (1977) 'Reassessment, 1977,' pp. xxv-lx in *Class and Conformity: A Study in Values*, 2nd ed. Chicago: University of Chicago Press.

Kohn, Melvin L. and Carmi Schooler (1969) 'Class, Occupation and Orientation,' *American Sociological Review*, vol. 34:659-78.

Kohn, Melvin L. and Carmi Schooler (1973) 'Occupational Experience and Psychological Functioning. An Assessment of Reciprocal Effects,' *American Sociological Review*, vol. 38:97-118.

Kohn, Melvin L. and Carmi Schooler (1978) 'The Reciprocal Effects of the Substantive Complexity of Work and Intellectual Flexibility: A Longitudinal Assessment,' *American Journal of Sociology*, vol. 84:24-52.

Lord, F. M. and M. R. Novick (1968) *Statistical Theories of Mental Test Scores*. Reading, Mass.: Addison-Wesley.

Mason, William M., Robert M. Hauser, Alan C. Kerckhoff, Sharon Sandomirsky Poss, and Kenneth Manton (1976) 'Models of Response Error in Student Reports of Parental Socioeconomic Characteristics,' pp. 443-94 in William H. Sewell, Robert M. Hauser, and David L. Featherman (eds), *Schooling and Achievement in American Society*. New York: Academic Press.

Miller, Joanne, Carmi Schooler, Melvin L. Kohn, and Karen A. Miller (1979) 'Women and Work: The Psychological Effects of Occupational Conditions,' *American Journal of Sociology*, vol. 85:66-94.

Otto, Luther B. and David L. Featherman (1975) 'Social Structural and Psychological Antecedents of Self-Estrangement and Powerlessness,' *American Sociological Review*, vol. 40:701-19.

Schooler, Carmi (1972) 'Social Antecedents of Adult Psychological Functioning,' *American Journal of Sociology*, vol. 78:299-322.

Schooler, Carmi (1976) 'Serfdom's Legacy: An Ethnic Continuum,' *American Journal of Sociology*, vol. 81:1265-86.

Sörbom, Dag (1975) 'Detection of Correlated Errors in Longitudinal Data,' *British Journal of Mathematical and Statistical Psychology*, vol. 28:138-51.

Spaeth, Joe L. (1976) 'Characteristics of the Work Setting and the Job as Determinants of Income,' pp. 161-76 in William H. Sewell, Robert M. Hauser, and David L. Featherman (eds), *Schooling and Achievement in American Society*. New York: Academic.

Werts, Charles E., Karl G. Jöreskog and Robert L. Linn (1973) 'Identification and Estimation in Path Analysis with Unmeasured Variables,' *American Journal of Sociology*, vol. 78:1469-84.

Werts, Charles E., Robert L. Linn and Karl G. Jöreskog (1971) 'Estimating the Parameters of Path Models Involving Unmeasured Variables,' pp. 400-09 in H. M. Blalock, Jr (ed.), *Causal Models in the Social Sciences*. New York: Aldine-Atherton.

Wheaton, Blair, Bengt Muthén, Duane F. Alwin and Gene F. Summers (1977) 'Assessing Reliability and Stability in Panel Models,' pp. 84-136 in David R. Heise (ed.), *Sociological Methodology*. San Francisco: Jossey-Bass.

Witkin, H. A., R. B. Dyk, H. F. Faterson, D. R. Goodenough and S. A. Karp (1962). *Psychological Differentiation: Studies of Development*. New York: John Wiley.

NOTES ON CONTRIBUTORS

Duane Alwin is Senior Study Director of the Survey Research Center, University of Michigan, where he is an Associate Professor of Sociology.

Edgar F. Borgatta is Professor in the Doctoral Program of Sociology and of Social Psychology and Personality at the Graduate School of the City University of New York, where he is also Research Director of the CASE Center for Gerontological Study. Dr Borgatta has written widely on sociological methods and statistics and is President of the Research Committee on Logic and Methodology for the International Sociological Association. His publications include *Aging and Society* (ed. with Neil G. McCluskey, Sage Publications, 1980).

Clifford C. Clogg is Faculty Associate at the Population Issues Research Center, Pennsylvania State University. He was formerly Assistant Professor at the University of Chicago. His publications include *Measuring Underemployment: Demographic Indicators for the United States* (Academic Press, 1979).

David R. Heise is Professor of Sociology at the University of North Carolina. He is a former editor of *Sociological Methodology* and current editor of *Sociological Methods and Research*. His publications include *Causal Analysis* (Wiley Interscience, 1975) and *Understanding Events* (Cambridge University Press, 1979).

Charles E. Holzer III is a member of the Depression Research Centre at Yale University.

William G. Howard is Director of Data Development and Research for the Central Texas Health Systems Agency, Inc. He was principal investigator for the *Data Sources Survey: Health Data in Texas* (Central Texas Health Systems Agency, 1979).

David J. Jackson is Deputy Chief, Population Research Section, Mental Health Study Center, National Institute of Mental Health, Adelphi, Maryland.

Karl G. Jöreskog is Professor of Statistics at the University of Uppsala. He is a past President of the Psychometric Society, a Fellow of the American Statistical Association and an elected member of the Academy of Sciences in Sweden. He has published numerous articles on factor analysis, covariance structure analysis, structural equation models and on analysis of longitudinal data and has given short courses on factor analysis and on causal model building in the social sciences at many places in the USA and Europe. Professor Jöreskog has been a Research Statistician at Educational Testing Service, a Visiting Professor at Princeton and Chicago and a Visiting Scientist at Stanford Research Institute.

Melvin L. Kohn is Chief of the Laboratory of Socio-énvironmental Studies at the National Institute of Mental Health, Adelphi, Maryland. He is author of *Class and Conformity: A Study in Values* (University of Chicago Press, 1977).

Alberto Marradi is Professor of the Methodology of Social Research at the University of Catania, Italy. He is the author of several papers on empirical and theoretical aspects of social research and (with C. Tullio-Altan) of a book on the values of Italian youth.

Bengt Muthén is Research Associate in the Department of Statistics at the University of Uppsala, Sweden.

Lynn Robbins is an Associate in Psychiatry at the University of Florida. She was formerly the Project Director of National Institute of Mental Health grants, evaluating southern mental health needs and services and the Community Mental Health Center Assessment Program. She is a co-author of *Planning for Mental Health Services: Needs Assessment Approaches* (1980).

Carmi Schooler is a Research Psychologist at the Laboratory of Socio-environmental Studies, National Institute of Mental Health, Adelphi, Maryland. Carmi Schooler's research focuses on the psychological consequences of occupational experience and the social structural determinants of both normal and abnormal adult functioning.

Dag Sörbom received his PhD from the University of Uppsala and is currently a Research Associate in the Statistics Department at Uppsala. He has published articles on statistical methodology for model building with latent variables, in particular, on models for group comparisons. He has worked on two major research projects 'Statistical Methods for Analysis of Longitudinal Data' and 'Structural Equation Models in the Social Sciences' with Karl G. Jöreskog as Project Director. Dr Sörbom is the master programmer of the computer programs EFAP, COFAMM and LISREL and has been on the staff on various workshops for teaching the uses of these programs.

Pablo Suárez is *Forskarassistent* (Assistant Professor) in the Department of Sociology at Uppsala University. Until 1973 he was Director of Research and Professor of Metasociology and of the Methodology of Social Research at the University of Chile. His publications include *Las Dimensiones de la Sociedad: Introducción a la Meta-Sociología* (Dimensions of Society: Introduction to Metasociology, Santiago, Chile, 1970) and *Praxiología, Planificación y Acción Social* (Praxiology, Planning and Social Action, Sinaloa, Mexico, 1978).